PENGUIN BOOKS

HALF AMERICAN

Matthew F. Delmont is the Sherman Fairchild Distinguished Professor of History at Dartmouth College. A Guggenheim Fellow and expert on African American history and the history of civil rights, he is the author of four books: *Black Quotidian*, *Why Busing Failed*, *Making Roots*, and *The Nicest Kids in Town*. His work has also appeared in *The New York Times*, *The Atlantic*, *The Washington Post*, and several academic journals, and on NPR. Originally from Minneapolis, Minnesota, Delmont earned his BA from Harvard University and his MA and PhD from Brown University.

* * *

Praise for *Half American*

Winner of the 2023 Anisfield-Wolf Book Award for Nonfiction
• A *New York Times* Notable Book •
A Best Book of the Year from *Time*, *Publishers Weekly*,
Booklist, *Washington Independent Review of Books*, and more!

"[A] poignant and unflinching account of how Black Americans helped the country defend its freedom even while regularly experiencing widespread racism, segregation, and violence at the hands of their fellow citizens."
—Cate Lineberry, *The New York Times Book Review* (editors' choice)

"Delmont is an energetic storyteller, giving a vibrant sense of his subject in all of its dimensions."   —Jennifer Szalai, *The New York Times*

"This book not only details historical wrongs committed against the Black press, it ardently honors the sacrifice of Black Americans who served in World War II."   —*The Wall Street Journal*

"*Half American* gives a detailed look at the dual battle Black service members waged, fighting fascism overseas and racism back home. . . . Fascinating."   —Amna Nawaz, *PBS NewsHour*

"Delmont shifts the spotlight to the wartime contributions of these often-overlooked heroes, crucially drawing attention to people who provided more 'behind the scenes' support."

—*Time* (The 100 Must-Read Books of 2022)

"Delmont makes a strong case that the unheralded work to which Blacks were assigned proved essential to Allied victory."

—Eric Foner, *London Review of Books*

"Civil rights expert Delmont has written what is sure to become the standard text on the experience of Black U.S. soldiers who fought in World War II. . . . While books have been written on the experiences of individual units and soldiers, this one takes a unique approach, making it one of the best and first truly comprehensive books on the subject. This is long overdue." —*Library Journal* (starred review)

"Revelatory . . . An eloquent and essential corrective to the historical record." —*Publishers Weekly* (starred review)

"The narrative provides important pages that have been missing from American history. A vital story well rendered, recounting a legacy that should be recognized, remembered, and applauded."

—*Kirkus Reviews* (starred review)

"Delmont's work restores these times to our collective memory."

—*Booklist* (starred review)

"A significant contribution to our knowledge of World War II history . . . *Half American* is more than an excellent introduction to this underappreciated chapter of military history. It is also a ground-breaking illumination of African American civilians' complex involvement in World War II." —*BookPage* (starred review)

"When I first learned about World War II, little was said about the role Black Americans played in the war effort. I wish *Half American* had been in my classrooms. Matthew F. Delmont's book is filled with compelling narratives that outline with nuance, rigor, and complexity

how Black Americans fought for this country abroad while simultaneously fighting for their rights here in the United States. *Half American* belongs firmly within the canon of indispensable World War II books."
—Clint Smith, author of *How the Word Is Passed: A Reckoning with the History of Slavery Across America*

"*Half American* is a triumph of eloquence and erudition. Historian Matthew Delmont sheds invigoratingly bold and new light on the dual struggle to end racial injustice at home and internationally during the Second World War. This expert distillation of the wartime struggle for Black dignity and citizenship reimagines the history of postwar American democracy. Through brilliantly moving personal histories that simultaneously touch the local, national, and global, *Half American* illuminates the depth and breadth of a 'Double V' campaign that, in many ways, never truly ended."
—Peniel E. Joseph, author of *The Third Reconstruction: America's Struggle for Racial Justice in the Twenty-First Century*

"Matthew F. Delmont's *Half American* is a bold, searing, and moving account of the courageous Black men and women who served during World War II. While their stories and contributions are too often sidelined in American popular narratives, Delmont's brilliant book skillfully weaves together insights from an array of archival records and military documents to place Black Americans at the center of the story. With rigor, passion, and depth of analysis, Delmont compellingly demonstrates that Black participation was absolutely essential to American victory during World War II. This is a must read for anyone interested in race, American democracy, and military history."
—Keisha N. Blain, coeditor of *Four Hundred Souls* and author of *Until I Am Free: Fannie Lou Hamer's Enduring Message to America*

"Matthew F. Delmont has opened up the conversation about World War II and civil rights in this artfully written book about the nuanced and complex relationship between Black soldiers and war supporters and visions of freedom abroad and at home. Through an absorbing series of narratives, Delmont reconsiders previously held notions of heroism to not only include the Black fighters often left out of stories of World War II but also include the myriad Black workers who staffed the nation's military industries and were subjected to racist attacks as they toiled. A brilliant piece of history, Delmont has ultimately challenged and transformed the definition of the Greatest Generation."

—Marcia Chatelain, Pulitzer Prize–winning author of *Franchise: The Golden Arches in Black America*

"Matthew F. Delmont has written a remarkable account of the shockingly oppressive conditions that African Americans—from the Tuskegee Airmen to the men of the 92nd Infantry to Black Marines—experienced during and after World War II. His research and ability to so eloquently describe those circumstances and the remarkable contributions that these men and women made in achieving our historic victories in Europe and Asia make this book a very compelling read. It ought to be mandatory reading for every member of Congress."

—Tom Daschle, former Senate majority leader

"This is an engaging, inspiring, and elegantly written history of the African American experience in World War II. Matthew F. Delmont illuminates the complex story of the two-front war fought by African Americans at home and abroad. Because of segregation and racism at home, Delmont shows how the 'Half Americans' were among the first to see the war as an existential struggle between forces of fascism pitted against the forces of freedom, democracy, and human rights—both domestically and globally. And Delmont never loses sight of the personal acts of courage, sacrifice, and patriotism that persevered despite harsh racial discrimination in wartime. This is an important book about what we can learn from African Americans in World War II—the warriors, the journalists and poets, leaders and home-front workers. A page-turning must read!"

—Dr. Gordon "Nick" Mueller, president and CEO emeritus, The National WWII Museum

"Meticulously researched and indispensable, this is the World War II book that every history buff and military history fan should be reading."

—*B&N Reads*

"Impeccably researched and deeply moving . . . Delmont weaves a breathless tale of Black men who heroically fought for their country but returned home to inequality, harassment, and joblessness."

—*BookBrowse*

"[A] comprehensive and compelling chronicle of the role of Black Americans in World War II."

—Dr. Glenn C. Altschuler, *Florida Courier*

"[*Half American*] is one of those books that fills in the blanks on the things you missed in history class—or the things you were never told in the first place. The stories in here are stunning and quite moving, but also frustrating, even ninety years after the fact. It's like sitting at the VFW, listening to old war stories that were told in a whisper but that need shouting."

—Terri Schlichenmeyer, *The Philadelphia Tribune*

"[A] superlative and sweeping history . . . Through his prodigious research and chronicling of myriad Black voices, Matthew Delmont shows readers 'what it means to dissent in a democracy.'"

—*Washington Independent Review of Books*

"In a time when questions regarding race in American are troublingly relevant, this meticulously researched retelling makes for necessary reading."

—*Coral Gables Magazine*

"Delmont has produced a thought-provoking and at times disturbing work. Delmont . . . pulls no punches."

—*The Active Age*

HALF

AMERICAN

THE HEROIC STORY *of* AFRICAN AMERICANS FIGHTING WORLD WAR II *at* HOME *and* ABROAD

MATTHEW F. DELMONT

PENGUIN BOOKS

PENGUIN BOOKS
An imprint of Penguin Random House LLC
penguinrandomhouse.com

First published in the United States of America by Viking,
an imprint of Penguin Random House LLC, 2022
Published in Penguin Books 2024

ISBN 9781984880413 (paperback)

THE LIBRARY OF CONGRESS HAS CATALOGED THE HARDCOVER EDITION AS FOLLOWS:
Names: Delmont, Matthew F., author.
Title: Half American : the epic story of African Americans fighting
World War II at home and abroad / Matthew Delmont.
Other titles: Epic story of African Americans fighting World War II at home and abroad
Description: [New York] : Viking, [2022] | Includes bibliographical references and index.
Identifiers: LCCN 2022010535 (print) | LCCN 2022010536 (ebook) |
ISBN 9781984880390 (hardcover) | ISBN 9781984880406 (ebook)
Subjects: LCSH: World War, 1939–1945—Participation, African American. | World War, 1939–1945—
African Americans. | World War, 1939–1945—Social aspects—United States. | United States—Armed
Forces—African Americans—History—20th century. | African American soldiers—History—20th century. |
African Americans—Civil rights—History—20th century. | Race discrimination—United States—
History—20th century. | Racism—United States—History—20th century. |
United States—Race relations—History—20th century.
Classification: LCC D810.B53 D45 2022 (print) | LCC D810.B53 (ebook) |
DDC 940.54/03—dc23/eng/20220328
LC record available at https://lccn.loc.gov/2022010535
LC ebook record available at https://lccn.loc.gov/2022010536

Printed in the United States of America
1st Printing

DESIGNED BY MEIGHAN CAVANAUGH

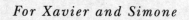

For Xavier and Simone

CONTENTS

INTRODUCTION

Shortly after the attack on Pearl Harbor in December 1941, James Gratz Thompson, a twenty-six-year-old Black cafeteria worker from Wichita, could not sleep. He had registered with the Selective Service the prior year, and now, with the U.S. declaring war on Japan and Germany, it was only a matter of time before he'd be drafted. The prospect of war was frightening for many civilians, but something else was on his mind on that cold Kansas night. Sitting in his family's home, in a vibrant Black neighborhood amid a segregated American city, Thompson wrote a letter to the editor of the *Pittsburgh Courier*, the nation's largest Black newspaper, expressing the concerns that he and many other Black Americans felt about joining a racially segregated military.

"Should I sacrifice my life to live half American?" Thompson asked. "Will things be better for the next generation in the peace to follow? Would it be demanding too much to demand full citizenship rights in exchange for the sacrificing of my life? Is the kind of America I know worth defending?"

Thompson's poignant questions about patriotism had an immediate impact. Hundreds of thousands of Black Americans read his letter printed in the pages of the *Courier*. The influential newspaper used the letter to launch the Double Victory campaign, with the aim of securing victory over fascism abroad and victory over racism at home. The *Courier* ran hundreds of stories, photographs, and cartoons to support this initiative. Double V clubs formed in communities across the country, and civil rights activists touted the slogan.

I have taught about World War II for more than a decade, but researching this book has forced me to see the war with fresh eyes. Taking the twin aims of the Double V campaign seriously—victory over fascism abroad and victory over racism at home—it is clear that the United States did not achieve a full victory in World War II. Although the Nazis were conquered on the battlefield, the racial ideas of white supremacy continued to flourish in America—then and today.

Half American aims to tell the definitive history of Black Americans and World War II. Nearly everything about the war—the start and end dates, geography, vital military roles, home front, and international implications—looks different when viewed from the African American perspective. For Black Americans, the war started not with Pearl Harbor in 1941 but several years earlier with the Italian invasion of Ethiopia and the Spanish Civil War. As soon as Adolf Hitler's regime rose to power in the 1930s, Black Americans recognized the significance of the Nazi threat and the similarities between the Third Reich's and America's racial policies. In the pages of newspapers and in activist refrains, Blacks argued that Nazi racial ideology was not solely a foreign problem. Describing a plan to segregate Jews on German railways, the *New York Amsterdam News* wrote that Nazis were "taking a leaf from the United States Jim Crow practices." The *Chicago Defender* noted that "the practice of jim-crowism has already been adopted by the Nazis" and proceeded to quote from the official newspaper of the SS, the Nazi paramilitary organization, on the American origins of Germany's railway ban on Jews.

In the days after Pearl Harbor, hundreds of Black volunteers were turned away by military recruiters. In a nation mobilizing for war, African Americans first had to fight for the right to serve in the military. Ultimately, over one million Black men and women served in World War II and hundreds of thousands worked in defense industries at home. The trailblazing Tuskegee Airmen, 92nd Infantry Division, Montford Point Marines, and 761st "Black Panther" Tank Battalion served bravely in combat, and Black troops shed blood in the iconic battles at Normandy and Iwo Jima, and in the Battle of the Bulge. Most Black troops, however, labored in unheralded but vital support jobs. Black newspapers highlighted the important roles these men and women played in lesser-known battles and war zones around the world, from New Guinea to Alaska, and from the Mediterranean island of Pantelleria to the mountains of the China-Burma-India theater.

When I started digging into the archival records and military documents regarding the work Black troops did during the war, it became clear to me not only that African Americans served bravely during the war, but that the United States would not have won World War II without the unsung contributions of Black troops.

A global war entailed logistics on a scale that surprised even America's military planners. Indeed, while fighting across the Pacific, Europe, North Africa, and Asia, the U.S. military required unprecedented amounts of food, fuel, medical supplies, ammunition, and other materials. Beyond being a battle of strategy and will, World War II was a battle of *supply*. Black Americans were engineers, quartermasters, construction workers, and supply troops who together formed the backbone of the U.S. military's logistical forces. Black truck drivers moved supplies from ports to the battlefronts; general service regiments cleared jungles, constructed roads, and built runways; navy construction battalions made ports and cleared beaches that enabled Allied invasions; and the Merchant Marine transported troops and supplies around the globe. Black troops fought courageously when given the opportunity in combat, but it was this behind-the-scenes support and supply work that helped the Allies win the war. These Black worker soldiers were largely invisible to white America, but Black journalists sung their praises during and after the war. "I can truthfully report that the record of the American Negro in World War II matches, if not surpasses that of any white man," *New York Amsterdam News* journalist Dan Burley wrote just after the war ended. "To him belongs the credit in winning the battle of supply."

As the popular memory of World War II took shape, the experiences of Black veterans remained peripheral. Years of movies and books focusing on D-Day and platoons in frontline combat have presented a misleading version of how the war was won. From *Life's* pictorial history of World War II in 1946 to *Saving Private Ryan* in 1998, white soldiers were presented as the iconic figures of the war. It's hard to overstate the depth of the disrespect to the Black veteran whose sacrifice has been redacted from history. "There are thousands of Black ex-GIs who will not talk about World War II because for the Black man it was humiliating, degrading, cruel—and not by accident," recalled Staff Sergeant David Cason Jr., a member of the 92nd Infantry Division, which saw combat in Italy. "The treatment of Black soldiers was deliberate, contrived, and planned as well as the Normandy invasion, only the invasion is over but the wounds of the Black soldiers are still raw."

After the war, Black veterans returned to cities and towns that were openly hostile to their presence. Hundreds of veterans were beaten and more than a dozen murdered for being too proud of their uniforms or insufficiently deferential to white people. "The veteran from Okinawa may well be lynched on the streets of a Georgia town if he does not step off the sidewalk when a white woman or man passes," Burley wrote. "He had better not wear his uniform or battle ribbons in Mississippi."

Despite this wave of violence, veterans returned from the war eager to fight for freedom at home. They moved from the "European Theater of Operations to the Southern Theater of Operations," as one veteran put it. For decades after World War II, Black veterans like Hosea Williams, Dovey Johnson Roundtree, Amzie Moore, and Medgar Evers fueled the civil rights movement and fought for the principles of democracy in America. For these veterans and millions of others, winning the war would be only a partial victory if the United States did not also overturn white supremacy and racial discrimination at home.

Of course, most white Americans understood the war to be *only* about defeating the Nazis and Japanese military, a "single V" abroad and the status quo at home. Indeed, many white Americans actively fought during and after the war to maintain white supremacy in the United States, while millions of others turned a blind eye to the injustices of racism while enjoying the benefits of their position atop the racial hierarchy. White politicians lobbied successfully for military bases to be built in their communities and then expressed outrage at the possibility of Black troops being stationed there. When the mayor of a Texas town heard that Black soldiers might be assigned to a local training base called Camp Swift, he asked his congressman to inform the president that he would "personally shoot the first one who came into town." White defense industry workers in Mobile, Philadelphia, and other cities organized "hate strikes," racially motivated walkouts, to protest the integration or promotion of Black defense workers. In Detroit, hundreds of whites carrying signs reading WE WANT WHITE NEIGHBORS IN OUR WHITE NEIGHBORHOOD blocked Black defense workers from moving in to a housing project. White police, bus drivers, and civilians vigorously maintained Jim Crow policies in the South, leading to hundreds of altercations with Black soldiers, some of which escalated, as in the murders of Private Henry Williams in Mobile in 1942 and Private Booker Spicely in Durham in 1944. "The whites think we are fighting a race war, on the streets, at work, and on the buses," wrote a Black staff sergeant stationed in Charleston, South Carolina.

It was not lost on Black Americans that their white countrymen understood the goals of World War II in very different terms. "White folks would rather lose the war than give up the luxury of race prejudice," quipped Roy Wilkins, National Association for the Advancement of Colored People (NAACP) secretary. Historian John Hope Franklin, who volunteered for service in the navy and army but was turned away despite having a PhD from Harvard University, wrote that World War II "raised in my mind the most profound questions about the sincerity of my country in fighting bigotry and tyranny abroad. And the answers to my questions shook my faith in the integrity of our country and its leaders."

As a historian, I am troubled by the collective amnesia in U.S. politics and media around racism. It permeates daily interactions in communities across the country. This ignorance has consequences. When Americans celebrate the country's victory in World War II but forget that the U.S. armed forces were segregated, that the Red Cross segregated blood donations, that Black World War II veterans returned to the country only to be denied jobs and housing, or that Black vets were attacked or murdered for violating the color line, it becomes all the more difficult to talk honestly about racism today.

It is high time that we reckon honestly with the history of World War II and the historical relationship between Nazism and white supremacy in this country. While many white Americans hold idealized notions of World War II as a "good war" fought by the Greatest Generation—an era when America was supposedly greater than it is today—the experiences of Black Americans tell a different story. During the summer of 1943, for example, race riots or rebellions raged across the country. There were more than 240 reports of organized racial violence in cities and at military bases, and most of these conflicts were sparked by police and deputized white civilians attacking Black citizens and soldiers. Then as now, this racial violence raised fundamental questions about America's commitment to democracy for all its citizens. "The treatment accorded the Negro during the Second World War marks, for me, a turning point in the Negro's relation to America," writer and war worker James Baldwin argued. "To put it briefly, and somewhat too simply, a certain hope died, a certain respect for white Americans faded."

Amid the battles over how to tell our national story, the World War II era has largely escaped the scrutiny commonly leveled at the history of slavery, and yet the history of World War II is every bit as fraught as that of the Civil War. The hypocrisy Black men and women faced in the service of their country was palpable. Black troops were forced to ride in Jim Crow railway cars en route to army camps in the segregated South. They drew the shades lest white townspeople pelt the trains with rocks. Soldiers and sailors frequently described feeling as though they were on a plantation. "It was as if we were the slaves and the white officers in our outfit were the overseers," recalled one Black sergeant—a sentiment shared by many. Even America's allies questioned how a nation that upheld racial apartheid at home could claim to fight for a free world abroad. As we grapple with parts of our nation's past that are too often ignored or distorted in textbooks and popular media, we must train our lens on the Greatest Generation.

In these pages you will find stories of Tuskegee Airmen leader Benjamin O. Davis Jr. and the yearslong fight to open the Air Corps to Black pilots; the truck drivers who landed in Normandy after D-Day and drove around the clock delivering critical supplies to General George Patton's 3rd Army as they pushed across France; the 761st "Black Panther" Tank Battalion who served for six consecutive months in four major Allied campaigns, including the Battle of the Bulge; the engineering troops who built the Alaska Highway and the thousand-mile-long Ledo Road between India and China; a Women's Army Corps (WAC) postal battalion that processed millions of letters to and from soldiers in the European theater; the Marines and quartermasters who fought the Japanese military and moved supplies in the Pacific; and many others. Similar to Ernie Pyle, the soft-spoken journalist whose reports from the front gave voice to average white soldiers, Black war correspondents such as Trezzvant Anderson, Ollie Stewart, and acclaimed poet Langston Hughes told the stories of ordinary Black troops and brought the triumphs and tragedies of the war home to Black readers.

Doris Miller, a navy messman who performed heroically at Pearl Harbor, is perhaps the best-known Black American from the war, but he was not the only Black messman whose name rang out after the attack. Julius Ellsberry, a twenty-year-old Mess Attendant First Class on the USS *Oklahoma*, was the first person from Birmingham, Alabama, to be killed in the war. The local Black newspaper compared Ellsberry to Crispus Attucks, the Black hero who was the first American killed in the American Revolution.

Seeing war zones abroad as closely connected to civil rights battlefronts at home also introduces characters who do not typically appear in military histories of the war. Thurgood Marshall, the head lawyer for the NAACP, barnstormed around the country seeking justice for Black troops who were catching hell on military bases. Labor leader A. Philip Randolph fought to integrate the defense industries and the military, rallying thousands in a demonstration of Black political power and proving a thorn in the side of Presidents Franklin D. Roosevelt and Harry Truman. Civil rights activist Ella Baker advocated for Black soldiers, veterans, and their families. Baker believed that ordinary Black people could be leaders and she nurtured these capacities through grassroots organizing and community workshops. The vision of leadership Baker realized was a direct rebuke of the U.S. military's belief that Black Americans lacked the intelligence, courage, and skill to succeed as leaders.

I ATTENDED HIGH SCHOOL at a military academy where the story of World War II was deeply woven into the school's history. The defining event of each year was the presentation of a saber named in honor of an alum and Marine pilot who earned the Medal of Honor for his heroism during the Battle of Midway. With more than four hundred young cadets in our dress uniforms standing at attention in company formation, it was a very moving ceremony. As one of only a handful of Black students, though, I always wanted to know more about how Black Americans experienced the war and fit into this larger story. National narratives of American identity and belonging seemed to include Black people only intermittently. Our textbooks discussed Black Americans during the Civil War and civil rights movement, but hardly anything in between. My mom taught me about the Tuskegee Airmen at an early age, but it was not until I became a professional historian and dug into researching this book that the full story began to emerge. After reading tens of thousands of archival documents, thousands more historical newspaper articles, and hundreds of books, it is clear that there is no history of World War II without Black Americans.

By the early 2020s, there were fewer than three hundred thousand living American World War II veterans, including approximately thirty thousand Black veterans. Their legacy and stories will endure for generations to come. These stories matter. Robert P. Madison, for example, paused his studies at Howard University to serve as a second lieutenant in the 92nd Infantry Division during the war, where he earned a Purple Heart in combat in Italy. After the war he earned architectural degrees from Western Reserve University School of Architecture and Harvard before returning to his hometown of Cleveland to establish a trailblazing architectural firm. Late in his life, Madison recalled a trip to a bookstore. "I saw this great big volume on World War II, and I leafed through it. I didn't see one reference to any Black soldiers or any Black airmen at all in the book. We were a forgotten group of people," he said. "I think we ought to show and represent everyone who fought in that war. And when I say fight, I don't mean were in battle, but who supported it, who were the ordnance, the quartermaster corps, the cooks . . . cause that is a record. That's our history."

My hope is that the Black veterans, war workers, and citizens who fought not only enemy armies but also their own countrymen to secure freedom and democracy will finally be recognized.

ONE

BLACK AMERICANS FIGHTING FASCISM IN SPAIN

If democracy is to be preserved in Europe, it must first be preserved in Spain. The world must rise to that issue or face an even greater offensive of the fascist powers.

—LANGSTON HUGHES

Several years before the United States officially entered World War II following the attack on Pearl Harbor, Black Americans were tracking the international spread of fascism closely. News relating to the Spanish Civil War, in particular, was especially captivating for them. In the pages of influential Black newspapers like the *Chicago Defender* and the *Baltimore Afro-American*, prominent Black journalists opined on the significance of the war for African Americans. Among such writers was Langston Hughes. Already internationally renowned at age thirty-five, Hughes followed the news in July 1936, as the Spanish military organized a coup against the popularly elected left-wing Republican government. General Francisco Franco, who viewed Nazi Germany as a model for Spain and went so far as to keep a framed picture of Adolf Hitler on his desk, emerged as the leader of the Nationalist forces. He appealed for military support from Nazi Germany and fascist Italy. Hitler and Italy's Benito Mussolini both quickly obliged, sending airplanes, tanks, troops, and supplies that gave Franco's army a decided military advantage over the Republican forces. Hitler and Mussolini saw Spain as a valuable ally. They were eager for their militaries to gain battlefield experience in preparation for a larger war in Europe, one that looked increasingly likely with each passing day. By August 1936, a headline in the *Chicago Defender* read WORLD WAR SEEN AS DUCE, HITLER AID FASCISTS IN WARTORN SPAIN.

For Langston Hughes, the coup was of interest not solely for what it signified for the progression of the war, the import of which was plain enough, but for the personnel it had drawn to resist it. Over thirty thousand international volunteers had come to the aid of the embattled Republican government. Three thousand of these volunteers were Americans, who, with many others, had risked their lives to serve in a civil war thousands of miles from home. And of this group, more than eighty men and women were Black. The Americans became known collectively as the Abraham Lincoln Brigade and fought side by side in racially integrated units that stood in stark contrast to the segregated U.S. military. While they were ultimately on the losing side in Spain—the Nationalists would win the war two years later—the Lincoln Brigade volunteers were clear-eyed about the threat Franco, Hitler, and Mussolini posed, and they were the first Americans to take up arms to stop the spread of fascism in Europe. Hughes wanted to tell their story.

But before he could write about the Lincoln Brigade, Hughes had to find a way to get to Spain. He had spent much of the 1930s traveling the globe after earning acclaim during the Harlem Renaissance a decade earlier. Eager for the attention his byline might draw to their paper, the *Baltimore Afro-American* hired him as a war correspondent. Assuming that press credentials would be a sure ticket to Spain, Hughes was disappointed to learn that the U.S. State Department did not think writers for the *Afro-American* merited them. Further complicating the matter, the State Department was not issuing passports for citizens to visit a war zone, so he could not travel directly to Spain. Instead, he planned to reach the country via France, following the path of like-minded writers, including Ernest Hemingway, George Orwell, John Dos Passos, and Hughes's friend Nancy Cunard, who were flocking to cover the civil war. He boarded an ocean liner called the RMS *Aquitania* in New York on June 30, 1937, and sailed for Paris, a city he'd fallen in love with a decade earlier.

In the City of Light, Hughes walked the cobblestone streets of Montmartre, the "little Harlem" of Paris. Nights were filled with jazz, drinks, and gossip; days were consumed with talk of the war in Spain. Hughes gathered with writers at the Second International Writers' Congress to debate what would happen if the military revolt in Spain was successful. Black people were intimately familiar with fascism in America, he argued, and proceeded to describe Jim Crow segregation in schools, theaters, and concert halls; dozens of horrific lynchings in the prior decade; and innocent Black defendants sentenced to jail or death by all-white juries. Hughes was not a bombastic speaker, but rather spoke in an even, assured tone. He could sometimes appear bored while reading his older poems for audiences, but when discussing contemporary events, his understated and direct speaking style conveyed passion and urgency. "Yes, we Negroes in America do not have to be told what Fascism is in action," he said. "We know. Its theories of Nordic supremacy and economic suppression have long been realities to us."

Hughes was building on a chorus of Black voices who recognized that the German Third Reich saw the American system of race law as a model and that Nazi ideology was not solely a foreign problem. "The racial policy of the Hitler movement is strikingly similar to that of the neo–Ku Klux Klanism of America," sociologist and public intellectual Kelly Miller noted three years prior, in 1933. Two years later, a *New York Amsterdam News* editorial argued, "If the Swastika is an emblem of racial oppression, the Stars and Stripes are equally so." Hughes received a rousing ovation in Paris for saying what many Black Americans were thinking at the time— that fascism was Jim Crow with a foreign accent.

After nearly a month in France, Hughes boarded a train from Paris to Barcelona with Cuban poet and journalist Nicolás Guillén. Crossing the border between France and Spain, the two men changed trains in the seaside town of Portbou. It was a quiet, sunny morning when they arrived. Children were swimming in the shimmering blue water of the Mediterranean. The view was idyllic. As Hughes looked around, however, the idyll was disturbed. The walls of the small customhouse were pocked by machine-gun bullets. Nearby, several houses lay in ruin, destroyed by aerial bombs. Signs reading REFUGIO pointed to mountain caves where people hid during the frequent air raids.

Leaving Portbou, they arrived in Barcelona in darkness, just before midnight. The train cars, station, and city were blacked out so fascist planes would not have easy targets. Hughes and Guillén followed the crowd as they departed the station, inching slowly in the dark toward the single lantern flickering at the end of the long platform. Guillén traveled light and helped Hughes carry his bags, books, records, and typewriter. They boarded a bus, and as the bus drove through pitch-black streets from the train station to the hotel, Hughes wondered what he had gotten himself into.

He'd barely managed to unpack and settle in for his first night in Barcelona when the realities of war were thrust upon him. In the middle of the night, he heard the low wail of an air-raid siren warning that fascist planes—German-made Junkers and Heinkels, as well as Italian-produced Savoia-Marchettis and Capronis—were approaching from Majorca across the Balearic Sea. Several loud explosions shook the walls of the hotel, and the lights went out. He jumped out of his bed, flung open the door to his room, and stumbled down a dark, crowded hallway. He descended the staircase to the lobby, where the flame of a candle provided the only light and cast shadows on the walls. The other hotel guests were in various stages of undress. Children cried while adults spoke frantically in Spanish, English, and French. His hands trembling, Hughes struggled to put his trousers on over his pajamas and light a cigarette. Outside, ambulance sirens wailed, and antiaircraft guns fired in loud, percussive bursts, driving the enemy planes away. Hughes did not sleep that night.

Two weeks later, venturing west to Madrid, Hughes arrived to find the city on edge, besieged by fascist batteries shelling nearly every day. "The crack of rifle fire, the staccato run of the machine-guns, and the boom of trench mortars and hand grenades can be heard so clearly that one finally realizes the war is only a few blocks away," Hughes wrote.

Despite being close to the front lines in Madrid, Hughes's accommodations were palatial. He was welcomed by the Alianza de Intelectuales Antifascistas (Alliance of Antifascist Intellectuals), a group that formed out of the International Writers' Congress. Led by Spanish poets Rafael Alberti and María Teresa León, the group occupied a house with dozens of rooms formerly owned by a marquis whose family had earned a fortune from the slave trade. The home was well appointed with antique furniture and medieval tapestries. Paintings by Francisco Goya and El Greco adorned the walls. Sometimes the writers and artists raided the closets for matador jackets and flamenco dresses. Hughes's jazz records provided the soundtrack for what became impromptu costume balls.

The meals were far less lavish. With no trains running into Madrid, all supplies came in on a single road, and food for the city's one million people was strictly rationed. Hughes and the other guests subsisted on two meals a day. Breakfast was a scant roll and coffee made from burnt grain. The cook worked what magic she could to make dinner appetizing, with meager rations of beans, onions, olive oil, and bread. On the rare occasions when there was fish or meat, each guest would get a thin slice in their soup. Between air raids, Hughes searched Madrid for bars serving tidbits with drinks. Hunger pains never abated, and Hughes lost fifteen pounds during the six months he was in Spain.

Hughes navigated between the different war zones in Spain based on reports from soldiers on leave from the front and leads from other journalists, such as *Chicago Daily News* correspondent Leland Stowe. One tip led him to the outskirts of Madrid, a couple of miles from the front, where Hughes finally caught up with the Abraham Lincoln Brigade. Their camp, hidden under trees, was barely visible from the road. Several hundred men were briefly at rest, but there was a rumble in the air.

Near a camouflaged tent painted zigzag green and brown, Hughes met Thaddeus Battle, a twenty-one-year-old who had paused his premed and political science studies at Howard University to volunteer. Battle was bespectacled and mild mannered, and his helmet and brown fatigue jacket fit awkwardly on his slight frame. As the two men smoked cigarettes in a tent on a chilly fall afternoon, they reminisced about how much they missed the street-corner diners in D.C. and Harlem with their steaks, hamburgers, and ice cream. Battle said he was not eager for war but felt that he had to leave school for Spain. "When we see certain things happening in Europe and Asia that may involve America in another world war, then . . . we see clearly the need for combatting such tendencies at home and abroad," he told Hughes. Battle's family had raised him to view books as precious and he was particularly outraged to witness Franco's fascist troops destroying schools and libraries.

As the afternoon faded, Hughes followed Battle to the cook tent for dinner. Among the Irish, English, and white American soldiers waiting for rabbit stew, Battle introduced Hughes to another Black volunteer, Bernard "Bunny" Rucker, the twenty-five-year-old son of a Christian minister. Rucker was good with his hands and worked on road construction projects during the Great Depression. Like Battle, Rucker now served as a truck driver in the Lincoln Brigade, transporting men and supplies to the front lines. It was dangerous work. Drivers often faced machine-gun fire and were sometimes strafed by German Condor Legion planes, Rucker explained. During the bloody Battle of Brunete in July, where Lincoln volunteers suffered more than three hundred casualties, Rucker was caught in heavy bombardment and a plane crashed into flames near his truck. This same man, who only a year prior had been living an ordinary life in Columbus, Ohio, was now having close brushes with death in a war zone. Hughes took notes.

With the temperature falling into the thirties, Hughes was shivering in a lightweight jacket, cursing the thoughtlessness with which he'd packed. When Rucker offered Hughes his wool overcoat, the poet was reluctant to take it, feeling the acute shame of being so underprepared, but the young truck driver insisted, saying that he could get another coat back at camp. And so Hughes wore the jacket during his winter in Spain and for years afterward.

Once the men finished dinner, Rucker borrowed one of the brigade trucks to give Hughes a ride back to his makeshift hotel in Madrid. Hughes was up late that night working on an article for the *Baltimore Afro-American* when he felt an artillery bombardment that was even more unsettling than the air raid he experienced in Barcelona. A shell whistled by his window and struck a building at the end of the block. Hughes's room shook so violently that his typewriter fell off his desk. "Sounded like the devil's 4th of July!" he wrote to a friend.

Days after Hughes met Battle and Rucker, the *Afro-American* started publishing his stories from Spain. "The Spanish situation is but a prophecy of what all Europe is approaching," the newspaper read, "and from this angle colored men and women here in America and throughout the world will be interested." Hughes's wartime articles did not disappoint. Each dispatch warned that a life-and-death struggle against fascism was under way in Spain and that Black Americans were among the first to try to stop Franco, Mussolini, and Hitler.

As Hughes tracked the war during the fall of 1937, the Republican forces met a series of military defeats at the hands of Franco's army, losing key territory along the northern coast and suffering thousands of casualties. Even seeming Republican victories, such as an offensive in the small town of Belchite that momentarily stalled Nationalist advances between Madrid and Barcelona, came at a tremendous cost in terms of tanks, aircraft, and men.

Hundreds of Lincoln Brigade troops were wounded in battle and many were cared for by fellow volunteers, medical professionals who had ventured to Spain. At a field hospital near the Madrid front, Hughes met one of these medical volunteers, a twenty-three-year-old nurse, Salaria Kea, whom he found particularly captivating. A native of Akron, Ohio, and a graduate of Harlem Hospital's nursing school, Kea was the first and only Black American nurse to serve in the Spanish Civil War. Kea did not consider herself to be political, but as a devout Catholic, she felt a calling to help people in need. When Mussolini's Italian army invaded Ethiopia in October 1935, Kea and a group of Harlem nurses raised enough money to send a seventy-five-bed field hospital to the besieged African nation. At New York University, where Kea took additional nursing courses, she met Jewish doctors who had fled from Germany. They described the terror of Hitler and the Nazi regime. She followed European war news in the pages of Black newspapers and was outraged to read about the bombings of churches and civilians. Going to Spain had felt all but inevitable. She volunteered for an American Red Cross mission only to be turned away. Her skin color made her more trouble than she was worth, they told her. There was room for her, however, among the ranks of the Lincoln Brigade.

When Hughes met Kea in late October 1937, she had been in Spain for six months, more than enough time to see the terror of modern warfare firsthand. She was no stranger to death. As the head nurse in the tuberculosis unit at Harlem Hospital, the only leadership role open to Black nurses, she had cared for hundreds of patients at the end of their lives. Still, she was shocked to see so many men, women, and children maimed in Spain. Bullets and shrapnel delivered horrible wounds, and bombing raids produced seemingly endless casualties. Lacking adequate supplies, due in part to the U.S. embargo against the Spanish government, the nurses had to wash and boil old bandages to sanitize them before wrapping them around new patients. Her medical unit traveled to various fronts, getting as close to the action as possible. At one battle, she could see Republicans and fascists lobbing hand grenades at each other and felt the hill quiver with each blast. She'd then watch and wait from barely a hundred yards away as newly wounded men would arrive at the mobile hospital. Her soft eyes and charming smile gave way to a look of focused determination. She cared for Black and white troops, all while under constant threat of attack. When she was working at a field hospital in Hijar, Spain, fascist troops broke through the front line and began bombing the hospital. With explosions shaking the ground, Kea dove into a nearby trench. She was knocked unconscious and buried under several feet of debris before fellow volunteers dug her out. Miraculously, she suffered only a sprained back, remarking later, "I guess my luck was good that day."

From Madrid, Hughes ventured 180 miles northeast to the International Brigades training base in Tarazona. He hitched a ride with a military convoy that traveled over shell-scarred roads shared by oxcarts and peasants on muleback. The truck, carrying soldiers and the poet, sped through countryside, past groves of oranges and olives, fields of wheat, and towns gutted by bombs. After surveying demolished eighteenth-century buildings in one small town, Hughes said it was "a kind of preview of what happened later to other larger and more famous European cities in World War II."

When Hughes arrived at the training base in November 1937, he was surprised to find a Black first lieutenant leading a staff of white officers and a diverse group of troops, including Black American, English, Irish, Jewish, Cuban, and Mexican volunteers. The officer was Walter Garland, a tall, handsome twenty-three-year-old from Brooklyn. Before volunteering for the Lincoln Brigade, Garland had enlisted and served two years in the U.S. Army and worked as a musical arranger for *Your Hit Parade*, a radio show sponsored by Lucky Strike cigarettes. He'd arrived in Spain as a private in January 1937 and saw combat the next month in the Battle of Jarama, just east of Madrid. He volunteered to carry ammunition to the front, past two lines of enemy fire, and suffered a bullet wound in the stomach. The cartridge boxes around his waist stopped the bullet from penetrating deeper and saved his life. Garland spent two months in the hospital and then attended the Republican army's Officers' Training School, earning a commission as a second lieutenant. A second wound at the Battle of Brunete forced

Garland to retire from combat. Now a first lieutenant, he was placed in charge of the training base in order to prepare the next cadre of volunteers. A white American volunteer credited Garland with building esprit de corps among the International Brigades and whipping untrained youth into warriors. "He instilled in me the conviction that we could go out there and take on the whole professional fascist armies and kick the shit out of 'em," the volunteer said.

Hughes timed his trip to the training base to coincide with a visit by two U.S. congressmen, John Bernard of Minnesota and Jerry O'Connell of Montana, who opposed the U.S. government's neutrality in the Spanish Civil War. In addition to a banquet and sports festival, a military parade was planned in honor of the guests. Wearing brown uniforms and steel helmets, the soldiers were led by Garland as they marched proudly in long ranks of three in the bright Spanish sunshine. Winding through the narrow village streets, they passed the reviewing stand and then stood at attention in the town square before the officers and dignitaries. Congressman Bernard praised Garland and the troops: "I have the greatest admiration for every one of you. . . . We know that you represent the cause of world democracy, the success of that cause will be a blow to Mussolini and Hitler." After marching, the American ranks started singing "The Star-Spangled Banner."

Seeing Garland in command of hundreds of men, Hughes was mesmerized. "I couldn't help but think about the army back home," Hughes wrote, "with its segregation of Negro troops, the difficulty Negroes have in securing military training, in entering the various National Guards, in being promoted to higher officerships, in being barred from Aviation and the Marines. But here in this antifascist army, Negroes and whites marched, trained, and fought together."

In contrast to Congressmen Bernard and O'Connell's advocacy in Spain, most Americans favored isolationism. In October 1937, President Franklin D. Roosevelt delivered a speech in Chicago calling for "quarantine" to check the expansion of aggressor nations and stop the present "reign of terror and international lawlessness." Roosevelt was referring to Germany, Italy, and Japan, though he did not cite these nations or their conquests by name. "Without a declaration of war and without warning or justification of any kind, civilians, including vast numbers of women and children, are being ruthlessly murdered with bombs from the air," Roosevelt said. "Innocent peoples, innocent nations, are being cruelly sacrificed to a greed for power and supremacy which is devoid of all sense of justice and humane considerations." Although the "Quarantine" speech was the president's strongest statement to date regarding the need for the international community to check the spread of fascism, the United States' policy of neutrality and nonintervention remained in place and was supported by Congress and the majority of Americans.

HUGHES WROTE CONSTANTLY IN SPAIN, often scribbling drafts in notebooks on the war front. His dispatches in the *Afro-American* profiled volunteers like Ralph Thornton, a thirty-five-year-old from Pittsburgh who stormed a fascist-held building in the Battle of Belchite; Abraham Lewis, a heavyset lieutenant from Cleveland who was in charge of clothing and feeding the volunteers; and Basilio Cueria, an Afro-Cuban former baseball star who led a machine-gun company. Hughes described how the Lincoln volunteers included Black

World War I veterans like Leroy Collins, Alonzo Watson, and Oliver Law, who proudly took up combat roles in the brigade that they were denied in the U.S. Army. The thirty-six-year-old Law was appointed commander of the Lincoln Brigade shortly before the Battle of Brunete, making him the first Black American to lead an integrated battalion. Law was trying to lead his troops up a ridge, waving his pistol to urge them on, when he was fatally wounded.

Each of these profiles was read by hundreds of thousands of people, thanks to the *Afro-American*'s distribution network. Circulation was highest in Baltimore, Washington, D.C., and the mid-Atlantic states, but dealers also sold the paper in cities like Cleveland, Houston, and St. Louis. His articles provoked discussions in barbershops, living rooms, on street corners, and elsewhere. Several friends and even a few strangers wrote Hughes to praise his dispatches from Spain.

Hughes also channeled what he witnessed during the war into poetry, adopting the persona and voice of a fictional Lincoln Brigade volunteer, "Johnny" from Alabama. In "Love Letter from Spain: Addressed to Alabama," he told a sweetheart back home that he was writing from a frontline trench in the mud and rain:

> Just now I'm goin;
> To take a Fascist town.
> Fascists is Jim Crow peoples, honey—
> And here we shoot 'em down.

These verses shortened the distance between Spain and the South. Hughes encouraged readers to see links between fascism abroad and at home. "Postcard from Spain: Addressed to Alabama" described the superior treatment Black soldiers received in Spain:

> Folks over here don't treat me
> Like white folks used to do.
> When I was home they treated me
> Just like they treatin' you.

Written in colloquial language, Hughes's poems and profiles presented the Black volunteers in Spain as relatable citizen soldiers. Readers could see themselves, their family members, and their neighbors in his portraits of the soldiers, truck and ambulance drivers, nurses, and cooks who volunteered in Spain. These types of personal connections across the ocean made war news in Europe urgently important for Black Americans.

At the same time, Hughes showed that these volunteers were part of a global fight. He described meeting "wide-awake men of color" from across the United States, the Caribbean, and Africa, "all of them here because they know that if Fascism creeps across Spain, across Europe, and then across the world, there will be no place left for intelligent young Negroes at all." Wearing uniforms with the insignia of various Republican and volunteer regiments, these soldiers, Hughes predicted, would soon be recognized internationally. Whereas the most prominent Black American ambassadors in Europe had been entertainers, Hughes felt that the Lincoln Brigade had a larger purpose. "These Negroes in Spain were fighters—*voluntary fighters*—which is where history turned another page," he wrote.

Hughes was putting a rosy spin on an increasingly dire situation for the Lincoln Brigade and Republican forces, which wanted for allies and weapons. Germany and Italy continued to support Franco's army, providing airplanes, tanks, artillery pieces, machine guns, and rifles, as well as tens of thousands of troops. The Italian Aviazione Legionaria and German Condor Legion flew hundreds of raids, bombing strategic targets in Barcelona, Madrid, and Valencia, killing and wounding both Republican fighters and civilians. International support for Spain's Republican government was significantly less robust. Mexico gifted the republic twenty thousand rifles, while Soviet leader Joseph Stalin directed his advisers to trade guns, tanks, and planes for Spanish gold. France, Great Britain, and the United States could have made similar deals to support a fellow democracy but continued to stay on the sidelines in Spain's civil war, believing that they could indefinitely postpone a confrontation with fascism. This imbalance in firepower was palpable on the battlefield, where the Lincolns' mission felt more quixotic by the day.

GIVEN THESE LONG ODDS, Hughes kept returning to one simple question in his conversations with the Black volunteers: Why did you come to Spain? What was true for people like nurse Salaria Kea held for many other volunteers, and many Black Americans in general; that is, that the war against fascism abroad started in October 1935 when Mussolini's Italian army invaded Haile Selassie's Ethiopia. When European powers colonized the African continent in the decades before World War I, Ethiopia's independence became particularly important for Black people around the world. After the Italian invasion, Black journalists warned that a monumental global conflict was imminent. "Unless there is a succession of miracles the first bomb that Italy drops on Ethiopia will be the signal for another World War," the *Norfolk Journal and Guide* predicted in 1935.

Organizations formed across the country to defend Ethiopia, and street corner speakers in Harlem urged Black people to give what they could to support the cause. "From New York to California, from Seattle through the everglades of Florida, there are more than eight million Black Men in America alone awaiting only transportation to rush to the defense of Ethiopia," the *Atlanta Daily World* maintained. Hughes's "The Ballad of Ethiopia," published in the *Afro-American*, also sounded this call:

> All you colored peoples,,
> Be a man at last.,
> Say to Mussolini,,
> No! You shall not pass!!

For the Black Lincoln volunteers, the desire to defend Ethiopia from fascism was realized in Spain. As volunteer Oscar Hunter explained in a short story, "I wanted to go to Ethiopia and fight Mussolini. . . . This ain't Ethiopia, but it'll do."

These soldiers saw fighting Spain as a proxy not only for defending Ethiopia, but also for combating racism in the United States. James Robinson, a volunteer from New York City, said he was convinced a fascist victory in Spain would embolden the Ku Klux Klan in America and "tighten more the chains of segregation and lynching that already engulf us." Hughes echoed these concerns. "Give Franco a hood and he would be a member of the Ku Klux Klan," he argued. "Fascism is oppression, terror and brutality on a big scale."

A soldier from New York said Spain presented a rare opportunity for Black people to go on the offensive, with guns and bullets, against racists. He considered himself lucky to be able "to strike a blow at the counterparts of those who oppress us at home."

WHEN HUGHES RETURNED HOME in January 1938 after a half year in Spain, he was broke. Fortunately, churches, colleges, and civic organizations across the country were eager to pay to hear him talk about the war in Spain. "If democracy is to be preserved in Europe, it must first be preserved in Spain," he told a crowd in Chicago. "The world must rise to that issue or face an even greater offensive of the fascist powers." The speech garnered boisterous applause, and crowds in Cincinnati, Milwaukee, Richmond, and other cities responded with similar enthusiasm.

In these lectures, Hughes also read poems that expressed his concerns for his country and the world, including "Song of Spain" and "Let America Be America Again." In the latter poem, Hughes expressed hard-earned bitterness about his country, while also calling for a new America to rise from the ashes of the Depression:

> O, yes,
> I say it plain,
> America never was America to me,
> And yet I swear this oath—
> America will be!

These poems were included in *A New Song*, a booklet published by the International Workers Order (IWO) in spring 1938. At only fifteen cents a copy, *A New Song* brought Hughes's poetry about the Spanish Civil War and American racism to thousands of readers.

When Salaria Kea returned to the United States from Spain in May 1938, she also embarked on a twenty-city speaking tour. The tour was organized by activist Thyra Edwards to raise funds to send ambulances and medical supplies to Spain. One hundred and fifty nurses and civic leaders welcomed Kea at the YMCA in Harlem. Edwards offered a warm introduction, saying that Kea's "slender brown hands have carried the banner of the Race people brilliantly and honorably on the war front in Republican Spain."

Kea described how, as her boat from Europe docked in New York City, she saw the Nazi flag fluttering from the smokestack of a German passenger liner. She began to cry. "Can you imagine that?" she said. "Here I have been out fighting for democracy and freedom for a whole year and come back to the United States to face that!"

The young nurse challenged the audience to take an active role in the fight against fascism in Europe. "What is happening there is not just a civil war, but in reality an invasion of Mussolini's and Hitler's fascist forces," she argued. "If those forces were victorious in Spain, it would be easy for them to invade France and eventually America." Kea commanded the crowd's attention. She urged her listeners to recognize the dire threat fascism posed. "Either you begin to fight now, or wait until the fight is brought to our very door," she warned. "And then, it might be too late."

She fell in love in Spain and married a volunteer ambulance driver, a quiet Irishman named John Joseph O'Reilly. Interracial marriages were illegal at the time in more than half of the United States. "I could not go South with him," Kea remarked of her new husband. Kea went on to serve in the U.S. Army Nurse Corps in World War II. Her husband became a U.S. citizen and fought in the U.S. Army during the war.

Kea, Walter Garland, and several dozen Lincoln Brigade veterans joined over fifteen thousand demonstrators for a peace march in New York City in August 1938. The fifth annual parade, sponsored by the American League for Peace and Democracy (formerly the American League Against War and Fascism), observed the anniversary of the start of World War I. The marchers chanted "Down with fascism, up with democracy" and "Lift, lift, lift the embargo on Loyalist Spain" as they made their way from Eighth Avenue and Fortieth Street to Madison Square Park. Kea marched alongside an ambulance, the side of which was painted to read FROM THE NEGRO PEOPLE OF AMERICA TO THE PEOPLE OF REPUBLIC SPAIN. The ambulance, sponsored by Paul Robeson, A. Philip Randolph, Hughes, and other prominent Black figures, was shipped to Spain shortly after the march. The crowd joined Reverend William Lloyd Imes, a civil rights activist and pastor of the city's St. James Presbyterian Church, in pledging to support the people of Spain, China, and Ethiopia facing fascist persecution. The marchers' voices echoed off buildings in Midtown Manhattan, sounding notice that despite the government's position of neutrality, many Americans were prepared to stand in opposition to fascism.

Meanwhile, the situation in Europe grew more ominous. Nazi Germany annexed Austria in March 1938 and then set its sights on democratic Czechoslovakia At a meeting in Munich on September 29 and 30, 1938, Hitler reached an agreement with Mussolini, British prime minister Neville Chamberlain, and French prime minister Édouard Daladier that Germany could annex the western region of Czechoslovakia, an area with over three million German-speaking people that had been part of Austria-Hungary prior to World War I. Since the League of Nations had failed to intervene when Italy invaded Ethiopia, another member state, and with Britain and France now acquiescing to Hitler's demands in the Munich Agreement, the Black press worried that democratic nations and institutions would do little to stem the tide of fascism in Europe. "Four gangsters met last week to divide the property of an innocent victim," the *New York Amsterdam News* argued. "Instead of making the world or even Europe secure they have only planted the seeds of further discontent which will lead to—war. . . . Ethiopia. Spain. Czechoslovakia. What's next?" Hughes wrote that Czechoslovakia had been "lynched on a swastika cross" and wondered, "Where will the long snake of greed strike again? Will it be here, brother?"

The Spanish Civil War led Hughes to reevaluate his commitments as a writer and to more forcefully challenge America to live up to its ideals. Speaking at Carnegie Hall, he described how the pain of lynching, Jim Crow segregation, and the humiliation of everyday discrimination made Black people a separate caste. As a writer, Hughes felt he had a crucial role to play in addressing apartheid in America. "We do not want any secondary Americans," Hughes said. "We do not want a weak and imperfect democracy . . . We want America to really be America for everybody. Let us make it so!"

As Hughes envisioned a truly democratic America, he could not ignore the escalating hostilities in Europe. Nazi persecution of Jews intensified, and in November 1938, paramilitary forces destroyed Jewish homes, schools, hospitals, stores, and synagogues, murdering dozens. This pogrom, known as Kristallnacht (night of the broken glass), received international news coverage and brought the terror of the Nazi regime into clearer focus for millions of people. In March 1939, Hitler's troops marched into Prague and laid claim to the Czech regions of Bohemia and Moravia, in violation of the Munich Agreement. Six months later, Hitler and Stalin, former arch-enemies, signed a neutrality agreement. The German-Soviet Nonaggression Pact allowed Hitler to invade western Poland and Stalin to control eastern Poland, and outlined plans for how the two powers would divide Eastern Europe. Nazi troops struck Poland on September 1, 1939, and two days later, Great Britain and France declared war on Germany. The Second World War had officially begun.

Hughes was shocked and humiliated by the Soviet pact with Nazi Germany. The Soviet Union had backed Republican Spain, trading military equipment and helping recruit thousands of volunteers from more than fifty countries. Hughes assumed the Soviet Union would be a bulwark against the spread of fascism in Europe. Although he was not a member of the Communist Party, Hughes treasured his travels to Russia in the early 1930s and quietly supported the Soviet Union throughout the decade, even as news of Stalin's brutal persecution of his foes came to light. Just a week before the pact, Hughes signed an open letter urging the United States to cooperate with the Soviet Union in the fight against fascism. As Hitler and Stalin divvied up Poland, Hughes felt like he had been duped and that the Lincoln Brigade had been betrayed. After the pact, Hughes grew more circumspect in statements on communism and the Soviet Union but remained fiercely and vocally opposed to racism in America and Nazism overseas.

In January 1939, Franco's forces, backed by Italy and Germany, seized control of Barcelona. Three months later, the Republican army surrendered. Overwhelmed militarily, the Republican forces also struggled during the civil war with infighting among their coalition of trade unionists, peasants, regional separatists, socialists, communists, and anarchists. Exhausted and dejected, the surviving members of the Lincoln Brigade returned to America in late 1938. Over a third of the American volunteers died in Spain, a higher proportion than that of the Spanish who fought for the Republican army. Eulogizing the American dead, Ernest Hemingway wrote, "No men ever entered earth more honorably than those who died in Spain."

The U.S. government, however, regarded all of the Lincoln veterans with suspicion, since many were members of the Communist Party and because the Soviet Union had backed Republican Spain. Lincoln veterans endured regular visits from the FBI for decades after they returned to the United States. Congressman Martin Dies, a Texas Democrat and first chair of the House Un-American Activities Committee, said the Spanish Civil War veterans were subversives because "if you were against Hitler and Mussolini before Dec. 7, 1941, you were a premature anti-Fascist."

James Yates recalled being detained by the FBI when he and other volunteers docked in New York. The FBI men "looked and acted as if they would have been more comfortable with the fascists we had been fighting in Spain," Yates wrote. They seemed baffled by what Black men from Alabama, Mississippi, and New York were doing fighting a war across the Atlantic.

Despite this official harassment, Yates and over 425 Lincoln veterans served in the American military during World War II, with a hundred more in the Merchant Marine. Bunny Rucker, the young truck driver who gave Hughes his overcoat, returned to Columbus,

Ohio, and helped found the Vanguard League, a civil rights group that fought to integrate community swimming pools and movie theaters. He was inducted into the U.S. Army in February 1942, along with his five brothers, and assigned to the segregated 92nd Infantry Division. Rucker fought in Italy in the Rome-Arno, the Northern Apennines, and the Po Valley campaigns, earning three Bronze Stars and a Purple Heart. Edward A. Carter Jr. fought for more than two years as a volunteer in Spain and then joined the U.S. Army shortly before Pearl Harbor. Originally assigned to a segregated quartermaster unit, Carter volunteered for infantry duty and saw combat in Germany as part of General Patton's 12th Armored Division. Carter was posthumously awarded the Medal of Honor for his heroism. Thousands more International Brigades volunteers from other nations also fought with the Allies.

The Black Americans who fought in the Spanish Civil War and those who followed the war through Hughes's accounts in the pages of the Black press had a very different origin story for the start of World War II than most white Americans. Years before Pearl Harbor, the stakes of fighting fascism were clear to Black Americans. As war clouds gathered over Europe, it was less clear that the United States military welcomed their service.

TWO

FIGHTING FOR A
CHANCE TO FIGHT

What, in the final analysis, do we ask? We plead, "Let us die for America if need be!" We are AMERICANS. This is our country which we would glorify before the entire world.

—ROBERT VANN, *The Pittsburgh Courier*
PUBLISHER AND EDITOR

Shortly after the end of the Spanish Civil War in the summer of 1939, Benjamin O. Davis Jr. arrived in Tuskegee, Alabama. Davis had graduated from the U.S. Military Academy at West Point in 1936. The son of a colonel, Davis was tall and boyishly handsome, with a military pedigree and bearing that rivaled those of any of his white contemporaries. The army, however, did not know what to do with him. Ever since he was a teenager and his father had brought him along for a ride with a barnstorming flier, Davis had desperately wanted to be a pilot. But when he applied for the U.S. Army Air Corps in his senior year at West Point, they rejected his application, citing that the Air Corps had no Black units. While nearly all his West Point classmates had received orders to lead troops, the army assigned Davis to be a professor of military science and tactics at the all-Black Tuskegee Institute. He had an officer's rank and uniform, but it appeared that there would be no real career for him in the army.

Davis knew that Black Americans had fought in integrated units in Spain and that at least one, James Lincoln Holt Peck, was commissioned as a pilot in the Spanish Republican Air Force. He found it galling that his own country denied him and other Black troops the same opportunities. On his current career path, Davis had a slim chance of leading men into combat, especially as a pilot. In a few short years he would be leading Black fighter pilots, the trailblazing Tuskegee Airmen, on missions in North Africa and Europe. But before these barriers would be broken, several battles lay ahead. If Black Americans were going to serve in World War II, they would have to fight for the right to fight.

Unsurprisingly, Davis's military peers and superiors dismissed his potential, as the army's official position was that Black servicemen were inferior as soldiers, officers, and human beings. Although Black Americans served bravely in every war fought by or within the United States, military leaders actively discouraged Black people from enlisting in the two decades after World War I. In 1925, for example, the Army War College published a report titled "The Use of Negro Manpower in War." The report drew on white officers' biased evaluations about how Black troops had performed in World War I, as well as on craniometry and other pseudoscientific theories, to argue that Black people lacked the intelligence, courage, and moral character to thrive as military leaders or soldiers. The report made dozens of outrageous claims:

> [The Black soldier] is mentally inferior to the white man. . . .
>
> The cranial cavity of the negro is smaller than the white; his brain weighing 35 ounces contrasted with 45 for the white. . . .
>
> The negro is profoundly superstitious. He is by nature sub-servient and naturally believes himself inferior to the white. He is jolly, tractable, lively and docile by nature, but through real or supposed harsh or unjust treatment may become sullen and stubborn. . . . He has not the physical courage of the white. He simply cannot control himself in fear of some danger in the degree that the white man can. . . .
>
> The negro is unmoral. He simply does not see that certain things are wrong. . . .
>
> An opinion held in common by practically all officers is that the negro is a rank coward in the dark.

These were not the isolated beliefs of a prejudiced individual or clique, but the official position of the U.S. Army on the worthiness of Black Americans. One generation of white army officers produced a profoundly racist assessment of Blacks in the military and passed their views on to the next generation of white officers, almost all of whom went on to serve in World War II.

The Army War College's guidance on Black troops echoed throughout America's military leadership. Colonel Ewart G. Plank, a West Point graduate who served in Britain during World War II, described Black soldiers as "akin to well-meaning but irresponsible children" who "generally cannot be trusted to tell the truth, execute complicated orders, or act on their own initiative except in certain individual cases." Henry Stimson, a World War I veteran who shaped military policy as the secretary of war during World War II, explained the lack of Black officers in his diary: "Leadership is not imbedded in the Negro race yet and to try to make commissioned officers to lead men into battle—colored men—is to work disaster to both."

General Thomas Holcomb, commandant of the United States Marine Corps from 1936 to 1943, was adamant that Black men were not welcome in his branch. "If it were a question of having a Marine Corps of 5,000 whites or 25,000 Negroes, I would rather have the whites," he said. Major General Edward Almond, who commanded the 92nd Infantry Division in Europe during World War II, thought poorly of the Black troops in his segregated division and firmly believed that racial integration would weaken the military. "There is no question in my mind of the inherent differences in races," Almond said. "This is not racism—it is common sense. Those who ignore these differences merely interfere with the combat effectiveness of battle units." These official views on Black troops trickled down to enlisted men. "White officers in general . . . have solidified false ideas about Black troops," argued Staff Sergeant Bill Stevens, a Black soldier who served in the 48th Quartermaster Regiment in World War II. "Their attitude toward Black soldiers is entirely different from that shown whites and these attitudes are immediately picked up by white enlisted men."

The army used these attitudes to justify reductions to Black military regiments during the 1930s and to transition Black combat units from World War I, like the 10th Cavalry, one of the original "Buffalo Soldier" regiments, to noncombat duty. As a result, the percentage of Black Americans in the army declined from around 10 percent in 1917 to less than 2 percent in 1937. When Davis arrived at Tuskegee, there were only 6,500 Black soldiers in the army's 360,000 troops. While one in every ten American citizens was Black, that proportion dropped to one in every fifty American soldiers.

Meanwhile, with war brewing internationally, President Roosevelt asked Congress in January 1939 for $300 million to enable the all-white Army Air Corps to grow from fourteen hundred to six thousand planes, plus the necessary spare parts, equipment, supplies, and aircraft hangars. Military leaders understood that the Air Corps, which Major General Frank M. Andrews described as a "fifth rate air force," would need to be enlarged and modernized if they were going to have any hope of competing with the German Luftwaffe. Congress approved the appropriation three months later, enabling a prodigious expansion of the American aerial forces.

Davis and other Black observers were outraged that the growth of the Air Corps meant more flying, training, and service opportunities for white Americans only. "This huge force of . . . war planes will cost a whole lot of money, and that money will come out of the pockets of everybody in this country," *The Pittsburgh Courier* argued. "Are Negroes going to fly those planes as well as pay for them?" The *Baltimore Afro-American* reprinted a rejection letter sent to Eugene Dixon, a Black Philadelphian who inquired about joining the Air Corps, advising him against filing an application at present. General Henry "Hap" Arnold, chief of the Army Air

Corps, was more explicit, telling his general staff that Black pilots could not serve in the Air Force because having Black officers command white enlistees would "create an impossible social condition." The *Courier* called the Air Corps a "lily-white" branch and demanded that Black citizens also be given the right to learn to fly.

While they initially made little headway with the Army Air Corps, advocates for Black pilots were successful in getting Representative Everett Dirksen, a Republican from Illinois, to add an anti-discrimination provision to the Civilian Pilot Training Act. Signed by President Roosevelt in June 1939, the act authorized the Civilian Aeronautics Authority to expand a civilian pilot training program. The program resembled civilian training programs already under way in Germany and Italy and was designed to rapidly increase the number of aviators in the United States.

Soon, a handful of Black colleges and training facilities, including Howard University, Tuskegee Institute, and Illinois's Coffey School of Aeronautics and North Suburban Flying School, were training hundreds of Black civilian pilots. The *Chattanooga News-Free Press*, a white daily, reported that 100 percent of the students in Tuskegee's aviation program passed in the first year, placing it ahead of segregated white technological schools like Georgia Tech, Auburn, and the University of North Carolina. Black leaders continued to push the Air Corps to train Black military pilots, not just civilian ones, and began jockeying over whether this training should take place on a segregated basis, as at Tuskegee, or at an integrated facility, like the Coffey School in suburban Chicago.

Teaching at Tuskegee Institute, Davis was only five miles away from Kennedy Field, where Tuskegee's civilian aviation program was based in 1940 and early 1941. As Tuskegee transformed into a hub for Black aviators, Davis envied the pilots who were soaring through the air near campus. His mind drifted back to that first experience in a barnstormer's plane. Wind whipped past him as the open-cockpit aircraft made steep turns and climbed into the clouds before diving low and returning to the safety of the dirt runway of Washington, D.C.'s Bolling Field. He experienced the same feeling of exhilaration as the passenger on a training ride while he was a cadet at West Point. The memories of these fleeting moments of flight came rushing back as he watched the Black pilots circling above Tuskegee. Despite his officer's rank, it seemed unlikely that he would ever realize his aspirations to fly for the army, and thus it was, for him, bittersweet.

AT THE SAME TIME that Davis's dreams of flying were fading, the NAACP and Black press were becoming vocal critics of the military's treatment of Black troops. Charles Hamilton Houston, the NAACP special counsel and a World War I veteran, visited several posts where Black units were stationed and wrote to General Douglas MacArthur to express his disappointment at the retrenchment of Black troops. "The Army has consistently discriminated, and is even now discriminating, against Negro officers and troops," Houston wrote. The War Department excluded Black Americans from newer arms of the service like the Air Corps, blocked Black officers from duty with troops, and reduced Black regiments to service battalions. He wrote to the White House to warn that if the United States went to war, Black Americans would "not again silently endure the insults and discriminations imposed on its soldiers and sailors in the course of the last war."

For Houston, the issue was deeply personal. He had served as an army first lieutenant in France during World War I and was one of more than 350,000 Black war veterans who returned home hopeful that their service in Europe would result in more racial equality in the United States. Instead, Houston was left disillusioned by the hate and scorn Black veterans experienced from their fellow Americans. In the first six months after World War I there were twenty-eight public lynchings, and at least seven Black army veterans were murdered while still wearing their uniforms. "The very uniform on a Negro was to the reactionary like a red rag thrown in the face of a bull," historian Carter G. Woodson wrote. "Negro soldiers clamoring for equality and justice were beaten, shot down, and lynched, to terrorize the whole Black population."

White violence against Black veterans was part of a larger campaign of terror designed to reinforce and strengthen the hold of white supremacy after the war. Over two dozen cities and towns witnessed organized anti-Black riots in the "Red Summer" of 1919, including Houston, Chicago, and Elaine, Arkansas. Twenty years later, as America edged closer to a new war, Houston resolved that the next generation of Black soldiers would be treated with respect.

Pittsburgh Courier editor Robert Vann was also ready to spill some ink in the fight for Black troops. Vann used Roosevelt's "Quarantine" speech and the prospect of an expansion of the armed forces to lobby for the formation of a separate Black division that would include combat units. *Courier* readers on February 19, 1938, found a headline calling for a "Campaign for Army, Navy Recognition" and an open letter from Vann to President Roosevelt. Vann stressed that Black Americans were eager to serve their country, but they were being denied this opportunity. "Even Negro combat troops have been made to feel that they are the domestic servants of the army in peace time," Vann argued. "This tends to stifle patriotism."

Vann gave ten reasons why Black Americans deserved equality in the army and navy. He highlighted the service of Black veterans in previous wars while arguing that Black Americans' taxes helped support the military, that Black Americans deserved to share in the educational benefits of service, and that Black troops would inspire the next generation of Black Americans. "What, in the final analysis, do we ask?" Vann wrote. "We plead, 'Let us die for America if need be!' We are AMERICANS. This is our country which we would glorify before the entire world."

The *Courier*'s campaign garnered support from Congressman Hamilton Fish, a Republican from New York who, as a white officer, served with a Black unit in France during World War I. Fish worked with Vann to write three bills, which Fish introduced in April 1938, appealing for an end to discrimination in the military, for the formation of a Black army division, and for the president to appoint two Black cadets to West Point every year. Vann lobbied tirelessly in support of this legislation, meeting with President Roosevelt in April and again in October. Vann described the president as being "very sympathetic" to the bills, but Roosevelt declined to voice support for the bills publicly because, as a Democrat seeking reelection, he did not want Republicans to get credit from Black voters for proposing the legislation.

NAACP leaders were divided over whether to support the *Courier*'s call for a separate Black division. NAACP secretary Walter White argued that such a unit would only entrench segregation in the army, and that the NAACP needed to "fight the evil of jim-crowism, past, present, and future." Roy Wilkins and Charles Hamilton Houston, however, shared Vann's more pragmatic analysis that real integration in the armed forces was not possible in the near term and that it was more important to get Blacks into all branches of the military.

The Vann-Fish bills ultimately died in the House Military Affairs committee, where twelve of the twenty-six members were Southern segregationists. Nonetheless, the *Courier* campaign led millions of Black civilians to focus their attention on military discrimination and laid the groundwork for the paper's Double V campaign during the war.

In the summer of 1940, Black leaders concentrated on Washington, D.C., where Congress was debating the Selective Service Act, the first peacetime draft in American history. The National Committee for Participation of Negroes in the National Defense, funded by Vann and the *Courier* and led by Howard University professor and World War I veteran Rayford Logan, urged lawmakers to add antidiscrimination provisions in the draft legislation. Logan told a congressional committee that Black citizens should be given a chance to serve equally in all branches of the military. He expressed frustration that Black citizens had to beg to bear arms in the nation's defense. Representing the NAACP, Charles Hamilton Houston testified that Black Americans "want some of the democracy they fought for in 1917 this time, and the sooner the better." The committee's campaign also prompted thousands of Black Americans to write to the War Department to ask about the military's policy for Black troops. The correspondence was so heavy that the adjutant general created form letters for replies.

Hamilton Fish and Senator Robert Wagner, also of New York, supported these efforts and proposed amendments to the draft bill to prohibit racial discrimination. Several Southern congressmen pushed back, arguing that such provisions would open the door to integration within and potentially beyond the military. Texas senator Tom Connally argued that it was unacceptable for Black soldiers to "serve in the same companies, sleep in the same rooms and eat at the same tables as white soldiers." Passing the draft bill with antidiscrimination amendments, he argued, would amount to a surrender to Black Americans "who want continually to agitate, disturb, stir up discussion, and raise the devil about what they speak of as their political and social rights."

Despite these objections, the Selective Service Act passed both the House and the Senate with the antidiscrimination amendments and was signed by President Roosevelt on September 14, 1940. Over sixteen million men between the ages of twenty-one and thirty-five were required to register for the draft and prepare for the likelihood of military service. As 1940 drew to an end, America inched closer to war.

AFTER TWO YEARS of continuous lobbying by the *Courier*, NAACP, and other civil rights advocates, the Selective Service Act had finally cracked open the door for more Black Americans to serve in the military. Yet the military's policy of segregation continued to limit these aspirations. The final version of the act included a provision, added at the request of military leaders, that no man would be inducted unless he was "acceptable to the land or naval forces for such training or service" and until "adequate provision could be made for shelter, sanitary facilities, medical care and hospital accommodations." This gave the army and navy grounds to reject potential volunteers and draftees they found unfit for service based on their own eligibility standards, while also ensuring that Black recruits would remain segregated. When the army announced a quota plan in which Black recruits would make up a percentage of the branch proportionate to their share of the total population (9 to 10 percent), they had neither enough regiments to which they could assign and train Black troops nor enough facilities for housing and feeding Black troops apart from their white compatriots. Thousands of Black Americans went to recruitment centers after President Roosevelt signed the Selective Service Act, only to be told that the army did not yet have space for them.

Draft boards also thwarted Black citizens from joining the military. Managed at the state and local levels, these drafts boards determined which men were fit or unfit for military service, as well as which men qualified for deferrals because their civilian work was essential to national defense. Local draft boards were ultimately where the Selective Service Act's antidiscrimination provisions were followed or flouted. Black Americans made up less than 1 percent of the over 25,000 people serving on 6,500 local boards. An NAACP survey in January 1941 found that seventeen states had all-white draft boards that were openly hostile to Black registrants. White recruiting officers frequently refused to serve induction notices to Black draftees who were classified as 1-A, "acceptable for military service." In the South, planters used their influence to get deferments for valued workers, keeping Black sharecroppers on farms and out of the military and defense industries.

The *Courier* reported that army officials ordered draft boards in New England to exclude Black Americans from the first draft. When Black ministers asked Tennessee governor Prentice Cooper to appoint Black representatives to local draft boards, he said, "This is a white man's country. America was settled by English, Scotch and Irish settlers who came here and shed their blood for it. White men cut down the trees, plowed the fields and developed America. The Negro had nothing to do with the settling of America." Cooper offered this distorted view of history to justify why only whites should be able to determine who was fit to serve in America's armed forces.

Many other Black applicants were turned away because they failed the Army General Classification Test, an early standardized test that purported to measure the intelligence and aptitude of recruits. A 1953 study by Columbia University professors found that 90 percent of these potential recruits attended segregated schools and were deprived of basic educational opportunities to learn how to read and write. In his diary, Secretary of War Stimson admitted that "the Army had adopted rigid requirements for literacy mainly to keep down the number of colored troops." Illiteracy rates were also high among white Southerners, but the War Department made exceptions to actively recruit them into the service.

Thousands of Black Americans volunteered to join the navy, but here, too, they met with unequal opportunities. Shortly after the Selective Service Act passed, Secretary of the Navy Frank Knox announced that Black volunteers would be segregated and could serve only as mess attendants aboard ships, where they would cook and clean for white officers. In the navy's view, segregation was necessary for general ship efficiency. "This policy not only serves the best interests of the Navy and the country, but serves as well the best interests of Negroes themselves," Knox argued.

Black messmen serving in the navy disagreed. Fifteen mess attendants aboard the USS *Philadelphia* stationed at Pearl Harbor wrote to the *Courier* to discourage other Black men from joining. Describing themselves as "sea going bellhops, chambermaids and dishwashers," the messmen said white sailors were advanced in rating after finishing training and given a pay increase to thirty-six dollars per month, while Black sailors were paid only twenty-one dollars a month and had limited opportunities for promotion. "With three months of training in making beds, shining shoes and serving officers completely, we are sent to various ships and stations of the Navy," they wrote. The men boldly signed their names to their protest letter and were quickly punished by the navy, which dishonorably discharged two of the sailors and gave undesirable discharges to the others.

In response, the National Committee for Participation of Negroes in the National Defense ran a large advertisement in the *Courier* urging readers to "REMEMBER THE THIRTEEN NEGRO MESSMEN OF THE U.S.S. PHILADELPHIA!," to organize mass protest meetings in their cities, and to write their congressmen. "White America is preparing for war," the ad warned. "All the plans, as they are put into practice, exclude Negroes. The War Department and the Navy Department plans for the coming war DEGRADE you. They would make war without you if they could. They would challenge your right to citizenship . . . Negros are Americans and you have a way to make known your wants."

The NAACP's Roy Wilkins also saw the navy's mess-attendant

policy as a fundamental challenge to Black citizenship. "There is more to all this than standing on the deck of a warship in a white uniform," Wilkins wrote in a powerful editorial in the NAACP's *The Crisis* magazine. "To be stigmatized by being denied the opportunity of serving one's country in full combat service in the Navy is humiliating enough. But the real danger and greater injustice is to deny a tenth of the citizens of this country any benefit whatsoever from the billions of dollars spent on our Navy." Black Americans paid taxes to support the Naval Academy and maintain naval bases, facilities, and training programs, from which they were excluded. The navy offered white sailors valuable job training, education, health care, character building, and travel, but denied Black Americans the same opportunities. "This is the price we pay for being classified as a race, as mess attendants only!" Wilkins argued. "At the same time we're supposed to be able to appreciate what our white fellow citizens declare to be the 'vast difference' between American Democracy and Hitlerism."

Complaints over racial discrimination in the military extended to the Air Corps as well. A cover of *The Crisis* featured a picture of an army fighter plane flying over Randolph Field, Texas, with a caption noting that this training was "FOR WHITES ONLY . . . Negroes are not being accepted and trained by the Army air corps at any field in the nation, despite all the talk of national unity and of the urgency of every group serving in national defense." Inside the magazine, an article by James Lincoln Holt Peck asked "When Do We Fly?" Peck, the Black pilot who saw combat with the Republican Air Force in the Spanish Civil War, praised the development of the United States' airpower. American factories were producing the finest warplanes in the world, and the army was training thousands of pilots to fly them. Mechanics, technicians, and maintenance workers, nearly two hundred thousand in all, were needed to keep the planes and pilots in the air. And yet Black Americans were being locked out of this buildup. "The issue becomes one of Negroes fighting for a chance to fight for the greatest democracy in the world," Peck contended. "We must lick a certain bigoted clique in Washington—and points north and south—before we can get at Adolf. And boy, how we want to get to Adolf! The battle on the 'home front,' however, is of more immediate import."

The *Courier* built on Peck's article with an editorial arguing that Black Americans "cannot FLY Uncle Sam's planes. They cannot SERVICE Uncle Sam's planes. They cannot MAKE Uncle Sam's planes. The only thing they CAN do and are compelled to do is to PAY for Uncle Sam's planes." Yancey Williams, a twenty-four-year-old Howard University engineering student who had completed primary flight training through the Civil Aeronautics Authority, sued the War Department on behalf of himself and other Black volunteers after being denied admission to the Army Air Corps. The *Chicago Defender* commended Williams's actions, writing, "The sooner we learn through official declaration whether Uncle Sam wants us to defend him or not, the better it will be for all concerned. We must make our stand now: Either we fight for democracy or we fight for segregation."

THESE FIGHTS OVER the military's racial policies and the draft played out against the backdrop of the 1940 election. While President Roosevelt led in the polls through the summer and fall, it was not a foregone conclusion that he would defeat Republican Wendell Willkie to win a third term or that he would carry the majority of the Black vote. Black migration out of the South meant that Black citizens formed key voting blocs in several cities in the Northeast and Midwest, and both parties saw military opportunities as an important issue for these voters. The Republican Party platform called for an end to discrimination in the army and navy, which the *Courier* deemed the "strongest plank in the history" of the party. For their part, the Democrats' platform mentioned Black Americans by name for the first time.

Roosevelt was trying to thread the needle by appealing to Black voters without alienating the Southern segregationist wing of the Democratic Party who felt threatened by Black political power. Senator Josiah Bailey of North Carolina said, "The catering by our National Party to the negro vote in Philadelphia, Chicago, New York, Boston and St. Louis is not only extremely distasteful to me, but very alarming indeed." A delegate from South Carolina similarly complained, "Our national party is being led around by the negroism of the North. I am mortally afraid of the negro in our national party." Republicans ran a full-page ad in the *Baltimore Afro-American* noting that President Roosevelt had promoted one hundred white colonels to the rank of brigadier general while skipping over Benjamin O. Davis Sr. "What chance have colored draftees when Roosevelt decrees . . . WHITE OFFICERS ONLY!" the ad read.

The week before the election, the president tried to make up lost ground. He promoted the sixty-three-year-old Colonel Davis to brigadier general, making him the first Black general in the U.S. Army. Roosevelt also appointed William Henry Hastie, dean of

Howard University School of Law, as civilian aide to Secretary of War Henry Stimson, and named Colonel Campbell C. Johnson, a professor of military science at Howard, as an adviser to the director of the Selective Service. The Black press generally praised these politically motivated appointments, while Stimson lamented in his diary that "the Negroes are taking advantage of this period just before [the] election to try to get everything they can in the way of recognition from the Army."

The younger Davis was thrilled when he learned of his father's promotion to brigadier general. He was proud that his father had broken another barrier in the military and, more selfishly, he saw the promotion as a chance to advance his own career. After spinning his wheels for two years teaching military science at Tuskegee Institute, Davis moved to Fort Riley, Kansas, to serve as an aide to his father, who was commanding the 4th Cavalry Brigade, composed of Black troops and white officers.

News of the war in Europe and Asia quickened the pace of life on the base, and the officers speculated about when the United States would be drawn into the conflict. Although Davis still could not use the all-white Officers' Club, the "lukewarm" reception he received at Fort Riley was an improvement over the "deep freeze" at West Point and Fort Benning.

Davis's stay at Fort Riley ended up being shorter than he anticipated. In early 1941, the chief of the Air Corps wrote to General Davis to request that his son be released for pilot training in a newly formed all-Black pursuit squadron at Tuskegee. The general quickly agreed, and Davis reported to Tuskegee Army Air Field in May to pursue his dream of becoming a fighter pilot.

For Davis, the five years after he graduated from West Point had been filled with fitful progress and frustration. He closely followed the campaign against military discrimination in the pages of the Black press. He took heart from the number of Black leaders and everyday citizens who spoke out against the shabby treatment the government offered Black soldiers and recruits. At the same time, he wondered if policies would change quickly enough to alter his career prospects. The facts on the ground did not look good. He saw only limited opportunities in the rigidly segregated military.

"In 1941 the Army still regarded all Blacks as totally inferior to whites," Davis recalled, "somewhat less than human, and certainly incapable of contributing positively to its combat mission." Still, the idea that Davis would be joining a training program for Black fighter pilots was almost unimaginable five years earlier. "For the first time I saw vague possibilities for a military career that could go far beyond assignments as a professor of military science and tactics at Black colleges," Davis wrote.

Although he was among the Black American elite, Davis's military career was a microcosm of the challenges faced by hundreds of thousands of other Black volunteers and draftees who found the military to be openly hostile to their presence. Black Americans were eager to serve their country, but the army, navy, and Marines were reluctant to harness this patriotism and manpower. It took organized campaigns for Black Americans to secure a foothold in the military, and from enlisted troops to officers like Davis, Black Americans understood their service to be an important battleground in the fight for full equality.

On the eve of America's entry into World War II, a parallel battle over discrimination in defense industries illustrated the power of Black protest. A. Philip Randolph, who founded and led the nation's first major Black labor union, rallied Black Americans to demand equal access to war jobs. Randolph proposed a bold tactic—a massive Black protest march on Washington—that would influence civil rights activism during the war and for decades to follow.

THREE

MARCH ON WASHINGTON

If Negroes are going to get anything out of
this National Defense which will cost the
nation 30 or 40 billions of dollars that we
Negroes must help pay in taxes as property owners and workers and consumers,
WE MUST FIGHT FOR IT AND FIGHT
FOR IT WITH GLOVES OFF.

—A. PHILIP RANDOLPH

Settling into his den at home in the Dunbar Garden apartments in Harlem, New York, A. Philip Randolph turned on
the radio. Like millions of Americans, Randolph was eager to
hear what President Roosevelt would say in his Fireside Chat that
December night in 1940. At 9:30 p.m. the president addressed the
nation. "My friends, this is not a fireside chat on war," Roosevelt
began, "it is a talk on national security, because the nub of the
whole purpose of your President is to keep you now, and your children later, and your grandchildren much later, out of a last-ditch
war for the preservation of American independence and all of the

things that American independence means to you and to me and to ours."

During the 1940 campaign, Roosevelt had promised that the United States would not declare war against the Axis powers unless the country was attacked. Now, weeks after being elected to an unprecedented third term, Roosevelt told Americans that it was crucial for America to provide military support to Britain and European allies. "The people of Europe who are defending themselves do not ask us to do their fighting," Roosevelt said. "They ask us for the implements of war, the planes, the tanks, the guns, the freighters which will enable them to fight for their liberty and for our security. Emphatically we must get these weapons to them, get them to them in sufficient volume and quickly enough, so that we and our children will be saved the agony and suffering of war which others have had to endure." Roosevelt argued that only American defense industries could stop the Nazis and other Axis powers who aimed to enslave and dominate the human race. "We must be the great arsenal of democracy," Roosevelt told the country. "For us this is an emergency as serious as war itself."

Unlike most Americans, Randolph expected to be able to convey his thoughts on the war directly to the president. At fifty-one years old, he led a union of over fifteen thousand Black railroad workers, which made him one of the most powerful Black people in the country. Over the prior fifteen years, Randolph had fought successfully to have the Brotherhood of Sleeping Car Porters (BSCP) recognized by the Pullman Company, the American Federation of Labor (AFL), and the U.S. government. He secured wage increases for the porters as well as a reduction in monthly work from 400 to 240 hours. "There was no other group of Negroes in America who constituted the key to unlocking the door of a nationwide struggle for Negro rights as the porters," Randolph said. "Without the porters I couldn't have carried on the fight for fair employment, or the fight against discrimination." These gains resonated nationally and established Randolph as a formidable advocate for Black workers.

Randolph's success as a labor leader and civil rights activist grew out of decades of exposure to radical Black thinkers. His parents raised him on stories of Frederick Douglass, Harriet Tubman, Nat Turner, and of the political power Black people briefly held during the Reconstruction era after the Civil War. His father, Reverend James Randolph, was an itinerant African Methodist Episcopal (AME) preacher who told his son about Henry McNeal Turner, an AME bishop, Civil War veteran, and politician who protested when white legislators attempted to expel newly elected Black state representatives. "I am here to demand my rights, and to hurl thunderbolts at the men who would dare to cross the threshold of my manhood," Turner said in 1868. "The Black man cannot protect a country if the country doesn't protect him; and if, tomorrow, a war should arise, I would not raise a musket to defend a country where my manhood is denied." Pointing to Turner and Black militants in history, the elder Randolph encouraged young Asa Philip to "speak the whole word," and to stand up for justice regardless of the consequences.

Randolph took this advice to heart when he moved from Jacksonville, Florida, to Harlem in 1911 at the age of twenty-two. He took free courses at City College, joined the Socialist Party, and became a soapbox speaker. Randolph was tall, dark-skinned, slender, and sharply dressed. He was also a gifted orator, with a speaking style that drew on his father's preaching and his own love of theater and Shakespeare. Crowds loved it. On Harlem's street corners, Randolph held forth on everything from the history of slavery to the French Revolution.

Alongside another young radical, Chandler Owen, Randolph started *The Messenger*, a monthly magazine where they sparred with Marcus Garvey and W. E. B. Du Bois, as well as elder Black leaders who they termed "the old guard." While he considered Du Bois's *The Souls of Black Folk* to be the most influential book he had ever read, Randolph opposed World War I and was incensed that Du Bois had published an editorial in *The Crisis* in July 1918 encouraging Black Americans "to forget our special grievances and close our ranks shoulder to shoulder with our own white fellow citizens and the allied nations that are fighting for democracy."

Randolph and Owen struck a very different tone that same year in an open letter to President Woodrow Wilson in the pages of *The Messenger*. "Lynching, Jim Crow, segregation, discrimination in the armed forces and out, disenfranchisement of millions of Black souls in the South," they argued, "all these things make your cry of making the world safe for democracy a sham, a mockery, a rape of decency and a travesty on common justice." After Randolph urged Black citizens to refuse military induction until the government stopped discriminating, federal agents arrested him for violating the Sedition Act. U.S. Attorney General A. Mitchell Palmer called Randolph and Owen "the most dangerous Negroes in the United States." For Randolph, the United States did not deserve the service of Black Americans in the First World War.

He initially felt the same way about World War II. In early 1940, he argued that Black Americans should oppose America's entrance into war because the "fingers of England and France [are] dripping with the blood of black, yellow and brown colonials." But as much as Randolph despised colonialism, he came to see Hitler as a different type of menace. The Nazi ideology that Blacks were subhuman changed his mind about the war. By the end of that year, when Roosevelt called for America to ramp up its defense production, Randolph was a member of the Committee to Defend America by Aiding the Allies and shared the president's sense of urgency about America supporting Britain. "If Britain loses, democracy and liberty lose," he wrote.

Randolph understood how much was at stake for Black Americans. Transforming the United States into the "arsenal of democracy" would mean millions of new jobs, but Randolph knew that if employers and unions continued to practice business as usual, Black workers would be left out of the defense industry boom. In Buffalo, New York, the Curtiss-Wright and Bell aircraft plants had no Black employees in production jobs. "While we are in complete sympathy with the Negro, it is against company policy to employ them as aircraft workers or mechanics . . . regardless of their training," the president of North American Aviation said. "There will be some jobs as janitors for Negroes." The head of Kansas City's Standard Steel vowed, "We have never had a Negro worker in twenty-five years and don't intend to start now."

Black newspapers and civil rights advocates fielded reports of racial discrimination from across the country at hundreds of manufacturers. Lester Granger, executive secretary of the National Urban League, described how experienced Black electricians, carpenters, bricklayers, and cement workers were blocked from defense industry jobs, despite labor shortages. "When these dark-skinned craftsmen moved forward to take their places at the hiring gates, they were met with outright refusal by contractors who, in the same breath, continued to shout for more workers," he wrote. The U.S. Employment Service (USES) asked a number of defense industries about their hiring practices and more than half said that they would not hire Black workers. Several made these policies explicit with signs advertising HELP WANTED, WHITE.

While defense work provided economic stability for many white Americans after the Depression, Black communities continued to face high levels of unemployment. From April to October 1940, the unemployment rate declined from nearly 18 percent to 13 percent for white workers but remained at 22 percent for Black workers. Randolph was as familiar as anyone with this data on employment discrimination, and the numbers were not encouraging. He knew that if Black Americans were going to participate fully in the arsenal of democracy, they were going to have to fight for it.

Just two weeks after the president's Fireside Chat, Randolph issued a bold call to action. "Negroes are not getting anywhere with National Defense," Randolph wrote in *The Pittsburgh Courier*. "The whole National Defense Setup reeks and stinks with race prejudice, hatred, and discrimination." The solution was to do something that would shock government officials. Randolph called for ten thousand Black people to march on Washington, D.C., with the slogan "WE LOYAL NEGRO-AMERICAN CITIZENS DEMAND THE RIGHT TO WORK AND FIGHT FOR OUR COUNTRY." He felt that this huge march was necessary because the regular and respectable methods of holding conferences and signing petitions had proved ineffective.

Rather than civility and negotiations, Randolph emphasized the importance of Black people recognizing and wielding their power to force the adoption of a given policy. In Randolph's estimation, this power flowed not from him or other Black leaders but from ordinary Black citizens. "Power is the active principle of only the organized masses, the masses united for a definite purpose," he argued. "If Negroes are going to get anything out of this National Defense which will cost the nation 30 or 40 billions of dollars that we Negroes must help pay in taxes as property owners and workers and consumers, WE MUST FIGHT FOR IT AND FIGHT FOR IT WITH GLOVES OFF."

RANDOLPH FORMED THE March on Washington Movement (MOWM) in January 1941 and, with eighteen regional coordinators and hundreds of grassroots activists, spread the word about the march. Several Black newspapers endorsed the idea of the march but were initially skeptical about its feasibility. "To get 10,000 Negroes assembled in one spot, under one banner with justice, democracy and work as their slogan would be the miracle of the century," *Chicago Defender* editors wrote. The proposed march gained traction because of Randolph's stature as a labor leader. "It was Randolph's immense prestige among all classes of Negroes that made this idea something more than a pretentious notion," said the Urban League's Lester Granger. Other high-profile Black leaders supported the march, including Mary McLeod Bethune, who led the National Council of Negro Women, and NAACP secretary Walter White.

The march idea gained momentum in the early months of 1941 thanks to a national network of organizers. Pullman porters promoted the march in Chicago, Detroit, Los Angeles, Oakland, and other cities. Young women sold buttons reading NEGROES MARCH FOR JOBS IN NATIONAL DEFENSE to raise money to charter buses and trains. Supporters posted bulletins explaining the march's goals in bars, pool halls, beauty parlors, and stores in Black neighborhoods. MOWM regional coordinators, such as former porter T. D. McNeal, rallied support after Randolph came through town on his speaking tour.

While others tended to the day-to-day logistics, Randolph ratcheted up the pressure on President Roosevelt and other Washington officials to racially integrate defense industries and the military. In March, he issued an official call for the March on Washington and set a date: July 1, 1941. "Let the Negro masses speak!" Randolph urged in the pages of *The Black Worker*, the magazine of the Brotherhood of Sleeping Car Porters. "Let the Negro masses speak with ten thousand Negroes strong, marching down Pennsylvania Avenue in the Capital of the nation." Randolph envisioned Black Americans from all walks of life marching in ranks, singing "John Brown's Body" and "Before I'll Be a Slave, I'll Be Buried in My Grave," carrying banners demanding defense jobs, equal employment and vocational training, and integration in all branches of the military.

Randolph pictured the march ending with a huge demonstration at the Lincoln Memorial. Two years earlier, Black contralto Marian Anderson had sung there in front of seventy-five thousand people after the Daughters of the American Revolution refused to permit her to sing in Constitution Hall. Like Anderson's open-air concert, the march would be a rebuke to Jim Crow policies in the nation's capital. "Is Jim-Crow in Washington?" Randolph asked. "What a question! Is water wet? Is fire hot? . . . Washington is not only the capital of the nation. It is the capital of Dixie. . . . There, crackerocracy is in the saddle. Ku Klux Klanism runs riot."

Beyond challenging racial segregation in Washington, D.C., Randolph saw the march as a call for the nation to live up to its ideals. "We are simply fighting for our constitutional rights as American citizens," he argued. "We hold no allegiance to an alien state. This is our own, our native land. Let us fight to make it truly free, democratic and just . . . We are Americans. We are patriots. We are fighting for the right to work! We are fighting for the right to live!"

For Randolph, Black patriotism was rooted in dissent and the desire to fight for full citizenship. "We will fight for Uncle Sam! We are opposed to totalitarian tyranny, Fascist, Nazi and Communist. We will fight for democracy! Yes, we will fight! Indeed, we would rather die on our feet fighting for Negroes' rights than to live on our knees as half-men; as semi-citizens, begging for a pittance."

Randolph made it clear that while the MOWM was not anti-white, it was important for Black Americans to carry out the march on their own. "We call not upon our white friends to march with us," he said. "There are some things Negroes must do alone. This is our fight and we must see it through. If it costs money to finance a march on Washington, let Negroes pay for it. If any sacrifices are to be made for Negro rights in National Defense, let Negroes make them. If Negroes fail this chance for work, for freedom and train-ing, it may never come again."

By calling on Black people to organize, Randolph challenged the military's official assessments that Black Americans lacked the in-telligence and courage to be leaders. The marchers would not only demand full equality, they would also demonstrate through their discipline and resolve that the beliefs white officials and citizens used to justify their second-class status were deeply misguided. While Benjamin O. Davis Jr. and other Black airmen, soldiers, and sailors fought against these racist stereotypes within the military, Randolph felt a civilian protest would exert even more pressure from the outside.

"Nobody expects 10,000 Negroes to get together and march anywhere for anything at any time," Randolph said. "They are supposed to be just scared and unorganizable. Is this true? I contend it is not." The *Afro-American* argued that the magnitude of Randolph's proposed march made it hard for white America to ignore. "One individual marching up and down Pennsylvania Avenue in front of the White House denouncing race prejudice is arrested as a crank and spirited away by policy," the editors contended. "Ten thousand persons get respectful attention. The public feels there must be something radically wrong when a crowd is moved to demonstrate against injustice."

By the end of May, it was impossible for Washington officials to ignore the March on Washington Movement. Randolph made sure of this by sending letters to the president, First Lady Eleanor Roosevelt, Secretary of War Henry Stimson, Secretary of Labor Frances Perkins, and others, inviting them to address the protesters on July 1. The First Lady told Randolph he was making a grave mistake and warned that the march would spark bitterness and backlash in Congress. The president and Sidney Hillman of the Office of Production Management sent memos to defense plants urging them to hire Black workers, but Randolph insisted that he would accept only an executive order.

Randolph also pressured the White House through the Black press. Pointing to Abraham Lincoln's issuing of the Emancipation Proclamation, Randolph challenged President Roosevelt to follow in Lincoln's footsteps "and take the second decisive step in this world and national emergency and free American Negro citizens of the stigma, humiliation and insult of discrimination and Jim-Crowism in Government departments and national defense." He also upped the ante, calling for ten times the number of Black marchers as originally planned to converge on Washington, D.C. The front-page headline in the *New York Amsterdam News* on May 31 read 100,000 IN MARCH TO CAPITAL.

Roosevelt agreed to meet with the march leaders but asked Randolph to stop preparations at once. Randolph demurred, telling the president via telegraph, "The hearts of Negroes are greatly disturbed . . . and their eyes and hopes are centered on this march, and the committee must remain true to them. We feel as you have wisely said: 'No people will lose their freedom fighting for it.'"

Randolph, Walter White, and T. Arnold Hill of the National Urban League met with the president, Secretary of War Henry Stimson, Secretary of the Navy Frank Knox, and other officials on June 18, less than two weeks before the march was scheduled to take place. "Hello, Phil," the president said, welcoming Randolph to his office. Roosevelt regaled the group with political anecdotes. Randolph was polite, but he was in no mood for small talk. He thought back to a meeting in the White House the prior September, when he, White, and Hill asked the president and military officials to end segregation in the military. Instead, Roosevelt issued a statement that the military's policy of segregation would continue and implied that the three Black leaders endorsed the plan. To make matters worse, Roosevelt referred to Black troops as "boys" and suggested the navy recruit Black sailors for "a colored band . . . because they're darn good at it."

Randolph was determined that Roosevelt would not outfox him again.

> "Mr. President, time is running on," Randolph interjected, when Roosevelt paused between stories. "You are quite busy, I know. But what we want to talk with you about is the problem of jobs for Negroes in defense industries. Our people are being turned away at factory gates because they are colored. They can't live with this thing. Now, what are you going to do about it?"
>
> "Well, Phil, what do you want me to do?"
>
> "Mr. President, we want you to do something that will enable Negro workers to get work in these plants."

Roosevelt replied that he would call the heads of several defense plants and ask them to ensure that Black job applicants were given equal consideration.

> "We want you to do more than that," Randolph said. "We want something concrete, something tangible, definite, positive, and affirmative."
>
> "What do you mean?" Roosevelt asked.
>
> "Mr. President, we want you to issue an executive order making it mandatory that Negroes be permitted to work in these plants."

Randolph understood what a bold request he had just made. No president since Lincoln had issued an executive order to specifically benefit Black Americans.

"Well, Phil, you know I can't do that," Roosevelt replied. "If I issue an executive order for you, then there'll be no end to other groups coming in here and asking me to issue executive orders for them too. In any event, I couldn't do anything unless you call off this march of yours. Questions like this can't be settled with a sledge hammer."

Randolph stood his ground and told the president that the march would take place as scheduled.

"How many people do you plan to bring?" Roosevelt asked.

"One hundred thousand, Mr. President."

Five months of organizing by MOWM activists across the country led to this moment. What started as a far-fetched idea was now plausible enough that Randolph could look Roosevelt in his eyes and threaten to march one hundred thousand Black demonstrators through the streets of the nation's capital. Roosevelt was alarmed and hoped that Randolph was bluffing. The president turned to Walter White, stared at him for several seconds, and asked,

"Walter, how many people will really march?"

White did not blink and replied firmly, "One hundred thousand, Mr. President."

"You can't bring 100,000 Negroes to Washington,"
Roosevelt replied. "Somebody might get killed."

Randolph assured the president that the marchers would be well
organized and disciplined and again encouraged him to address the
gathering.

"Call it off and we'll talk again," Roosevelt said curtly.
The President encouraged Randolph and White to work
with his assistants to solve the problem with defense contractors.

"Not defense contractors alone," Randolph interrupted.
"The government too. The government is the worst of-
fender." Roosevelt was frustrated and told Randolph that
he would not be bullied by the president of the porters'
union.

"Then I shall have to stand by the pledge I've made to
the people," Randolph replied.

With the meeting at an impasse, Roosevelt asked his diplomatic
adviser Aubrey Williams, defense labor adviser Anna Rosenberg,
and New York mayor and head of the Office of Civilian Defense
Fiorello La Guardia to show Randolph, White, and Hill to an an-
teroom and hammer out a solution. After several more hours of
discussion, the Black leaders left the White House with the promise
that Roosevelt's advisers would work with Randolph to draft an
executive order for the president to sign. Joseph Rauh, a young lawyer in the Office for Emergency Management, was assigned the task
of writing the executive order and was given the simple directive:

"you gotta stop Randolph from marching." Rauh prepared several drafts but Randolph considered them too weak and sent each
one back.

Finally, after six days, a draft emerged that was acceptable to
both Randolph and the White House. Randolph called off the
march and Roosevelt signed Executive Order 8802 on July 25 with
no fanfare, ceremony, or speeches. The executive order forbade discrimination in defense industries and job training programs, and
established a new, temporary agency, the Fair Employment Practices Committee (FEPC), to enforce the order. The executive order
was silent about discrimination and segregation in the military, however. It was not everything Randolph wanted, but it was more than
any Black leader and movement had extracted from a president in
generations.

EXECUTIVE ORDER 8802 was warmly received by most Black
Americans and established Randolph as a leader to be reckoned
with. "This order—executive order 8802—has given new meaning, new vitality to the Emancipation Proclamation," said attorney
and World War I veteran Earl Dickerson. "Lincoln's proclamation
of 1863 freed us physically; Roosevelt's proclamation of 1941 is the
beginning of our economic freedom." Mary McLeod Bethune wrote
to Roosevelt, praising the order as "a refreshing shower in a thirsty
land." New York congressman Adam Clayton Powell Jr. described
the order as "the most significant gain ever made by Negroes under
their own power," while NAACP assistant secretary Roy Wilkins
said, "Never in the history of the United States has the President issued an Executive Order which is at once a condemnation of racial

discrimination as a policy and a powerful aid, economically, to the well-being of Negro citizens." The *Amsterdam News* praised Randolph as "the nation's No. 1 Negro leader" and noted that "already he is being ranked along with the great Frederick Douglass."

This optimism turned to frustration, though, once it became clear that the FEPC was virtually powerless to enforce Executive Order 8802. Roosevelt asked *Louisville Courier-Journal* editor Mark Ethridge to lead the FEPC, and he was joined by three white committee members, Radio Corporation of America head David Sarnoff, Philip Murray of the Congress of Industrial Organizations (CIO), and William Green of the American Federation of Labor (AFL), as well as two Black members, BSCP vice president Milton Webster and Dickerson. A part-time staff made up of recruits from labor unions, law schools, civil rights organizations, and universities worked out of a small office in the Social Security Building in Washington, D.C. While the staff believed in the FEPC's mission, they were completely overwhelmed when the office received more than sixteen hundred discrimination complaints between October and December 1941.

Nationally, Black applicants continued to be turned away from defense jobs at alarming rates. In fall 1941, the U.S. Bureau of Employment Security revealed that 51 percent of defense job openings barred Black workers, and that the rejection rate was much higher in Michigan (82 percent), Ohio (84 percent), and Indiana (94 percent). The government's report found that the plants manufacturing aircraft, tanks, shells, and ammunition had acute shortages of skilled and semiskilled labor but still refused to hire Black workers.

When Black workers did make it through the doors of defense industries, they often faced resistance from their white compatriots.

In September 1941, for example, 250 white autoworkers at Packard Motor Car Company in Detroit staged a sit-down strike when two Black workers were promoted to the metal polishing department. Two months later, nearly seventy white tool and die makers at Curtiss-Wright Corporation in Columbus, Ohio, walked out to protest the hire of a single Black machinist. These white workers organized to protect their privileged access to defense jobs, and the money and dignity these jobs provided.

With an initial staff of eleven and a budget of eighty thousand dollars, the FEPC lacked the people and resources to investigate more than a fraction of the racial discrimination cases that were reported, much less the untold acts of discrimination that never reached their office. The FEPC also lacked the power to fine or subpoena defense contractors that violated the executive order. Without this authority, they relied on what FEPC officials called "quiet persuasion" to encourage employers not to discriminate based on race, creed, color, or national origin. They also launched a publicity campaign that included mailing thousands of posters of Executive Order 8802 to war plants and hosting public hearings in targeted cities, including Los Angeles in October 1941, and Chicago, New York, and Birmingham in 1942, to collect evidence and educate the public about the FEPC and the executive order.

Despite these limited powers, Southern segregationist politicians attacked the FEPC vociferously throughout the war. Georgia senator Richard Russell later called the FEPC "the most dangerous force in existence in the United States today . . . it is a greater threat to victory than 50 fresh divisions enrolled beneath Hitler's swastika or the setting sun of Japan." What scared Russell and other FEPC opponents was that the federal government acknowledged that employment discrimination was wrong and started taking steps, however haltingly, to investigate and remedy this discrimination. In doing so, Executive Order 8802 and the FEPC threatened a segregated labor system that dictated that certain jobs were suitable only for whites and other jobs only for Blacks. As Howard University historian Charles Wesley noted during the war, "the presence of the Negro raises objection whenever he comes as an equal. As long as he is an inferior—a porter, a nurse, a sexton, a servant—he is tolerated."

Randolph's battle for equal access to defense work therefore also struck at the heart of America's racial caste system that treated Black Americans as second-class workers and citizens. Civil rights activist Pauli Murray understood the FEPC's shortcomings, but still argued, "This victory cannot be overestimated. It was the first national wedge in discrimination in employment and MOWM's greatest contribution to the goal of equal rights for all."

For Randolph and millions of other Black Americans, the lesson from the March on Washington Movement was that ordinary Black citizens possessed a tremendous amount of political potential. The key was to harness it to fight for specific goals. "You possess power, great power," Randolph said. "In this period of power politics, nothing counts but pressure, more pressure and still more pressure."

With America's entry into the war looking more likely by the day, Black citizens' long-simmering anger with racism became more prominent. Although Randolph canceled the planned march, far more than a hundred thousand Black people took action against discrimination across the country. In big cities and small towns, in defense factories and restaurants, on army bases and navy ships,

Black Americans fought policies and people that demeaned them. "A New Negro has arisen in America," Mary McLeod Bethune said. "Militant in spirit," committed to democracy, and willing to "save America from itself." Looking back years later, Randolph put it simply: "The Negro masses awakened in 1941."

Black soldiers and sailors stood prominently among these awakened masses. Stationed predominantly in the South, they encountered racist hostility at army camps and in neighboring towns. Many Black troops feared they would be killed in their own country before they ever deployed. With each passing day it became increasingly clear that the military's policy for Black troops, shunting them into segregated camps in segregated towns, was fueling a war on the home front.

FOUR

AT WAR DOWN SOUTH

Unless some action is taken in this matter,
this threat against our democratic form of
government will go unpunished and will certainly give courage to other mobs to show
similar disrespect for the uniform of the
United States Army.

—THURGOOD MARSHALL

When he arrived at the NAACP's New York City headquarters at 69 Fifth Avenue on a cool autumn morning in 1941, Thurgood Marshall was exhausted. As
the chief lawyer for the nation's largest civil rights organization, he
had traveled nearly fifty thousand miles over the prior year, visiting
local NAACP chapters, trying cases, and lobbying politicians in
Washington, D.C. Voting rights, school segregation, and antilynching legislation dominated his agenda, but recently, a new issue had
emerged.

Opening the door to his office, Marshall found his cluttered desk as he had left it. Copies of the *Baltimore Afro-American*, *The Pittsburgh Courier*, and *The New York Times* lay atop tall stacks of law books and legal files. On the corner of the desk was a tidy pile of new letters that had arrived since Marshall was last in New York.

These letters, which were from Black troops stationed at places like North Carolina's Fort Bragg, Mississippi's Camp Shelby, and Louisiana's Camp Livingston, worried Marshall. What started as a trickle of mail had exploded in recent months. Reading dozens of letters from soldiers each week, Marshall understood that a new civil rights battlefront had emerged on the nation's rapidly expanding military bases. The success of the campaign to open the military to more Black Americans, from the Selective Service Act to the new all-Black air squadron in Tuskegee, came at a terrible cost.

"I am taking it upon myself to write to you in the hope that something may be done to put a stop to the treatment of the Black troops now stationed at Camp Lee, Virginia," wrote Sydney Rotheny, a member of the 9th Quartermaster Regiment. "The situation is getting very serious and I can truthfully say for myself and the other two thousand Black men now at Camp Lee, that we are getting very tired, so tired that we are ready to take things into our own hands." Rotheny described a series of indignities: White officers slapped and threatened to kill Black enlisted men. On the bus into town, white soldiers demanded that Black soldiers give up their seats. To get back from town, white military police made Black soldiers wait in a separate line until all white soldiers boarded the bus. This meant Black soldiers sometimes waited an hour or more as bus after bus filled with white troops and motored back to camp. At the segregated post exchange, an overzealous white second lieutenant took it upon himself to ban the sale of Black newspapers.

Throughout Camp Lee, Black soldiers were called racial epithets daily.

"Aren't we supposed to be men?" Rotheny asked. "Yet we are treated like dogs." The majority of Black troops at Camp Lee were drafted from cities in the north and west and were struggling to adjust to the Southern system of racial segregation they found on and off base. "It would be a pleasure soldiering for Uncle Sam if we were treated like humans," he concluded, "but as things stand now, all we want is out, out of the Army and back to our homes."

MARSHALL SAW SEEKING JUSTICE for these soldiers as part of his calling as a lawyer. Since he was young, his parents had told him stories of his grandfathers and their military service. Isaiah Olive Branch Williams, his maternal grandfather, was born free in Maryland and worked as a captain's steward on a Union warship during the Civil War. His navy service continued after the war, as he sailed on ships patrolling the coasts of Peru and Chile. Thorney Good Marshall, Thurgood's paternal grandfather, escaped slavery in Virginia, and after the Civil War, joined the all-Black 24th Regiment of the U.S. Cavalry, one of the famed Buffalo Soldier units.

When Marshall was a teenager at Baltimore's Colored High and Training School, his favorite teacher and mentor was his debate coach, Gough Decatur McDaniels. A World War I veteran, McDaniels was a leader of the Baltimore branch of the NAACP. Thurgood enjoyed hearing McDaniels and his uncle, Cyrus Marshall, describe their service during the Great War. These stories were always tinged with pain, though, because neither veteran felt like the country valued their service.

Marshall heard a similar mix of pride and pain when his mentor, Charles Hamilton Houston, talked about his service as a second lieutenant in France. Although he did not yet have formal legal training, Houston served as a military lawyer in Europe during the war, representing Black soldiers facing misconduct charges. The racism Houston experienced during and after World War I fueled his desire to study law and fight for Black Americans. After the war, Houston gained admission to Harvard Law and was the first Black student elected to the *Harvard Law Review* editorial board. Houston was the dean of Howard University School of Law in 1930 when the twenty-two-year-old Marshall matriculated. Houston dramatically raised the academic standards at the school and had high expectations for his students.

Houston's goal was to make Howard Law the "West Point of Negro Leadership," and Marshall became one of his prized pupils. After graduation, Marshall toured the South with his mentor, investigating school segregation for the NAACP. Marshall had wanted to be a lawyer since he was a teenager, but Houston gave him a new sense of the professional power and responsibility this entailed. "Houston made public statements that Black lawyers he trained at Howard would become social engineers rather than lawyers," Marshall said. "That was our purpose in life." Houston left Howard in 1935 to become the NAACP's lawyer and recruited Marshall to join the legal staff the following year. They shared an office for two years, until Houston left New York to run his family's law firm in Washington, D.C. Marshall, now thirty years old, became the NAACP's top lawyer in 1938.

Being a civil rights lawyer in this era was not an office job. Marshall traveled as much as nine months out of the year, riding Jim

Crow trains to Southern towns where white hotels and restaurants would not serve him. Countless Black people opened their homes to him, offering a place to sleep and a seat at their dinner tables. While the meals were modest, they nourished him. As he talked with people in poor, rural communities across the South, Marshall understood the urgency of fighting segregation and racism.

Because the NAACP had not previously prioritized fieldwork, Marshall's appearance in these small towns was an event. People would travel miles to see him in court, and he cut an imposing figure. Standing six feet two, he wore sharp double-breasted suits, chain-smoked, spoke in a booming voice, and laughed even louder. Years before he won the *Brown v. Board of Education* case at the Supreme Court in 1954 or became the first Black U.S. Supreme Court justice in 1968, Marshall was already a household name in Black America. He was to the courtroom what heavyweight champion Joe Louis was to the boxing ring. In communities across the South, two words signaled that Black citizens would have at least a fighting chance against an unjust legal system: "Thurgood's coming."

ONE OF THE LETTERS on Marshall's desk was from the men of the 94th Engineer Battalion, who desperately wanted Thurgood and the NAACP to investigate their treatment in rural Arkansas. Originally based at Fort Custer, Michigan, the fifteen hundred members of the 94th came mostly from Detroit and Chicago. They traveled to Arkansas in early August 1941 to take part in field maneuvers with the 2nd Army. These war games were designed to show troops, most of whom had been civilians just a few months prior, how to advance to contact and attack an enemy, how to organize a defensive position, and how to withdraw. The 94th Engineers' role in the war games was not glamorous, but the battalion was eager to practice for possible deployment—building and repairing roads and bridges. Unexpectedly, their combat experience started even before the field maneuvers began.

After a brief stop in Little Rock, the engineers traveled ninety miles southwest and set up a temporary camp outside the small town of Gurdon, Arkansas. The field maneuvers transformed Gurdon (population two thousand) into a buzzing post town, with over seventy thousand soldiers coming through the area in the summer of 1941. The townspeople were excited and a bit alarmed to see so many tanks, trucks, and artillery pieces. Lumber crews cleared swaths of oaks, hickories, and maples to make space for the war games.

On the night of August 11, two hundred of the engineers received passes to visit town. When they arrived, the white military police restricted the soldiers to the two-block "Negro district." Milling outside of the two small bars they were allowed to patronize, the soldiers were harassed by white motorists who shouted insults and veered close to them at crosswalks.

Tensions mounted as a rumor spread among the soldiers that the military police had arrested and beaten a member of the battalion. The rumor proved false, but when it was time to enforce the ten p.m. curfew, several military police pulled their revolvers and threatened the soldiers if they did not head back to the bivouac area. The troops were agitated but ultimately complied and walked the four miles back to camp. The engineers' voices, loosened by drink, echoed in the humid night air.

Sensational stories spread overnight among the white citizens of

Gurdon that their town was being invaded by Black northern soldiers. In the morning, the town marshal started swearing in new
deputies to bolster the police force. Just after sundown, the state police drove to the bivouac area to let the 94th know they were not welcome in Arkansas. They verbally and physically assaulted the Black
camp guards, who had rifles but no live ammunition, per the army's
field maneuvers policy.

That same evening, a group of soldiers tried to find recreation in
the neighboring town of Prescott but were turned away by a large
group of armed white civilians. The next night, several troops ventured to another small town, Hope, to attend a dance organized by
the Black community. After the first song, the state police burst in,
hit the men and women with their nightsticks, and ordered the
soldiers back to camp.

When military officials got word of these incidents, they declared Gurdon and neighboring towns off limits to Black troops
and directed the white officers who led the 94th to move the battalion's bivouac area farther away from Gurdon. On August 14,
hundreds of soldiers marched along Highway 67 en route to a new
temporary campsite deeper in the woods. Rain soaked their boots
and fatigues. After hiking over four miles, they encountered several
cars full of state police and white civilians. The police and civilians
jumped out and aimed rifles, sawed-off shotguns, and revolvers at
the soldiers. Hurling racial epithets, the police yelled at the army officers to get their men off the highway and into the ditch, which was
now filled with knee-deep muddy water.

Unlike many white army officers, the leaders of the 94th had
the respect of the Black troops in their command and they tried to
stand up to the state police. "These are not 'damn niggers,' they are

soldiers, representing the United States Army," said Lieutenant Donald Curry of Madison, Wisconsin. A Gurdon police officer slapped Lieutenant Curry, called him a "damned Yankee," and told him his rank did not mean anything in the South. Another police officer jabbed his shotgun into the stomach of a white company commander and dared him to move. Three truckloads of white military police arrived during the altercation but did not intervene. Furious, Curry and the other officers ordered the soldiers into a gully, where they marched the remaining miles to their new campsite. "We had to walk either in the ditch or in the brush behind the ditch, being forbidden to put our Black feet on the white man's highway," Sergeant Eugene Gaillard remembered.

As they made camp in the woods of rural Arkansas, in a marshy area swarming with mosquitos, chiggers, and venomous water moccasins, the Black troops of the 94th were angry, demoralized, and scared. They had been drafted or had volunteered to serve in the U.S. Army. Now, just days before they were supposed to be practicing field maneuvers in preparation for war, their lives had been threatened in their own country by fellow Americans. The troops stayed up late that night, clutching flashlights and army-issued knives, fearing that white townspeople would attack their new campsite.

As midnight came and went, the soldiers debated what they should do. One group argued that they needed to fight back. They told stories of an all-Black World War I infantry regiment who marched on Houston in August 1917 to stop the police from harassing Black civilians and soldiers. These soldiers had clashed for two hours with white police and civilians. Twenty people died, dozens of soldiers were court-martialed, and thirteen of the soldiers were later hanged. But even if the 94th wanted to emulate this bloody example, they lacked ammunition for their rifles.

Another group of soldiers argued that they should flee Gurdon and try to make it back up north to Fort Custer, Michigan. The troop detail who stayed behind to clean up the old bivouac area described being approached by a band of white civilians who threatened to hang the soldiers if they were in Gurdon after sundown. The men reasoned that if local whites could strike a white army officer with impunity, they would not hesitate to kill Black soldiers. The uniform of the U.S. Army offered them no protection, or worse; the sight of a Black person in uniform seemed to inflame many white people, making Black troops a target.

Several men mentioned the example of Felix Hall, a nineteen-year-old private who had been found hanging by a noose tied to a sapling in a ravine near Fort Benning, Georgia, five months earlier. Hall's feet were bound in wire and his hands were tied behind his back. He was wearing his green army uniform. The soldiers had read about this lynching in the *Chicago Defender* while they were still at Fort Custer. Now it seemed like an ominous example of the fate they might encounter if they stayed in the Arkansas woods.

By daybreak, over two hundred soldiers had decided to leave camp and take their chances. Knowing that a large cluster of Black soldiers would attract too much attention, they changed out of their uniforms into fatigue overalls, broke up into small groups, and started walking in different directions away from Gurdon. Clarence Woods Jr., a private from Detroit, hopped a freight train to Texarkana, Texas. He changed trains a dozen times, winding his way through west Texas, New Mexico, and Arizona, before reaching California on August 23. In Los Angeles, he told the local NAACP and *The California Eagle* newspaper about what his battalion experienced in Gurdon. Several trains and over two thousand miles later, he arrived at Fort Custer on September 2.

Sergeant Lester Duane Simons, a former swimming star at Ann Arbor High School, rode a boxcar north from Arkadelphia to Missouri, where a friendly white family took him in for a night and fed him. When he and the other AWOL soldiers made it to Fort Custer, they turned themselves in to Major Theophilus Mann, a Black lawyer attached to the 184th Field Artillery.

THURGOOD MARSHALL LEARNED about Gurdon when letters and telegrams started to stream into NAACP headquarters from members of the 94th and their family members. One soldier wrote that the battalion faced "an unholy alliance of state police, southern white MPs, and southern sheriffs." Another soldier noted, "It's odd that the U.S. Govt. would let a small town of a few thousand people rule them like that." The brother of two members of the 94th wrote that it was "an appalling situation when the United States Army can no longer give protection to its soldiers."

Within the NAACP office, Marshall handled the legal aspects of the case, while secretary Walter White managed the public relations. Marshall instructed the Detroit NAACP branch to take sworn testimonies from as many of the soldiers who fled Arkansas as possible, so that these affidavits could later be used in their defense. He lobbied the Department of Justice and the War Department to investigate the violence the Black troops encountered in Arkansas. "Unless some action is taken in this matter, this threat against our democratic form of government will go unpunished and will certainly give courage to other mobs to show similar disrespect for the uniform of the United States Army," he wrote.

While the wheels turned slowly in Washington, D.C., the local NAACP chapter in Detroit organized a mass meeting at the Bethel African Methodist Episcopal Church, where Walter White was the featured speaker. Activists handed out flyers reading "Stop Army Brutality!! Riots, Mistreatments and Murder Must Cease!" Several hundred people attended the meeting, many of them mothers and fathers concerned about how their sons were being treated in the army. The meeting raised two hundred dollars for the NAACP's legal effort.

Beyond Detroit, Black newspapers across the country picked up the story. TERROR REIGN SWEEPS NATION'S ARMY CAMPS, NEGROES GO AWOL, the *New York Amsterdam News* headline read. "The wave of beating and killing of Negro soldiers encamped in southern communities should be checked without delay and the guilty persons brought to trial," the *Defender* editors wrote. "It is bad enough for the Negro soldier to be Jim-Crowed. He should not have to endure insults, humiliation, and death at the hands of irresponsible and prejudiced white trash."

The Pittsburgh Courier published an open letter to President Roosevelt calling out the gap between America's wartime rhetoric and the reality of racism. The *Courier* noted that FDR had recently signed the Atlantic Charter, which outlined the United States' and the U.K.'s aspirations for the postwar world and affirmed the rights of nations to choose their own government, while Black troops faced violence in the South. "While you were on the high seas, Mr. President, joined with Prime Minister Churchill in setting up a declaration of principles to give hope to the subjugated, oppressed and exploited peoples of the world, the forces of hate, unreason and prejudice were busy in America trampling those principles in the mire." In addition to calling for investigations of racial violence at army bases and a fair trial for the soldiers who fled Gurdon, the NAACP and Black press renewed the call for desegregation of the military.

For their part, military leaders continued to insist that the problem was Black soldiers, not segregation. General Benjamin Lear, commander of the U.S. 2nd Army, spoke to the 94th Battalion just after dozens of their members fled Gurdon for Fort Custer. "I am ashamed of you," he told the Black troops. "You are the ones who have started all of this trouble. You are a disgrace to your race, to yourselves, and the 2nd Army. You know you are down here in the South and you will do as they want you to." Lear replaced the white commander of the 94th, arguing that he had been "too easy with his men." Major General Robert Richardson, who led the 7th Corps, blamed the northern troops for not "understanding the attitude of the Southerner." And despite the fact that Marshall had applied particular pressure to his mentor and former Howard law professor William Hastie, who was the civilian aide to the secretary of war, Henry Stimson, Stimson argued that the difficulty in Arkansas would not have occurred without the "unjustified demonstration" by Black troops.

By October 1941, six members of the 94th were being held in the guardhouse at Fort Custer. They were court-martialed and accused of starting trouble in Gurdon and leading their fellow troops who went AWOL. If convicted, they could be sentenced to hard labor or confinement, or given dishonorable discharges, which would make them ineligible for veterans' educational, employment, and health benefits.

Marshall worked with the Detroit NAACP branch to support the troops' defense, which was led by Major Theophilus Mann. The troops were fortunate to be represented by Mann, the first Black lawyer to serve as defense counsel in an army trial. Mann believed that the soldiers who ran away from Gurdon had reason to fear for their lives and was able to persuade the officers on the court-martial board of this fact. Thanks to Mann's skill in the courtroom and Marshall's work behind the scenes, the soldiers were freed and returned to their battalion.

Two years after surviving Gurdon, the 94th Engineers were in Italy, repairing railroads and building bridges that enabled the Allies to move troops, trucks, artillery, and supplies through the Volturno River and Naples areas. Like Black Americans in different military branches and theaters of war, the 94th soldiered on despite the racism they encountered.

While Marshall and his allies achieved an important victory on behalf of the 94th, the Gurdon incident and wave of violence against Black troops at army camps in 1941 raised serious doubts among Black Americans about the value of fighting for inclusion in the war effort. Each week brought news of Black soldiers being forced to ride segregated buses and use segregated latrines, or being beaten or killed if they refused to comply with this system of Jim Crow apartheid. As thousands of young Black men were being drafted and volunteering for the military, the parents, spouses, siblings, children, and friends who cared for them were left to wonder if the home front was actually a war zone.

THE STAKES OF Black military service became even more clear aboard the American destroyer USS *Reuben James*. The vessel was one of a group of U.S. Navy destroyers tasked with escorting convoys of Allied merchant ships carrying supplies and equipment from the United States to Great Britain. Nearly a year after President Roosevelt declared that America would be the arsenal of democracy, and months after he signed the Lend-Lease Act, which allowed the U.S. to supply military aid to foreign allies without formally entering the war, the *Reuben James* helped keep vital shipping lanes open. This was dangerous work. German U-boats hunted like wolf packs across the Atlantic, with groups of submarines firing torpedoes at Allied ships. While the United States was still officially neutral, for all intents and purposes the *Reuben James* was at war in the Battle of the Atlantic.

In October 1941, while the 94th Engineers regrouped at Fort Custer, the *Reuben James* steamed from Newfoundland to Iceland. Three Black American messmen—twenty-five-year-old Raymond Cook, from Warner, Virginia; twenty-three-year-old Nebraska Dunston, from Spring Hope, North Carolina; and twenty-six-year-old Joseph Johnson, from Elm City, North Carolina—sailed among the enlisted crew. Like their shipmates, these messmen understood that their lives were on the line. In the prior weeks, the crew received word that German submarines had attacked two destroyers—the USS *Greer* and the USS *Kearny*—killing eleven men on the latter. Unlike their shipmates, these Black sailors were not allowed to serve in combat roles aboard the *Reuben James*. Naval policies dictated that Black Americans could be drafted or volunteer only for the messmen branch, where they would serve and feed white officers.

The three Black messmen had just awoken on the morning of October 31, 1941, when a German U-boat fired two torpedoes that struck the *Reuben James*'s port side. The impact ignited the forward magazine, tearing the ship in half. The front part of the ship lifted into the air and immediately began to sink. The sailors who survived the blast scrambled topside and had only minutes to try to evacuate, as the aft part of the ship slipped into the sea. The men launched three rafts and jumped into the frigid waters of the Atlantic Ocean. As the sailors thrashed and bobbed in the oily water, one of the ship's depth charges, which had become unsecured during the attack, exploded, launching men and debris into the air along with an enormous column of water. Just as the men began to get their bearings, another depth charge went off, knocking some men unconscious and tearing others apart. The two blasts killed dozens of sailors who had survived the initial German strike. The other ships in the convoy rescued forty-four survivors, who were so coated with oil that they looked like seals.

The *Reuben James* was the first U.S. Navy ship sunk by enemy fire in World War II. Ninety-three enlisted men and all seven officers died aboard the *Reuben James*, including Raymond Cook, Nebraska Dunston, and Joseph Johnson. While the U.S. had not officially declared war, these Black messmen were among the first Americans killed in action in the war.

British prime minister Winston Churchill cabled President Roosevelt after the attack, writing, "I am grieved at the loss of life you have suffered with Reuben James. I salute the land of unending challenge." While Churchill hoped the incident would finally prompt

Roosevelt to ask Congress to declare war, the president and press were measured in their response and Congress remained divided on the issue. Folk singer Woody Guthrie eulogized the sailors in "The Sinking of the Reuben James":

> *Have you heard of a ship called the good Reuben James*
> *Manned by hard fighting men both of honor and fame?*
> *She flew the Stars and Stripes of the land of the free*
> *But tonight she's in her grave on the bottom of the sea*
> *Tell me what were their names, tell me what were their names*
> *Did you have a friend on the good Reuben James?*

News of the *Reuben James* came and went in the mainstream press and did not capture the attention of most white Americans.

Black Americans saw the *Reuben James* differently. Annie Johnson had just come home to her modest house in tiny Elm City, North Carolina, and turned on the radio when she heard the announcer describe the sinking of the *Reuben James*. While details on casualties and survivors were still sketchy, she had a terrible feeling that her son, Joseph, was among the dead. After his father died, Joseph had taken over the work on his family's small farm. He volunteered for the navy in 1940 because it paid more than a Black man could earn in Elm City. Joseph visited his mother and younger sister in the summer of 1941, while he was on furlough. They drove fifty miles to a Black-owned photo studio in Raleigh so he could have his picture taken in his uniform. He looked handsome in his navy whites. Now, as the radio broadcast news of the *Reuben James*, Annie Johnson looked at her son's picture and wept.

The sinking of the *Reuben James* put the absurdity of the navy's racial policies in sharp relief. Even though the navy assigned Black Americans to subservient roles, messmen were still very much at war. "Nazi torpedoes make no distinction between admirals and messmen," the *Courier* argued. "Death drew no color line against them but the Navy does." The *Courier*'s front page on November 15 featured photographs of Cook, Dunston, and Johnson in their uniforms with the headline FIRST AMERICAN NEGROES TO DIE DEFENDING NATION. The paper also published the Western Union telegrams the men's families received from the navy notifying them of their deaths, as well as pictures of Dunston's grandparents and Johnson's mother and sister reading the telegrams. "The color of their skin doesn't lessen their grief," the caption noted.

Three weeks later, when navy officials expressed frustration that recruitments had slumped after the sinking of the *Reuben James*, the *Courier* contended that the navy had only its own policies to blame. "The Navy has made flunkies of Negroes," the paper argued on December 6, 1941. "It has set up an exclusive class of whites in the Navy who are made to feel that the job of fighting belongs to them and the job of flunkeying belongs to the Negroes."

THURGOOD MARSHALL READ about the sinking of the *Reuben James* on the road. During November 1941, he visited Dallas, Houston, New Orleans, Birmingham, and West Palm Beach, meeting with local branches to discuss legal cases involving school discrimination and voting rights. Marshall's speeches increasingly invoked America's democratic ideals, arguing that Nazi racial ideology and Jim Crow segregation were two sides of the same coin.

In Houston, Marshall spoke with Lonnie E. Smith, a forty-year-old dentist from the city's Fifth Ward. Smith had attempted to vote in the prior year's Democratic primary in Harris County, but was denied a ballot. The all-white primary system in Texas and other Southern states disenfranchised Smith and millions of other Black voters. Writing back to Walter White, Roy Wilkins, and his colleagues at NAACP headquarters in New York, Marshall said the meeting with Smith went well, and that he was hopeful that this case would finally be the one that got the Supreme Court to find the all-white primary system unconstitutional. Marshall stressed that the NAACP would need to raise more money to pay for their legal efforts and that the organization needed to improve their work in the field, meeting more local people, encouraging the creation of more branches, and signing up more dues-paying members. He approached the immense struggle that lay before them with a sense of humor, introducing his reports as an "installment in that stirring saga of unselfish devotion to a great cause, 'Saving the Race,' by Thurgood Marshall."

When Marshall arrived back in New York City in the first week of December, he was energized by the important work he was doing to ensure that Black Americans could go to equal schools, exercise the right to vote, and serve their country without being degraded by their countrymen. After weeks on the road, Marshall was eager to read the latest letters and newspaper clippings that had amassed in his absence. Soldier complaints predominated, and one letter in particular caught his attention:

> I am complaining of how the mess attendants are treated in the U.S. Navy. . . . Sometimes officers curse the colored men who cannot make any reply. . . . It is awful enough

for these men to have to shine officers' shoes, make up officers' bunks and serve them meals, without having to take insults. . . . I want all Race boys to know how we are treated in the U.S. Navy. Please don't come in here!

These sentiments were similar to those he had heard from army soldiers at Fort Bragg, Fort Benning, and elsewhere, but this sailor was not writing from the South. Marshall did not recognize the name of the base, so he jotted it down: *Pearl Harbor.*

FIVE

REMEMBER PEARL HARBOR, REMEMBER SIKESTON TOO

> Is it fair, honest or sensible, that this
> country . . . . should continue to bar Negroes
> from service except in the mess department
> of the Navy, when at the first sign of danger
> they so dramatically show their willingness
> to face death in defense of the Stars and
> Stripes?
>
> —*The Pittsburgh Courier*

Shortly before eight a.m. on December 7, 1941, Mess Attendant Second Class Doris Miller was in the galley of the USS *West Virginia* gathering dirty laundry when he heard the low drone of dozens of planes flying over Pearl Harbor's Battleship Row. Miller, a Black messman from Waco, Texas, was about to distinguish himself as a hero during the attack that drew the United States into World War II.

Miller was startled by a bugle call for a fire-and-rescue crew and several explosions, distant but getting closer. Initially, he thought it was a drill, but then remembered that it was Sunday morning, an unusual time for so much commotion. As Miller struggled to comprehend what was happening, a torpedo struck the *West Virginia*, dislodging the rudder and sending a giant geyser of water over the ship's stack and crashing down on the deck. Minutes later, more torpedoes pounded the *West Virginia*, knocking out the electricity and causing the ship to list rapidly to port.

The general alarm sounded, and Miller rushed to his battle station in the middle of the ship. When he arrived, he saw that his station had been destroyed by the barrage. Amid the explosions and antiaircraft fire, Miller heard officers calling for all available men to go topside. A former high school football player and shipboard boxing champion, the twenty-two-year-old Miller was strong and athletic, but he had trouble navigating his six-feet-three-inch, two-hundred-pound frame through the dark, smoke-filled passageway of the tilting and flooding ship. Torpedoes and bombs continued to rock the vessel, tossing those below deck into hard metal walls and flinging men above deck into the flaming, oil-choked harbor water.

When Miller finally made it topside, the morning's chaos came into clearer view. The planes bore the Empire of Japan's red sun symbol. From the deck of the *West Virginia*, he could see flames and giant plumes of smoke coming from the nearby USS *Arizona* and USS *Oklahoma*. The *West Virginia* had been stationed at Pearl Harbor for months to guard against a potential attack, and Miller knew Black messmen on the other ships. On shore leave the messmen would swap stories about ports they had visited in the Caribbean and South America and about the indignities, large and small, of cooking and cleaning for white officers. They wondered when the United States would officially enter the world war. Now, with smoke blotting out the sun over Oahu, they had their answer.

Miller had little time to process the horrible realities of war unfolding before him. On the upper deck, Lieutenant Commander Doir C. Johnson spotted Miller and enlisted the powerful Texan to help him carry the ship's commander, Captain Mervyn Bennion, whose abdomen had been sliced open by a piece of metal from a bomb explosion. Using a makeshift stretcher, Miller helped move his mortally wounded captain to a sheltered spot below the navigation bridge. Lieutenant Frederic White then ordered Miller to quickly follow him to a pair of unmanned .50-caliber antiaircraft machine guns.

Despite having no training on the ship's weapons, Miller loaded ammunition and fired at the Japanese planes that continued to buzz overhead. "It wasn't hard," Miller later recalled. "I just pulled the trigger and she worked fine. I had watched the others with these guns. I guess I fired her for about fifteen minutes. I think I got one of those Japanese planes. They were diving pretty close to us."

Their ammunition spent, Miller and White used a fire hose to beat back the flames on the deck and pulled several sailors out of the burning water. With the *West Virginia* sinking into the harbor, Miller and his surviving shipmates descended a rope suspended from a boat crane and jumped into the water. They swam nearly a quarter mile to shore, dodging patches of flaming oil as the bodies of their fallen countrymen floated past.

The damage to the navy's Pacific Fleet was devastating. The attack killed 2,403 service members and wounded over 1,100 more. Six ships were sunk or destroyed along with over 160 U.S. Navy and Army Air Corps planes. Black American mess attendants stationed in Hawaii died in equal proportion to their numbers on the battleships. On the *Arizona*, for example, 24 Black messmen lost their lives.

The next day, President Roosevelt addressed a joint session of Congress and a nationwide radio audience. Calling December 7, 1941, "a date which will live in infamy," Roosevelt told Americans that Japan had attacked not only Pearl Harbor, but also U.S. and British bases in Malaya, Hong Kong, Guam, the Philippines, Wake Island, and Midway Island. "No matter how long it may take us to overcome this premeditated invasion, the American people in their righteous might will win through to absolute victory," the president said. "I believe that I interpret the will of the Congress and of the people when I assert that we will not only defend ourselves to the uttermost but will make it very certain that this form of treachery shall never again endanger us." The president continued his call to arms: "There is no blinking at the fact that our people, our territory, and our interests are in grave danger. With confidence in our armed forces—with the unbounding determination of our people— we will gain the inevitable triumph—so help us God."

Congress quickly voted to declare war on Japan (82–0 in the Senate and 388–1 in the House, with pacifist congresswoman Jeannette Rankin casting the lone dissenting vote). Roosevelt signed the declaration before the sun set on December 8. Three days later, on December 11, Germany and Italy declared war on the United States, which immediately entered the war against the European Axis powers.

In the days and weeks after Pearl Harbor, thousands flocked to recruitment offices to volunteer for service. People purchased war bonds in lieu of Christmas gifts and towns organized drives for paper, rubber, and scrap metal. Cities along the Pacific and Atlantic seaboards held regular air-raid and blackout drills to prepare for an attack on the U.S. mainland. The federal Office of Price Administration mandated food and gas rationing. Bandleader Sammy Kaye's "Remember Pearl Harbor" played on radios and jukeboxes across the country:

> *We will always remember*
> *How they died for liberty*
> *Let's REMEMBER PEARL HARBOR*
> *And go on to victory*

WITH PEARL HARBOR changing seemingly everything in America, Black leaders hoped the military's policy of segregation would also be upended. The NAACP wired Secretary of the Navy Frank Knox shortly after the attack to ask that the navy not limit Black volunteers to the messman branch. "These men want to fight, not cook," the *Chicago Defender* added. While Roosevelt was asking Congress for a declaration of war on December 8, editors from a dozen Black newspapers met with War Department officials at the Munitions Building in Washington, D.C.

The meeting, scheduled weeks earlier by William Hastie to discuss the treatment and morale of Black troops, took on a new sense of urgency now that the United States was officially at war. The editors responded positively when the army chief of staff, General George C. Marshall, opened the meeting by announcing plans for a Black division to be formed at Fort Huachuca, Arizona, and admitting that he was not "personally satisfied" with the army's progress on racial issues.

The meeting soured when Colonel Eugene R. Householder, representing the Adjutant General's Department, read his prepared remarks. "The Army did not create the problem" of racial segregation, Householder told the editors. "The Army is made up of individual citizens of the United States who have pronounced views with respect to the Negro. . . . Military orders, fiat, or dicta, will not change their viewpoints." The colonel said the army would not engage in experiments to meet the demands of race champions. "The Army is not a sociological laboratory," he concluded.

The editors were appalled and found the "sociological laboratory" line particularly insulting. The army was already engaged in a vast sociological project, they contended, by taking hundreds of thousands of civilian volunteers and draftees and transporting them around the country to newly built or recently expanded bases. As the army grew rapidly, new practices and policies were being adopted and adapted every day. "The War Department has been arbitrary in adopting the modes of prejudices of Georgia, Florida and other Southern States, and has forced such prejudices upon the rest of the country," the NAACP's Roy Wilkins argued. The army brought Jim Crow segregation to camps in California, Michigan, and New Jersey, and required Black troops from the north to endure Southern bases and towns where racial hatred ran hot. By embracing Jim Crow segregation, not only did the army force Black troops to suffer as second-class soldiers, they gave a federal stamp of approval to the South's system of racial apartheid. The claim that "the Army is not a sociological laboratory" was another way of saying "segregation is here to stay," one editor remarked.

This anger flowed through the pages of the Black press after Pearl Harbor. AWAKE WHITE AMERICA, THE HOUR IS AT HAND! read the front-page headline in the *Chicago Defender*'s first national edition after the attack. "White America must learn now—especially those who inhabit the South—that a Negro in the Armed service of his country, in the uniform of his government, must be respected as a defender of democracy," the *Defender* argued. "He cannot be insulted in this uniform that now represents a sacred cause; he must not be spat upon, jailed, beaten, cursed and otherwise abused and tormented as the case has been, then called upon to sacrifice his life for those who hold his patriotism so cheaply." The newspaper called for white Americans to "bomb the color line" before striking back against Japan.

The *Defender*'s front page also profiled three young Chicagoans who heeded the radio appeals from army recruiters to "Remember Pearl Harbor" and attempted to volunteer for military service. Twenty-one-year-old Edgar Davis, nineteen-year-old Lewis Grady, and twenty-year-old Mitchell Jordan stood in line with hundreds of other men but were turned away by the recruiting officer because the army did not have enough all-Black units to accommodate them. "Don't you accept American citizens in this army?" Davis asked.

In the editorial page of *The Crisis*, Roy Wilkins argued that thirteen million Black Americans were fighting for "a new world which not only shall not contain a Hitler, but not Hitlerism . . . a world in which lynching, brutality, terror, humiliation, and degradation through segregation and discrimination, shall have no place—*either here or there*." Reflecting his frustration over the War Department meeting, Wilkins charged that the fight against Hitlerism must begin in Washington, D.C., and must attack the military's system of racial segregation. "A lily-white navy cannot fight for a free world," he argued. "A jim crow army cannot fight for a free world. Jim crow strategy, no matter on how grand a scale, cannot build a free world. So we fight the Great Fight, not against Germany, Italy and Japan, but for the Great Peace. And we begin here, and now."

The NAACP and Black newspapers also pressed their case from another angle, arguing that the bravery Black mess attendants demonstrated during the Pearl Harbor attack showed the folly of the navy's racial policies. While Doris Miller would not be publicly identified for several weeks, by late December, reports circulated of a Black messman who performed valiantly during the attack. Walter White wrote to Secretary Knox and President Roosevelt to suggest that the unidentified hero be recognized with a Navy Distinguished Service Medal. The editors of *The Pittsburgh Courier* agreed that this hero from the galley should be honored. "Is it fair, honest or sensible," they asked, "that this country . . . should continue to bar Negroes from service except in the mess department of the Navy, when at the first sign of danger they so dramatically show their willingness to face death in defense of the Stars and Stripes?"

The sacrifices Black messmen made at Pearl Harbor were nowhere more evident than in the communities that mourned them. In Birmingham, Alabama, more than three hundred people filled the pews at Sixteenth Street Baptist Church for a memorial service to honor Julius Ellsberry, the twenty-year-old Mess Attendant First Class on the USS *Oklahoma*. Ellsberry had volunteered for the navy as soon as he turned eighteen, and on the morning of December 7 he helped several shipmates reach safety before he was killed. As his parents and six younger siblings sat in the church's front row, his mother thought of how Julius had written her just days before the attack to apologize for missing Christmas for the second year in a row. He enclosed a money order to buy presents for the family. The next letter she received was an official telegram from the navy saying that her son was lost in action in the line of duty and in the service of his country. She was devastated to lose her son. Nothing could bring Julius back, but she took pride in seeing his navy picture displayed prominently in homes and businesses throughout Black Birmingham with the message "Remember Pearl Harbor." *Birmingham World* editor Emory O. Jackson compared Ellsberry to Crispus Attucks, the Black hero who was the first American killed in the American Revolution. "No man not even an admiral can give more to his country than his life," Jackson wrote.

In Beaufort, South Carolina, navy veteran Adam W. Bush mourned the loss of his son, Samuel Jackson Bush, who perished on the USS *California*. Similar scenes took place at memorials for other Black mess attendants, such as Moses Anderson Allen in New Bern, North Carolina; Irwin Corinthia Anderson and Donald Monroe in Norfolk, Virginia; and Andrew Tiny Whittemore in Nashville, Tennessee. Each of these men was among the first Americans in their towns to die in World War II.

The memorial for Private Robert Brooks made it clear that the military could not always police racial boundaries, despite their best efforts. Brooks, a tank driver with 192nd Tank Battalion, had just arrived at Clark Field in the Philippines when Japan's Pacific attack began. A Japanese bomb killed him early in the afternoon of December 8, making him the first U.S. Armored Force casualty of the war. Commanding General Jacob Devers, chief of the Armored Force, ordered that the main parade ground at Kentucky's Fort Knox be renamed Brooks Field in honor of the fallen private. Devers invited Brooks's parents, sharecroppers in rural Sadieville, Kentucky, to attend the dedication ceremony on December 23. It was an impressive event, with six generals in attendance and a bugler sounding taps in the tank driver's honor.

It was not until the parents arrived at the dedication ceremony that Devers and the army learned that Brooks was Black. The draft board had recorded him as white and the light-skinned Brooks declined to correct their error. Devers remained generous in his praise of Brooks. "In death there is no grade or rank," the general told the crowd. "And in this, the greatest democracy the world has ever known, neither riches nor poverty, neither creed nor race, draws a line of demarcation in this hour of national crisis." Devers delivered his bold speech without a sense of irony at a segregated base in a segregated army in a segregated state. Still, the *Norfolk Journal and Guide* wished that the army and navy would print the speech and post copies at every camp and on every ship.

Black soldiers stationed at the military camps around Alexandria, Louisiana, would have welcomed some of the democracy General Devers described. A sleepy town in central Louisiana, Alexandria's population boomed when the war started, as troops flooded into three nearby army camps (Claiborne, Livingston, and Beauregard) and airfields (Alexandria, Esler, and Pollock). More than sixteen thousand Black troops were stationed there, including members of the 758th Tank Battalion, the first Black armored unit. Each weekend, thousands of soldiers descended on the town to unwind and carouse. As in Gurdon, Arkansas, and other Southern towns, white military and local police restricted Black soldiers to the four-block Lee Street district, in the Black part of town.

Saturday, January 10, 1942, was shaping up to be a regular weekend night until a white motorist honked her horn at a Black soldier crossing the street and yelled for him to get out of the way. "Would you run over a soldier?" he snapped back. The woman flagged down a white city police officer, who arrested the soldier. When other Black troops attempted to intervene, several dozen white MPs arrived on the scene and the two groups traded insults and blows. The situation escalated as state police and MPs fired indiscriminately and Black troops fought back with bottles, rocks, and sticks.

"You would think Japan had made it to Lee St. it was so much shooting," said a member of the 91st Engineers. A Black waitress who witnessed the brawl and was struck by a stray bullet called Lee Street "Alexandria's Little Pearl Harbor."

When the fighting stopped, twenty-nine Black troops were wounded, three of them critically. Rumors swirled in the Black community that police had killed as many as a dozen Black soldiers. In a letter to Secretary of War Stimson, the NAACP's Walter White charged that Alexandria was yet another example of how the army's policy of segregation hurt the morale of Black citizens. "The Army has taken thousands of Negro men from northern and eastern states, and placed them in localities whose traditions and practices are designed deliberately to humiliate and insult them, and even to maltreat and kill them," White wrote. While the army insisted that it was not a sociological laboratory, Black troops felt like they were living through a terrible experiment.

————————

TWO WEEKS LATER, a civilian killing brought fresh outrage. In the early morning hours of Sunday, January 25, 1942, word spread through Sikeston, Missouri, that a white woman, Grace Sturgeon, was in grave condition after being slashed in her home. The police went looking for the unknown Black assailant and found Cleo Wright, a twenty-six-year-old Black oil mill worker, two miles from Sturgeon's house. Wright's pants were covered in blood and the police found a bloodstained knife in his pocket. On the way to the police station, Wright allegedly pulled a second knife from his boot and stabbed the marshal, who shot Wright several times at point-blank range. The police officer drove Wright, now bleeding profusely, to a local white hospital, where he received cursory bandages and sutures, before driving Wright to the jail at city hall.

When the police cruiser carrying Wright arrived at the jail just after daybreak, a crowd of angry whites had already formed outside. They were certain that Wright was guilty of attempting to rape and kill Sturgeon, whose husband was an army man stationed in Bakersfield, California. By late morning, the mob had grown to several hundred. They entered the jail, pushed aside police officers, and seized Wright, whose bullet wounds had left him barely conscious and clinging to life. Several men pulled Wright feet-first down the concrete steps of city hall and tied his legs to the bumper of a car. They dragged their captive over a mile through Sunset Addition, Sikeston's Black community. The car stopped just north of the Missouri Pacific Railroad tracks, between Lincoln Street and Fair Street, and the men cut Wright loose.

As a crowd of nearly four hundred whites jeered and cursed at

Wright, one man doused him with five gallons of gasoline and another tossed a match to set him ablaze. Wright let out a ghastly cry and raised his arms to the sky. His body burned in view of two Black churches, where parishioners were in the midst of Sunday services. Dozens of white men, women, and children drove or walked to Sunset Addition after their own church services ended to view Wright's charred remains. Postcards commemorating the lynching were displayed in white Sikeston homes, businesses, and schools.

Coming less than two months after Pearl Harbor, the lynching of Cleo Wright sent shock waves throughout the country. The NAACP's Walter White sent an urgent telegram to President Roosevelt as soon as he heard the news, calling for a federal investigation in Sikeston. Dozens of ordinary Black citizens also wrote the president, including a Brooklyn father who asked, "Is this the Democracy that we are trying to teach the world?" A Black army draftee wrote to the *New York Amsterdam News* encouraging his fellow soldiers to "remember Cleo as we die for democracy." *The New York Times* suggested that the lynching gave "comfort to Nazis," while the Cleveland *Call & Post* wrote that the Missouri mob "proved to America and the world on last Sunday that they could out-Hitler Hitler in brutal savagery." Several papers stressed the lynching's international implications, noting that Germany and Japan used Sikeston as anti-American propaganda.

In Missouri, local NAACP branches organized a mass rally in St. Louis on February 1, 1942. Over 3,500 people filled the YMCA gymnasium and lobbies and listened to speakers call for federal antilynching legislation. Protesters carried signs reading REMEMBER PEARL HARBOR! REMEMBER SIKESTON TOO! This slogan caught on and was repeated at protest meetings and in Black newspapers across the country over the next several months. Thurgood Marshall met with Justice Department officials about the case and U.S. Attorney General Francis Biddle authorized a federal investigation into Wright's lynching. Although the investigation produced no indictments, it was the first time a federal grand jury convened for a lynching case.

In Detroit, tensions boiled over days after the Cleo Wright lynching, when white protesters attempted to block Black defense workers from moving into the Sojourner Truth Housing Project. Carrying American flags, clubs, stones, and signs reading WE WANT WHITE NEIGHBORS IN OUR WHITE NEIGHBORHOOD, the pro-segregation demonstrators harassed the Black families. Black counterprotesters carried signs reading REMEMBER PEARL HARBOR and FIGHT HITLERISM HERE AND ABROAD. Another sign read NEGROES HAVE LANDED IN AUSTRALIA, WHEN DO WE LAND IN SOJOURNER TRUTH?, referring to a contingent of Black army engineering troops who arrived in Melbourne in late January.

Several young Black men tore up their draft cards after the Sojourner Truth incident. "I will take my fighting and dying, if necessary, right here on the streets of Detroit for some democracy for my own people," one man said. Over two thousand state troops and local police were eventually called in to defend the two hundred Black families that moved into the homes. The *Courier* saw the Sojourner Truth episode as evidence that the pressure campaign led by the NAACP, the Black press, and ordinary Black Americans worked. "Detroit serves as a lesson to those timid Negroes who always denounce agitation for citizenship rights as 'likely to cause trouble,'" the editors argued. "Militant Negroes organized and intelligently agitated and demonstrated until they won."

Just weeks after Pearl Harbor, the stakes of World War II were clear for Black Americans. Defeating the Axis powers was an important national priority for which thousands of Black people would risk their lives, but defeating fascism on foreign battlefields was only half the fight. Victory would be incomplete unless it also uprooted white supremacy in America. These dual war aims coalesced under a slogan that came to define the Black American experience during the war: Double V.

SIX

DOUBLE VICTORY

White folks would rather lose the war than
give up the luxury of race prejudice.

—ROY WILKINS

Pearl Harbor and Sikeston were fresh in the mind of James
Gratz Thompson, the twenty-six-year-old from Wichita who
had written to the *Courier* in January 1942 questioning
whether he should sacrifice his life to live half American. He wondered whether winning the war would make things better for Black
people and whether his country was willing to change. Thompson
continued:

> I suggest that while we keep defense and victory in the
> forefront that we don't lose sight of our fight for true de-
> mocracy at home. The V for victory sign is being dis-
> played prominently in all so-called democratic countries
> which are fighting for victory over aggression, slavery and

tyranny. If this V sign means that to those now engaged in this great conflict then let we colored Americans adopt the double VV for a double victory. The first V for victory over our enemies from without, the second V for victory over our enemies from within. For surely those who perpetrate these ugly prejudices here are seeking to destroy our democratic form of government just as surely as the Axis forces.

The *Courier* seized on Thompson's idea and in the next issue launched the Double V campaign.

The historical roots of Double Victory ran deep. When Frederick Douglass encouraged free Blacks to join the army in 1863, he described the Civil War as a "double battle, against slavery in the South and against prejudice and proscription in the North." In 1919, W. E. B. Du Bois encouraged the nearly 350,000 Black Americans who served during World War I to "battle against the forces of hell in our own land." He wrote, "We return. We return from fighting. We return fighting. Make way for Democracy! We saved it in France, and by the Great Jehovah, we will save it in the United States of America, or know the reason why." Black Americans, and especially Black World War I veterans, carried this sentiment with them as they fought white supremacy in the 1920s and '30s.

The Double V slogan was powerful not because it was new, but because it was old. It was deeply rooted in the lived experiences of generations of Black Americans who had fought for full citizenship. The Double V articulated the hopes, frustrations, and demands of millions with clarity and urgency: *This war will be different. This war has to be different.*

This clarity about war aims, however, was not necessarily shared by white Americans. In 1942, World War II was not yet the "Good War," and beyond the charge to "Remember Pearl Harbor," the question of what the war was about was still inchoate. Six months after the nation entered the war, 53 percent of Americans polled did not have a clear grasp of war aims. Sociologist Samuel Stouffer, who led the U.S. Army's Research Branch and conducted hundreds of surveys on the attitudes of American soldiers during the war, found that the average GI believed that the United States had to win the war after the Japanese attack on Pearl Harbor, but was not motivated to fight by ideology or idealism. *Life* magazine noted "the bewilderment of the boys in the armed forces concerning the meaning of the war."

Writer Arthur Miller found a similar sense of confusion with war workers in the Brooklyn Navy Yard. Miller felt that among the men he worked with fourteen hours a day, only his fellow Jewish coworkers comprehended what Nazism meant. Others seemed ignorant of, or untroubled by, Hitler's ideology of Aryan racial superiority. For these men, Miller said, "we were fighting Germany essentially because she had allied herself with the Japanese who had attacked us at Pearl Harbor." While he was in North Africa, war correspondent Ernie Pyle confided to another journalist, "You, who have roots in Europe, can work up a real hate about this thing, but I can't. When you figure how many boys are going to get killed, what's the use of it anyway." Poet Randall Jarrell was stationed at bases in Texas, Illinois, and Arizona as a member of the U.S. Army Air Corps. In a letter to a friend, he wrote, "99 of 100 people in the army haven't the faintest idea what the war's about. Their strongest motives are (a) nationalism . . . and (b) race prejudice—they dislike Japanese in the same way, though not as much as, they dislike Negroes."

While Black Americans were fighting against white supremacy, many white Americans were fighting to uphold and strengthen a racial caste system where they held the dominant position. Edward Moe, a federal investigator who surveyed racial attitudes early in the war, found that many white Southerners believed that World War II was about preserving things "as they have been in America" and had "revolting visions of what the new socie; may be like" if racial hierarchies were upended. These white citizens had a fundamentally different vision for postwar America. "White men are so fixed in their emotional attitudes [about race] that their morale may seem to depend upon the maintenance of those attitudes," argued Jonathan Daniels, the liberal Southern editor of the Raleigh *News and Observer* and a Roosevelt adviser on racial issues. "Sometimes it is easier to ask people to give up their lives than to give up their prejudices."

The flip side of the Double V campaign was that most white Americans understood the war to be only about defeating the Japanese and the Nazis militarily, a "single V" abroad that maintained the status quo at home. It was not lost on Black Americans that their white countrymen understood the war in very different terms. "White folks would rather lose the war than give up the luxury of race prejudice," the NAACP's Roy Wilkins quipped.

Military segregation made no sense for a nation trying to win a war; it made sense only for a nation trying to appease white racial prejudices. At the same time army and navy recruiters pleaded for volunteers after Pearl Harbor, they continued to turn away Black college graduates, doctors, language specialists, tradesmen, and others with skills that would aid the war effort. The navy, Wilkins charged, "would rather not have a vital radio message get through than to have it sent by Black hands or over equipment set up by Black technicians." The military's policy of segregation was costly and inefficient because it required the construction and maintenance of separate and redundant training facilities, as well as additional logistical planning for troop transportation and deployments. At training camps across the country, white commanders forced black troops to use separate and unequal barracks, mess halls, and hospitals, among other facilities. As federal property, military installations were not subject to Jim Crow state laws, yet segregation was the norm even though it served no strategic or tactical purpose.

Similarly, the Red Cross's policy of segregating blood from Black donors had no scientific basis, and it required additional time and effort to separately track, store, and ship "white" and "colored" blood. Black Americans saw the policy as an affront. Dr. Charles Drew, the Black pioneer who developed the process to store blood plasma and led the first large-scale blood banks in the United States and Great Britain, resigned from the Red Cross military blood bank program in protest. Civil rights activist Pauli Murray boycotted the blood-donor program in Los Angeles, calling it a "policy which rivals Hitler's for its official approval of 'racial superiority.'" In a poem dedicated to Doris Miller, poet Gwendolyn Brooks expressed her frustration with the blood ban in verse:

> In a southern city a white man said
> Indeed, I'd rather be dead.

Indeed, I'd rather be shot in the head
Or ridden to waste on the back of a flood
Than saved by the drop of a Black man's blood.

SINCE THE DOUBLE VICTORY CAMPAIGN demanded more than simply military victory, it was regarded as radical by many white officials and citizens. Presidential adviser Jonathan Daniels called the Double V campaign "extortion" and considered the idea of "two victories or none" to be evidence of the conditional loyalty of Black Americans. *Richmond Times-Dispatch* editor Virginius Dabney called Double V "a war against our enemies and against the whites at home," while *Birmingham Age-Herald* editor John Temple Graves II warned, "The Negro must not regard [the war] as a shining opportunity to right his wrongs."

FBI director J. Edgar Hoover charged that the Double Victory campaign and the Black press's wartime coverage of racism were seditious because they could be used for enemy propaganda. Shortly after Pearl Harbor, Hoover tried to indict *Baltimore Afro-American* editors under the Espionage Act for publishing person-on-the-street comments that were sympathetic to Japan. His FBI agents openly subscribed to Black newspapers, made frequent field visits to question editors and reporters, and kept an extensive collection of Black press clippings in an effort to catch the editors in acts of disloyalty. *Pittsburgh Courier* editors shot back at Hoover in March 1942, charging that FBI actions were "an obvious effort to cow the Negro press into soft-pedaling its criticism and ending its forthright exposure of the outrageous discriminations to which Negros have been subjected."

President Roosevelt shared many of Hoover's concerns about sedition, and in his April 28, 1942, Fireside Chat he promised Americans that "this great war effort . . . must not be impeded by a few bogus patriots who use the sacred freedom of the press to echo the sentiments of the propagandists in Tokyo and Berlin." In a cabinet meeting the following month, the president directed Attorney General Biddle to meet with Black editors "to see what could be done about preventing their subversive language."

To make matters worse, influential syndicated columnist Westbrook Pegler also attacked the Black press. Pegler accused the *Chicago Defender* and the *Courier* of "exploiting the war emergency" in order to "push the aspirations of colored people." He charged that the Black press was inciting violence among Black soldiers and was as dangerous as radio priest Father Charles Coughlin, whose weekly paper and broadcast program reached more than thirty million people and espoused profascist and anti-Semitic views. Pegler's smear of the Black press was read by millions of white Americans, most of whom had little direct exposure to Black newspapers and therefore were easily persuaded that the Black press was unpatriotic. Black editors felt as though they were caught in a vise, with the White House, Justice Department, FBI, and white journalists squeezing from all sides.

Chicago Defender publisher John Sengstacke did not wait for Biddle to summon him. In June 1942, he flew to Washington, D.C., and asked Mary McLeod Bethune, civil rights activist and special adviser to Roosevelt on Black American affairs, to help him secure a meeting with the attorney general. When Sengstacke arrived at the Department of Justice, he was ushered into a conference room where Biddle was seated at the head of a long table. In front of the attorney general, a dozen copies of the *Defender*, *Courier*, and *Afro-American* were spread on the table, each one with headlines detailing racial violence at military bases that spring. Biddle told Sengstacke the articles were a disservice to the war effort and "came very close to sedition." The Justice Department was watching the papers closely, he said, and if they continued down this path he was "going to shut them all up."

Sengstacke did not shrink from this threat. He told the attorney general the Black press was urging readers to support the war, but they were also duty bound to speak out when Black people's love for their country was not reciprocated. He described how *Arkansas State Press* publishers Lucius and Daisy Bates had endured several FBI visits and feared being shut down by federal officials for their criticism of segregation in the South. Gesturing to the papers arrayed before him on the table, Sengstacke said this crusading against racism did not start with the war. Black newspapers had been fighting racism for generations and they were not about to stop.

Sengstacke looked Biddle in the eyes and took a long pause. "You have the power to close us down, so if you want to close us, go ahead and attempt it." Biddle shifted uncomfortably in his seat. Sengstacke, his eyes still trained on the attorney general, said he hoped it would not come to this and that he saw a way to compromise. The Black press needed access to War Secretary Stimson and other government officials, he said.

"Nobody will talk with us," Sengstacke said. "So, what do you expect us to publish? We don't want to publish the wrong information. We want to cooperate with the war effort. But if we can't get the information from the heads of various agencies, we have to do the best we can."

"Well, I didn't know that," Biddle replied, his firm tone beginning to soften. "Well, look, I'll see if I can help you in that way. And what I'll do is make arrangements for you to see some of these people."

Biddle picked up the phone and called Frank Knox and arranged for Sengstacke to meet with him later in June. The attorney general and the *Defender* editor kept talking for more than an hour. Biddle promised that the Justice Department would not bring sedition charges against the Black press, as long as they did not release anything more critical than what they had already published. Sengstacke said that while he could not guarantee other publishers would tone down their coverage, if they were granted interviews with government officials they would be glad to back the war effort.

When Sengstacke met days later with his fellow Black publishers, they were relieved to hear that sedition indictments were being held at bay and pleased to have more access to government officials. Their relief compounded when the Justice Department cracked down on more than two dozen anti-Semites and white supremacists, including publishers of extremist newspapers, for taking part in "a nation-wide conspiracy to destroy the morale of our armed forces through systematic dissemination of sedition." While Hoover and the FBI continued to hound Black editors and reporters during the war, Biddle was true to his word and did not indict the Black press.

For their part, Black editors felt the burden of selling their readers on supporting the war effort. While government officials believed the newspapers were stoking animosity, the editors knew that many average Black Americans were deeply skeptical of the war abroad and that Black press headlines were mild in comparison to the opinions shared every day in Black neighborhoods. When more than forty Black leaders met in early 1942, the vast majority agreed with the assessment of William Hastie, civilian aide to the secretary of war, that Black Americans were "not whole-heartedly and unreservedly all-out in support of the present war effort." Roy Wilkins confided to Hastie that he believed Black Americans were cynical and disillusioned. Their enthusiasm for the war effort was tepid because they saw the Allies as the lesser of two evils. *Philadelphia Tribune* publisher E. Washington Rhodes agreed, arguing that "many Negroes felt that the present war is a 'white man's war,' and that Negroes had nothing to fight for. It was the Negro Press which has changed this attitude by insisting that Negroes are American citizens and as such have the duty to fight, work and die for America."

When Morehouse College graduate Lewis Jones chose to go to jail rather than join the army, the *Afro-American* sent a reporter to try to change his mind and, when he refused, condemned his decision as irresponsible. Forty Howard University students wrote an angry reply to the Baltimore paper arguing that thousands of Black men and women would count Jones as a "hero" and "will rank him with Frederick Douglass and A. Philip Randolph."

THE DOUBLE VICTORY CAMPAIGN was in full swing when the navy released the name of the heroic Black messman from Pearl Harbor. Almost overnight, Doris Miller became one of the most famous Black Americans, even if many reports misspelled his first name. "To Dorie Miller . . . a real sailor, an American fighting man, no longer an 'unnamed hero' . . . America salutes you!" the *Courier* wrote. Comparing the mess attendant to heavyweight champion Joe Louis, the *New York Amsterdam News* wrote, "Dorie Miller's act of heroism at Pearl Harbor did more than all the talking and writing we could do for the next 20 years to change the Naval attitude toward us." The Black press led a campaign for the navy to honor Miller's courage. Attorney General Biddle sent President Roosevelt a stack of clippings about Miller from Black newspapers and advised, "You may wish to urge the award of a medal." FDR forwarded the memo to Frank Knox and several days later ordered that Miller be awarded the Navy Cross.

After Pearl Harbor, Miller was transferred to the USS *Indianapolis*, which engaged Japanese forces in the waters off New Guinea in the spring of 1942. En route to the Aleutian Islands in the North Pacific, the *Indianapolis* stopped briefly in Hawaii. On May 27, Miller received the Navy Cross from Admiral Chester Nimitz, the commander of the U.S. Pacific Fleet, on the flight deck of the aircraft carrier USS *Enterprise*. The wreckage from Pearl Harbor was still visible nearby. Miller stood proudly before Nimitz, as dozens of officers and sailors, all white, looked on. Pinning the medal to Miller's chest, Nimitz said, "This marks the first time in the present conflict that such high tribute has been made in the Pacific Fleet to a member of his race and I am sure that the future will see others similarly honored for brave acts."

Miller became a powerful symbol because his actions proved that Black Americans could fight heroically if only they were given the chance. His story also resonated because even after his bravery at Pearl Harbor earned him the Navy Cross, he was still a mess attendant tasked with serving white officers. In the months after Pearl Harbor, thousands of Black Americans deployed to distant war sites, such as Australia and Alaska, and found themselves in service roles in the army and navy. They and their loved ones could relate to Miller's story. They toiled behind the scenes and would never get the national recognition Miller earned, but they did the dirty work that would help win the war.

SEVEN

DIRTY WORK IN DISTANT LANDS

When some people decry the passing of
American spirit, I think of the boys who
hacked a road through a wilderness as track-
less as that crossed by the covered wagons
which went to Oregon in 1850. I think of the
Negro soldiers from the Deep South who
drove trucks at forty-five degrees below zero.

—CAPTAIN RICHARD NEUBERGER,
CORPS OF ENGINEERS

This war is a new kind of war," President Roosevelt told the nation in a Fireside Chat in February 1942. "It is different from all other wars of the past, not only in its methods and weapons but also in its geography. It is warfare in terms of every continent, every island, every sea, every air-lane in the world." Take out a map and spread it before you, Roosevelt urged. The battle lines of this world war extended far beyond America's borders. "We must all understand and face the hard fact that our job now is to fight at distances which extend all the way around the globe."

In his chat, the president tried to assure the public that despite Pearl Harbor and the string of Japanese victories in the Pacific, America would use its resource and production advantages to win a war of attrition against Japan. Roosevelt referenced the anniversary of George Washington's birth and urged Americans to remember that General Washington and the Continental Army also met "formidable odds and recurring defeats," and to show the same "moral stamina" as "Washington's little army of ragged, rugged men."

Privately, though, Roosevelt and military leaders worried about how the Allies could stem the tide. In the months after Pearl Harbor, the Imperial Japanese Navy and Army asserted their dominance across the region. Japan seized key strategic sites in the Philippines, the Dutch East Indies, Singapore, and the Malay Peninsula, taking tens of thousands of Allied troops as prisoners of war and gaining control of important oil and rubber supplies. With subsequent conquests of large parts of New Guinea and the Solomon Islands (colonial possessions of Australia and Britain, respectively), Japan gained a defensive perimeter in the South Pacific and a launching pad for attacks on mainland Australia. "The Pacific situation is now very grave," Roosevelt cabled Churchill after the Japanese conquest of Java in March.

While Australia desperately needed Allied support to fend off Japanese attacks, their government maintained immigration-restriction policies that barred non-Europeans from the country. With this "White Australia" policy in place, Australia asked the United States not to send Black troops down under. American officials were reluctant to disrupt racial norms in an Allied nation, but felt that the war emergency demanded a quick ramp-up in the region. They sent thousands of Black American troops to Australia in the early months of 1942, though military leaders assured the Australian government that they would station them in remote areas and away from cities.

The Black troops in the 96th Engineer General Service Regiment arrived in Australia in the midst of this convoluted compromise. Near Townsville on the northeast coast of Queensland, the engineers cleared four turf runways, each over a mile long, that enabled Allied planes to patrol the air over the Coral Sea. The battalion moved to Port Moresby near the end of April 1942, becoming the first American troops to land in New Guinea. They immediately got to work building landing strips and bridges, laying macadam roads, and installing pumps and water mains. "We did some of just about everything to be done," said Private Leon Thomas of New Orleans. The engineers performed this grueling labor while Japanese planes strafed and bombed the island day and night.

The work was urgent because American military intelligence had intercepted and deciphered messages suggesting that the Japanese were planning a major offensive on Port Moresby in early May. While the 96th fortified the southeastern tip of New Guinea, four U.S. Navy aircraft carriers and dozens of warships descended on the area to thwart the invasion. The American and Japanese fleets played a game of cat and mouse in the Coral Sea. The Japanese sank an American tanker and destroyer, while both sides searched for their opponents' carriers, before finally engaging directly on May 8.

Aboard the USS *Lexington* during the Battle of the Coral Sea, mess attendant Elvin Bell fought fires amid explosions of gasoline vapors and ammunition and ventured belowdecks to rescue three trapped shipmates. The twenty-year-old former foster child from Jamaica, Queens, in New York City was awarded the Navy and Marine Corps Medal for his heroism. The Battle of the Coral Sea was a draw, but it stopped the Empire of Japan's unchecked advance across the region. A month later, the U.S. Navy scored a decisive victory at the Battle of Midway, turning the tide in the Pacific war.

Fighting in the Pacific was laborious and brutal. The Allies sought to seize key islands, kill, capture, or drive out Japanese soldiers, and build airstrips and ports. The goal of this island-hopping strategy was to bring the war closer and closer to Japan. From New Guinea to the Solomon Islands, Black troops played a crucial role in the Allies' success. "You've had a part in the building and upkeep of all our airfields; and thus you've helped make possible the destruction of the [Japanese] convoy in the Bismarck Sea, the flying of the infantry over the mountains . . . you've contributed your share to every crack we've taken at the [Japanese]," Brigadier General Hanford MacNider told the 96th Engineers. "You've carried out important work projects, even unloaded ships so we could eat and fight. You've built roads and the mains which give us power and light. You're one of the workingest outfits in this man's Army. All of us here are proud of you. All America will be proud of you when your record gets into the histories."

THE PACIFIC WAR WAS VAST, like the ocean itself. At the same time as the Battle of Midway was taking place, the Japanese navy bombed American military bases two thousand miles north on Dutch

Harbor and seized Attu and Kiska, two of the Aleutian Islands that stretch like a tail southwest of Alaska. The Aleutian Islands were an important transportation route in the North Pacific and the bombing raid raised fears that attacks on the West Coast of the United States would follow. The attack also heightened the sense of urgency for the Black troops who were building the Alaska Highway to connect the territory to the contiguous United States across Canada.

Shortly after Pearl Harbor, President Roosevelt identified Alaska as a strategic priority and directed Congress and the military to find a way to build an emergency supply route. "The effective defense of Alaska is of paramount importance to the defense of the continent against attack from the west," the administration's report argued. A highway would provide a secure inland route that was not exposed to attack from the sea. It would prove to be a costly and challenging slog through treacherous terrain.

With work on the highway set to begin in spring 1942, the general in charge of defending Alaska wanted Black troops sent to the Last Frontier only under specific conditions. Brigadier General Simon Bolivar Buckner Jr., named after his father, who served as a Confederate general in the Civil War, planned to retire in Alaska after the war. He wrote to his West Point classmate Brigadier General Clarence Sturdevant to express his concern that Black soldiers would "remain and settle [in Alaska] after the war, with the natural results that they would interbreed with the Indians and Eskimos and produce an astonishingly objectionable race of mongrels which would be a problem from now on." Buckner continued, "We have enough racial problems here and elsewhere already. I have no objections whatever to your employing them on the roads if they are kept far enough away from the settlements and kept busy and then sent home as soon as possible." In Alaska, as in Australia and, later, in the European theater, racial prejudice competed with military necessity in decisions about where to deploy Black troops.

Sturdevant, too, did not want Black troops working on the road. As the assistant chief of the Corps of Engineers charged with overseeing construction of the military highway, however, his need for labor ultimately outweighed his animus against Black Americans. It quickly became clear that the four white engineer regiments he initially tapped for the job would not be able to complete the work quickly enough. He apologized to Buckner for the need to assign Black troops to the region but promised that they would be hard at work around the clock in out-of-the-way places and would be sent back to the mainland before the end of the year.

When they boarded a train from Camp Livingston, Louisiana, early on an April morning, the 93rd Engineer General Service Regiment did not know where they were headed. Five days later they arrived in Prince Rupert, British Columbia. From there they boarded a ship to Skagway, Alaska, and set up a temporary camp at an airfield outside of town, away from local residents and apart from the white army engineers. They did not know why they had been sent to this remote territory, only that they had traveled over four thousand miles from one Jim Crow camp to another. By summer, three more Black units—the 95th, 97th, and 388th Engineer General Service Regiments—joined the 93rd in Alaska. Totaling more than thirty-six hundred troops, the Black engineers made up a third of the U.S. soldiers working on the highway.

The highway project had an old-fashioned flavor to it. Armed with axes, handsaws, picks, and shovels, the engineers pushed through swamps and forests, across rivers and over mountains. They guided bulldozers and trucks through mud and muck in the summer and over ice and snow in the winter. It was grueling labor and the men sang as they fought the road mile by mile—work songs that their parents and grandparents had sung back in Alabama, Georgia, and Mississippi.

"It was modern-day slavery," said Joseph Haskin from Lafayette, Louisiana, who volunteered to join the 93rd Engineers before Pearl Harbor. "The racism displayed toward Blacks by the white officers in command, made it an almost intolerable situation," said Paul Francis, another member of the 93rd. "We were treated like convict labor." A white officer in Alaska made this connection explicit in a letter that referenced the cruel slave owner from Harriet Beecher Stowe's novel *Uncle Tom's Cabin*. "Have trouble getting them to work and get up on time," the officer wrote of Black troops, "so just like Simon Legree I ride them."

Despite the harsh weather and racist attitudes of white officers, the Black engineers played a critical role in successfully completing the highway in only eight months. The road stretched over sixteen hundred miles from Dawson Creek, British Columbia, to Delta Junction, Alaska, farther than the distance from Seattle to Los Angeles or from New York to Miami. The road was "a sword pointed at our enemies in Japan," said Brigadier General James O'Conner.

The news from Alaska also captured the imaginations of other Black Americans. Claude Albert Barnett, founder of the Associated Negro Press, called the highway "the world's greatest monument to Negro labor" and praised the engineers for "demonstrating the faith, loyalty and patriotism of Black Americans for flag and country." Several Black newspapers carried a photo of Corporal Refines

Sims Jr., a Black engineer from Philadelphia, shaking hands with Private Alfred Jalukamet, a white engineer from Texas, after their bulldozers completed the road's last link. The picture marked a rare moment of racial unity and equality in a segregated and deeply unequal army.

The papers marveled that the engineers averaged eight miles of road per day, crossed more than two hundred streams, reached an altitude of more than four thousand feet, and bridged one river in only three days. War correspondent Herbert Frisby visited the Yukon Territory and asked *Baltimore Afro-American* readers to "try to imagine a modern highway the base of which is wood, and over which now travels the heaviest kinds of trucks and freight, twenty-four hours a day." Frisby said he met several Alaskans who referred to the military highway as the "Negro road" as a tribute to "our engineers."

Fighting a global war required a colossal logistical undertaking to link the continental United States to battlefronts around the world. On a map, these supply lines looked neat and orderly, so many air, land, and sea routes crisscrossing the globe. On the ground, it was clear that building, maintaining, and defending these supply lines entailed a tremendous amount of work. Starting early in the war, Black troops played a vital role across the Pacific, building runways, roads, and other critical infrastructure. It was a preview of the dirty work Black troops would do later in the war, transporting vital war supplies inland from the beaches of Normandy and building the thousand-mile-long Ledo Road between India and China.

EIGHT

TUSKEGEE TAKES FLIGHT

> The nation can no longer afford to fight a
> total war with only part of its resources
> whether this is in equipment or in man-
> power. It can no longer afford to appease
> southern racial sensibilities when this will
> mean the difference of hitting its foes with
> a sledge hammer instead of a pop gun . . .
> [Black pilots] stand courageously ready to
> join their white brothers in blasting the com-
> mon enemy out of the sky.
>
> —*Chicago Defender*

As Black engineers built the Alaska Highway, another group of Black Americans were building a new world five thousand miles away in Tuskegee, Alabama. Benjamin O. Davis Jr. read about the Black engineers in New Guinea and Alaska with mixed emotions. He was proud that his fellow soldiers, his Black countrymen, were distinguishing themselves in the Pacific. At the same time, he was frustrated that he and the other Tuskegee pilots were still waiting for their opportunity to join the fight.

Nearly six years had passed since he graduated from West Point, the first Black man to do so in over four decades. Unlike at West Point, he was not alone at Tuskegee. Four other Black pilots survived advanced classroom and flight training to join Davis at the graduation ceremony on March 7, 1942.

These five men, the first Black aviators in the U.S. Army Air Corps, took different routes to Tuskegee. Howard University graduate Lemuel Custis was a police officer from Hartford, Connecticut; Charles DeBow hailed from Indianapolis and studied business at Hampton Institute in Virginia; George Spencer Roberts grew up in rural West Virginia and graduated from West Virginia State College when he was eighteen; and Mac Ross was one of ten children of a Dayton, Ohio, postal worker. As a West Point grad and son of the first African American general, Davis had a military pedigree that set him apart, but he was happy to be one of a cohort of pioneers.

Major General George Stratemeyer, commander of the Southeast Air Corps Training Center, gave the graduation address. Stratemeyer was a West Point classmate of Dwight D. Eisenhower and Omar Bradley. The class of 1915 was heralded as the "class the stars fell on" because a third of them reached the rank of general, a record for the academy. While he was part of the old guard, Stratemeyer spoke movingly about what lay ahead for the Tuskegee Airmen.

"In past wars, American Negro soldiers have done their full duty with combat units of the ground forces," the general said. "In this war, the American Negro is destined to take his place in the defense of his country by performing combat duties in the air." Stratemeyer told the graduates and their families that airpower would play a pivotal role in the war.

The pilots did not need convincing. They had gravitated to flying because it was the most glamorous and thrilling opportunity the military offered. It required a mixture of intelligence, skill, and daring. When the base commander pinned silver wings on the pilots' uniforms it was a powerful symbol that Black Americans had joined an elite echelon of the army.

Just beyond the walls of the post theater, a world of skilled Black military men and women was taking shape at Tuskegee Army Airfield. More than a dozen Black nurses were assigned to the base hospital. Led by First Lieutenant Della Raney, the first Black woman commissioned in the Army Nurse Corps, the nurses offered medical care to the pilots and ground personnel. The aviators would not have gotten off the ground without the expertise of mechanics who performed daily maintenance on the BT-13 Valiant, PT-17 Stearman, and AT-6 Texan trainers. In March 1942 alone, more than eight hundred mechanics and other ground crew arrived at the airfield, forming the nucleus of the 366th Material Squadron. While the Tuskegee pilots received the lion's share of attention, the Tuskegee air base was a hub of Black expertise and excellence during the war.

It was also a Jim Crow base in a Jim Crow town. William Hastie opposed segregated flight training at Tuskegee from the outset. He lobbied Secretary of War Henry Stimson and other military and civilian officials, arguing that more Black pilots could be trained if they were spread out across multiple air bases in northern states, and that more pilots would persist if they were trained in these less hostile environments.

Hastie's concerns were well founded. Colonel Frederick von Kimble, who took over as Tuskegee air base commander in January 1942, strictly enforced segregated living quarters and dining facilities. The

Black personnel hated him. Many of the Black enlisted men had trained previously at Chanute Field in Illinois under relatively integrated conditions. They found von Kimble capricious and the rigid segregation at Tuskegee abrasive. A pair of enlisted men staged a sit-in in the "whites only" section of the post restaurant, and others tried to forcibly desegregate base facilities. Davis and the other Black officers chafed at the signs posted on bathroom doors reading FOR COLORED OFFICERS and FOR WHITE OFFICERS. They wondered what kind of army would not allow a person, even an officer, to use a certain bathroom because of the color of their skin. Worse still, von Kimble ordered white officers not to socialize with their Black counterparts and refused to assign Black officers to jobs that matched their qualifications.

Davis described the air base as a "prison camp for Black servicemen and their families," while his wife, Agatha, called Tuskegee a "hell of a hole." Airman George "Spanky" Roberts married his sweetheart, Edith, the same day he earned his wings. They moved off base, but with no one willing to rent them a house, they were forced to move in with a local Black family.

Tensions mounted shortly after the graduation ceremony when local police tried to seize a soldier who had been arrested by a Black military policeman for disturbing the peace in town. More than a dozen heavily armed white civilians crowded around the Black MP, who pulled his pistol and refused to hand over the soldier. Word of the standoff spread quickly, and soon a large group of Black soldiers and civilians were on the scene. Two Alabama Highway Patrol officers and a Macon County deputy sheriff provided backup for the local police. They forcibly disarmed the Black MP and proceeded to beat him with billy clubs, severely enough that he required treatment at the nearby VA hospital.

When news of the beating reached the base, the pilots and mechanics were irate. Several airmen armed themselves and hopped a truck heading into town. Director of Flight Training Noel Parrish, a white officer whom the Black personnel respected, stopped the truck and persuaded the men to return to the base. Von Kimble's solution to this near racial clash was to prevent Black MPs from carrying weapons, enforce a curfew on Black troops, and promise his superiors that he would "ferret out" the small number of "radically inclined" personnel.

Despite this pervasive racism, Davis and his fellow Tuskegee pilots found joy in the air. They soared over verdant forests, streams, and orderly farmland that looked like a checkerboard from the air. They guided their powerful planes through loops, rolls, stalls, and forced landings. They worked their way up to chandelles, steep climbing turns to change direction at maximum attitude. Flying was exhilarating and offered the airmen a freedom they were denied on the ground.

It was also hard work, particularly for Davis. He was not a natural flier and unlike his classmates George Roberts and Lemuel Custis, he had not completed a Civilian Pilot Training program. The precise military bearing that enabled Davis to survive West Point initially made him too conscientious and stiff in the air. With determination and practice he honed the skills and instincts he needed to be a successful pilot. Flying in formation at night, with stars glistening in the Alabama sky, Davis believed for the first time that he would someday fly on a real mission.

The question was when. Rumors swirled that the airmen could be deployed at any time. The first five Tuskegee air base graduates were the nucleus of the unit, but it would take several more months for enough pilots to complete advanced training before the fighter squadron would reach full strength. As spring gave way to the hot and humid summer months, Davis and his fellow airmen trained and waited. They acquainted themselves with their P-40 Warhawks and imagined using the plane to outmaneuver German or Japanese foes in combat. In their downtime, the pilots would go to the post exchange and pick up copies of *The Pittsburgh Courier* and the *Baltimore Afro-American*, alongside copies of magazines like *Time* and *Life*. In these pages they followed the war in the Pacific and Europe and drew inspiration from the stories they read about Black troops who had already deployed.

The fifth class of Tuskegee pilots graduated in August 1942, bringing the 99th Fighter Squadron to its full strength of thirty-three pilots, and the army declared the unit ready for combat the following month. Now the commander of the 99th, Davis tried to keep morale up among his restless pilots. While white peers from other air bases rushed into combat after completing just five weeks of training, the Tuskegee Airmen repeated the same flying exercises over and over. The army seemed to have no idea where to send their first unit of Black pilots.

While the airmen bided their time, work at the air base continued apace, with Black women playing a central role. Marcelle Phyllis Reid of Atlanta drew maps for the pilots' cross-country flights, while Cecilia Dixon, an Alpha Kappa Alpha soror during her days at West Virginia State, guided air traffic on the runway. Adelle McDonald, a housewife from Tuscaloosa, Alabama, repaired dam-

aged airplane wings, rudders, and ailerons. Air base news and bulletins were typed and printed by women such as twenty-year-old
Gertrude Williams of Chicago and Lillian Register of Pensacola,
Florida. Like Williams and Register, many of the women at Tuskegee had brothers in the service as well. They were among the thousands of Black American families with multiple loved ones serving
in the military during the war.

For the crucial weather information they needed to fly, the pilots
turned to Black meteorologists like Wallace Patillo Reed. Reed came
to Tuskegee after completing a mathematics degree at the University
of New Hampshire and specialized meteorology training classes at
Massachusetts Institute of Technology. He led a detachment of nearly
a dozen weather forecasters, all of whom excelled in math, science,
and engineering. Many of the recruits aspired to be pilots themselves, but poor eyesight or age led them into the weather service.
The weather detachment collected and recorded weather conditions
and briefed the airmen every day. Without the weathermen, the airmen could not safely take flight.

The women and men at the air base were giving their all for the
war effort, but no amount of patriotism, academic preparation, or
grit could buffer them from what Davis described as the "unfair-
ness, demeaning insults, and raw discrimination" of daily life in
Tuskegee. The ever-present reality of racism meant conditions on
the base were always tense. In September 1942, the base was even
more on edge after the 99th suffered their first casualty when Lieutenant Faythe McGinnis crashed on a routine flight.

A week later, Lieutenant Norma Greene, a nurse from Elkins,
West Virginia, was shopping in Montgomery, Alabama, in preparation for her deployment overseas. After she finished shopping, she

purchased a bus ticket for the forty-mile trip back to Tuskegee. When she boarded, the driver told her that the bus was for whites only and she would need to wait for a later coach. Lieutenant Greene needed to get back for her shift at the air base hospital and she refused to leave the bus. The driver called the city police and the four officers forcibly removed Greene from the bus, then hit and arrested her. She spent the night in jail before the police turned her over to military authorities. She returned to work on the air base, bruised and shaken by the ordeal.

News of the arrest and beating spread quickly around the base and to the NAACP's offices in New York. "The race question is getting worse than ever down here and something must be done about it," one of Greene's nursing colleagues wrote in an urgent letter. A local civil rights activist wrote to Walter White, explaining that the bus assault was a commonplace experience for Black people in Alabama. "This incident is only one of many that have confronted Negroes seeking bus transportation in this area," he wrote. "Several instances are known locally of respectable, law-abiding, colored citizens who have been insulted or threatened."

The pattern of racial discrimination at Tuskegee produced dangerously low levels of morale among Black officers and enlisted personnel. "They are soul-sick over the relentless impact on their lives of the hatred of white Alabama in general and the little town of Tuskegee in particular," *The Pittsburgh Courier* argued. "Their morale is low because they feel that the Command at the post has tried to placate the hatred of a poor, insignificant, little Southern town like Tuskegee, rather than assert the authority of the United States Army and protect the men [and women] at any cost. If a soldier has got to feel that his is the best army in the world, how is he going to feel that way if his army can't lick a Tuskegee, Alabama?"

When William Hastie and Thurgood Marshall read the news from Tuskegee, they were alarmed that the violence by white police and civilians against Black troops and military personnel continued unabated. They recorded the bloodshed since Pearl Harbor: Sergeant Thomas Foster in Little Rock, Arkansas; Private Charles Reco in Beaumont, Texas; Private Willie Jullis in El Paso, Texas; Private Henry Williams in Mobile, Alabama; Private Larry Stroud in Columbia, South Carolina; Private Raymond Carr in Alexandria, Louisiana. All were shot and killed by police or, in Williams's case, by a bus driver authorized to carry a firearm and exercise police power. The Justice Department and the War Department chronically failed to investigate these cases. The Black pilots, nurses, and ground crew at Tuskegee knew these names thanks to the Black press, as did Black troops on bases in other parts of the country and as far away as New Guinea.

For the Tuskegee Airmen, all of these stories made them even more eager to deploy. They reckoned they would be safer in a war zone than staying in the Jim Crow South.

IN EARLY NOVEMBER 1942, more than one hundred thousand American and British troops landed on the coasts of French Morocco and Algeria. The North African invasion had been debated in Washington, D.C., for months. President Roosevelt viewed the operation as a first step toward American forces engaging the Nazis in Europe, while most of his military advisers opposed the idea. General George Patton, who commanded the troops under Supreme Allied Commander General Dwight D. Eisenhower, called Roosevelt's decision to authorize the invasion "about as desperate a venture as has ever been undertaken," because of the coordination, cooperation, and logistical complexity it involved.

Roosevelt wrote a letter that was delivered to all the soldiers and sailors in the U.S. Expeditionary Force on the eve of the invasion, called Operation Torch. "You have embarked for distant places where the war is being fought," he wrote. "Upon the outcome depends the freedom of your lives: the freedom of the lives of those you love—your fellow-citizens—your people. Never were the enemies of freedom more tyrannical, more arrogant, more brutal." Operation Torch marked the largest American troop deployment to date in the Atlantic and Mediterranean and the first major joint military operation between the United States and the United Kingdom.

Roosevelt's strategic gamble paid off. The French troops in Morocco turned against the Vichy French and their Nazi commanders and joined the Allies. Days later the British-led Allied forces completed a successful push to drive Nazi field marshal Erwin Rommel and German-Italian forces out of Egypt.

The victories changed the military outlook in Europe. The Allies gained access to key Mediterranean shipping lanes and secured bases from which to launch attacks on Italy. More important, with the Americans committed to the defense of Europe, the Allies could defeat the Nazis.

"Now this is not the end. It is not even the beginning of the end," Winston Churchill told the British people. "But it is, perhaps, the end of the beginning. Henceforth Hitler's Nazis will meet equally well armed, and perhaps better-armed troops. Henceforth they will have to face in many theatres of war that superiority in the air which they have so often used without mercy against others." The prime minister ordered church bells to be rung all over Britain.

When Benjamin O. Davis read about the victories in North Africa he knew that his unit could receive orders to go overseas any day. Rumor had it that the 99th would be sent to a nonwhite country to minimize objections from local officials. He hoped the squadron would soon be part of the air superiority Churchill described, and he did his best to keep up morale among the pilots. "The success of the combat unit will prove to be the opening wedge for the air minded youths who aspire to the field of Aviation," he told the 99th in late November. "My greatest desire is to lead this squadron to victory against the enemy."

While Davis tried to rally his squadron, William Hastie reached his breaking point. He resigned his position in the War Department in January 1943. In his resignation letter he singled out Army Air Corps officials who created and maintained what he considered an untenable segregated situation at Tuskegee. "The racial impositions upon Negro personnel at Tuskegee have become so severe and demoralizing that, in my judgment, they jeopardize the entire future of the Negro in combat aviation," he told Secretary of War Stimson. "Men cannot be humiliated over a long period of time without shattering of morale and destroying of combat efficiency."

Hastie said the army's unrelenting racial discrimination made him question "the sincerity and depth of our devotion to the basic issues of this war," as well as America's "ability as a nation to maintain leadership in the struggle for a free world." Now free to express himself as a private citizen, he attacked the army's racial policies in the pages of the Black press and in a pamphlet published by the NAACP titled *On Clipped Wings: The Story of Jim Crow in the Army Air Corps.*

Hastie's anger with the military grew in proportion to the number of Black people who were serving their country. As 1943 began, there were nearly five hundred thousand Black Americans in the armed services, including fifty-five thousand Black soldiers and sailors overseas. Tuskegee Army Airfield was home to over three thousand Black men and women, including more than one hundred Black pilots.

The men and women at Tuskegee wanted to be able to do their jobs and contribute to the war effort without being degraded. The desire was common among Black Americans engaged in war work, both within the military and in the defense industries. As airmen, mechanics, and nurses fought discrimination at Tuskegee, hundreds of thousands of Black Americans fought for jobs in the factories that were making airplanes, munitions, and countless other war materials.

NINE

WAR WORK

We want the whole world to know that the
Ford Motor Company is flagrantly violating
the executive order of President Roosevelt,
No. 8802. We feel that this is every man's war
regardless of race. We are fighting for Democracy abroad. We want Democracy at home
as well. Mr. Ford, Negro women and men
will and must play their rightful part in helping win this war.

—PROTEST FLYER, DETROIT

When A. Philip Randolph looked out over the giant
crowd at Madison Square Garden, he could hardly believe his eyes. Nearly twenty thousand people trekked
from Harlem and Brooklyn to Midtown Manhattan on the night
of June 16, 1942, to be part of what one newspaper called the largest Black mass meeting in history. The crowd sang along when the
band played "We Are Americans Too." More than a dozen Black
leaders urged the crowd to fight for equal rights and justice. "We

have grown tired of turning the other cheek," educator and activist Mary McLeod Bethune said. "Both of our cheeks are now so blistered they are too sensitive for further blows."

Randolph entered the arena to a standing ovation, in a procession of over one hundred uniformed Pullman porters and maids. Black Americans, he said, must "kill Jim Crow in America and bury him in the grave with Hitler's Nazism, Mussolini's Fascism and Hirohito's militarism." Three years earlier, twenty thousand Nazi supporters had filled the same arena to celebrate a whites-only vision of America. On the stage that night a thirty-foot-tall banner of George Washington was flanked by American flags and swastikas. Now, on a humid summer night in the Garden, Randolph had succeeded in staging a powerful rejoinder. He asked the crowd to think of the Black troops who were already deployed and declared, "Surely Negroes can't be expected to fight for democracy in Burma, when they don't have it in Birmingham."

Drawing the largest crowds of his career, Randolph wanted to keep the heat on the Roosevelt administration and ensure that Black Americans had equal access to defense industry jobs. His threatened March on Washington a year earlier had persuaded President Roosevelt to pass Executive Order 8802, forbidding discrimination in defense industries and job training programs. The order became even more important after Pearl Harbor, when the United States officially entered the war. Black Americans desperately wanted the steady paychecks and respect that came with producing ships, planes, tanks, trucks, and other war materials. For these war jobs to become a reality, the government would have to take unprecedented steps to investigate and stamp out employment discrimination.

Randolph had good reason to doubt that the government was up to this ambitious task. The Fair Employment Practices Committee (FEPC), the temporary agency Roosevelt created to enforce Executive Order 8802, was floundering, caught in political crossfire. The FEPC held public hearings in Los Angeles, Chicago, and New York, which revealed widespread racial discrimination by employers and labor unions. "We found unfair employment practices only slightly removed from the Hitler pattern," one committee member said. These hearings earned the FEPC many enemies. Companies and unions did not like being investigated by the agency, and Southern politicians resented what they saw as a federal intrusion into regional employment and social practices. The FEPC's critics became increasingly vocal during 1942, urging the president to restrict the agency's authority.

These tensions came to a head at the FEPC hearing in Birmingham, Alabama, in late June 1942, just days after Randolph's rally at Madison Square Garden. Committee member and *Louisville Courier-Journal* editor Mark Ethridge opened the meeting and tried to mollify his fellow white Southerners. He argued that Executive Order 8802 was a "war order, and not a social document," a claim that echoed the military officials who insisted the army was not a sociological laboratory. Ethridge said the order did not require the desegregation of war jobs and that the FEPC had no position on the segregation of workers. He took aim at Black leaders like Randolph, who interpreted 8802 as a second Emancipation Proclamation, for giving Black people false hope that the federal government could legislate an end to racial segregation.

"There is no power in the world—not even in all the mechanized armies of the earth, Allied and Axis—which could now force the Southern white people to the abandonment of the principle of social segregation," Ethridge argued. "It is a cruel disillusionment, bearing the germs of strife and perhaps tragedy, for any of their leaders to tell them . . . that they can expect it as the price of their participation in the war." Taking Ethridge at his word meant that Jim Crow was a more imposing and unbending power than Nazi Germany, fascist Italy, and the Empire of Japan combined.

Ethridge sent a copy of his remarks to the White House, saying he hoped they would "ease the tension" in the South. The president's advisers praised Ethridge for offering "sound and constructive" advice. When Randolph got word of what happened at the Birmingham hearings, he was livid. "The old slave masters said the same thing about slavery but slavery was abolished," he fumed. Chicago alderman Earl Dickerson, one of two Black FEPC members, said the hearing showed "very definitely that the South is still more interested in 'keeping the Negro in his place' than in winning the war for democracy."

While Randolph and Dickerson called for Ethridge's resignation, Roosevelt dealt a severe blow to the FEPC's already limited powers. At the end of July, he transferred the FEPC to the War Manpower Commission, where the agency would be under the supervision of former Indiana governor Paul McNutt. Whereas the FEPC had previously reported to and received its budget from the president, the transfer put the agency's budget at the discretion of Congress, where Southern politicians could restrict or deny its funding. An FEPC field representative in the South described the move as similar to the "deal of 1876" that ended federal protection of Black civil and political rights following the Civil War, a compromise that marked the end of the Reconstruction era and led to the establishment of Jim Crow laws. Now, the FEPC field rep charged, the president was again willing to "let the South settle 'the Negro problem' in traditional ways." Randolph called the transfer "a complete surrender to the Ku Klux spirit."

Randolph had reason to be angry. McNutt slashed the FEPC's budget and refused to hire more staff workers to investigate the avalanche of discrimination complaints the agency received. In January 1943, McNutt announced that at the president's direction, he was indefinitely postponing public hearings on discrimination. Randolph called the move a "slap in the face" and said it proved that the "FEPC was just a sop, an appeasement . . . to stop the March on Washington for jobs and justice." Charles Hamilton Houston, Thurgood Marshall's mentor, resigned from the committee and said McNutt was making a mockery of the nation's war aims. It was clear "the four freedoms do not cover the Negroes," Houston argued, "and the Atlantic Charter takes effect for Negroes at the bottom of the Atlantic Ocean."

While Randolph led a Save the FEPC Conference in February 1943, the decimation of the agency took the wind out of his sails. Executive Order 8802 was the signature policy achievement of Randolph's March on Washington Movement, but with the FEPC in shambles the order had no teeth. As Randolph regrouped, local activists continued the fight to end segregation and discrimination in war work. This patchwork of pickets and sit-ins gathered strength during the war and laid the foundation for the growth of the civil rights movement after the war.

IN THE SUMMER OF 1942, more than two hundred Black women marched on the U.S. Employment Service office in Los Angeles to demand that the agency open aircraft production jobs. "This is our war [but] we cannot win it in the kitchen, we must win it on the assembly line," said one protester. In St. Louis, more than five hundred Black men and women affiliated with the local chapter of the March on Washington Movement picketed the Carter Carburetor plant, a facility that made artillery and bomb fuses. Carter had a million-dollar defense contract and employed three thousand people, all white. The protesters marched behind a large American flag and carried signs reading RACIAL DISCRIMINATION IS SABOTAGE; FIGHT THE AXIS—DON'T FIGHT US; and OUR BOND DOLLARS HELP PAY CARTER'S PAYROLL, WHY CAN'T WE WORK THERE?

In Detroit, a coalition of local civil rights activists and Black union leaders called for Ford to hire Black women at the company's River Rouge and Willow Run plants. After a Ford personnel director rejected their demands, claiming that such a move would create a disturbance in the plant because white women there refused to work with Black women, they staged a four-hour protest at the Ford employment office. "We want the whole world to know that the Ford Motor Company is flagrantly violating the executive order of President Roosevelt, No. 8802," the rally flyer read. "We feel that this is every man's war regardless of race. We are fighting for Democracy abroad. We want Democracy at home as well. Mr. Ford, Negro women and men will and must play their rightful part in helping win this war."

In the defense industry, workers and activists fought plant by plant and town by town to ensure Black Americans gained equal access to war work. The barriers were immense: U.S. Employment Service (USES) offices were administered locally, and in the South and border states, the USES operated separate offices for white and Black workers. Employment offices across the country used prewar discriminatory labor patterns to justify recommending whites for skilled and semiskilled jobs and Black Americans for unskilled jobs. Many union locals refused to admit or train Black members, or allowed them to join only second-class auxiliary unions, which deprived them of seniority rights and grievance protections. Meanwhile, most industry management believed that white and Black labor could not work together.

The barriers to defense work began to crack thanks to local protests and the diminished, but still tangible, threat of FEPC action. These were often small victories—Ford hired two dozen Black women at Willow Run as a result of the protests, for example—but they added up. As the draft drew more white men into military service, several regions and industries experienced labor shortages, which opened doors further for Black workers. In 1940, Black Americans held less than 0.2 percent of aircraft industry jobs. By 1944, they made up 6 percent of the industry, with more than a hundred thousand Black workers making airframes, engine components, propellers, and other aircraft parts. Black employment in shipbuilding increased from less than 5 percent to more than 12 percent over a similar time period; tank manufacturing from less than 2 percent to more than 7 percent.

Black workers also made important breakthroughs in skilled and semiskilled war industry jobs. Black men held 5.9 percent of these jobs in 1940 and 10.1 percent by 1944; Black women's share increased from less than 5 percent to more than 8 percent, with thousands leaving domestic service jobs in white homes for war work.

Overall, more than one million Black Americans, including six hundred thousand Black women, held defense jobs during the war.

Each of these numbers was a life transformed by war work. Ella Jackson was one of the millions of Black Americans who fled the South during the war. "The shipyard people came to Louisiana offering $1.20 an hour to work in California," she said. "I'd worked for as little as 25 cents an hour, 50 cents an hour, and thinking I was doing pretty good. Had I ever seen a ship? I imagine I had not. I didn't even know what a ship looked like. But they were hiring, so we went." Ruth Wilson, a young mother whose husband was in the army, quit her job as a maid and laundress and moved to Philadelphia. She found a job as a sheet metal worker at the Philadelphia Navy Yard, where she helped build an aircraft carrier. "That experience changed my life because I made more money and became independent," she said. "The War made me live better," agreed Fanny Christina Hill, who was hired at North American Aviation in Inglewood in 1943. "My sister always said that Hitler was the one that got us out of the white folks' kitchen."

LIKE THESE BLACK "Rosie the Riveter"s, more than six thousand Black women contributed to the war effort by volunteering for the Women's Army Corps (WAC). Congress established the Corps as an auxiliary in May 1942, and it was converted to active-duty status in the army the following year. Mary McLeod Bethune led recruiting efforts for Black American WACs. WACs took on a variety of roles, such as switchboard operators, mechanics, truck drivers, stenographers, and postal clerks. They wore uniforms and drilled in military formation.

A *Chicago Defender* profile of the first cohort of thirty-nine Black WAC trainees at Fort Des Moines, Iowa, marveled at their precision. With their heads high, chests out, and marching in unison, the WACs are "breathing defiance to Hitler, Hirohito, Mussolini and all they represent," the *Defender* proclaimed. When the trainees snapped to the commands of twenty-six-year-old Myrtle Anderson—"eyes right" and "salute the reviewing officers"—the paper said their marching would have made a male army platoon commander proud. "They carry themselves as West Pointers. In every sense of the word they are soldiers with the single exception that they don't handle arms."

The Women's Army Corps was the first time women served in the army in a large-scale capacity other than as nurses, and it was a particularly important milestone for Black women. "I wanted to prove to myself, maybe the world, that we would give what we had back to the U.S. as a confirmation that we were full-fledged citizens," WAC veteran Elaine Bennet recalled. Speaking to the national convention of Congress of Industrial Organizations (CIO) women's auxiliaries, Lieutenant Mildred Osby said, "We WACs are rich women and poor women—we are doctors, lawyers, teachers, social workers, stenographers, factory and domestic workers, housewives, we are widows of Bataan and Corregidor with one motivation—to make the most direct personal contribution possible to winning the war and the peace."

Like their male counterparts, Black women battled the army's official policies of segregation, racism from white officers, and discriminatory practices that assigned them to the lowest and dirtiest jobs. Charity Adams, commanding officer of the WACs at Fort Des Moines and later of the 6888th Central Postal Directory Battalion in Europe, remembered the humiliation of arriving at the army camp. After traveling by train from Ohio to Iowa with a racially integrated group of recruits, the first thing she heard when she exited the train was a uniformed officer shouting, "Negroes on one side! White girls on the other."

Black WACs were allowed to use the post's swimming pool for only one segregated hour each week, after which white personnel immediately drained the pool. Many of the women were familiar with these petty racist tactics from their civilian lives, but it was humiliating all the same. At the WAC officer ceremony, all the white candidates' names were called before Adams and the other Black graduates received their commissions. The WACs also endured the intertwined harms of racism and sexism, what civil rights activist Pauli Murray termed "Jane Crow." Adams argued that many men, including Black soldiers, resented the presence and successful performance of Black women in the military. "I survived in a state of pleasant belligerency," Adams recalled. "I had no chip on my shoulder, I kept it slightly below the shoulder."

The gains Black Americans made in defense industries and the Women's Auxiliary Corps were as tenuous as they were hard-fought. Black workers vied to win the war while knowing that peace would likely bring a return to the prewar status quo of employment discrimination. Workers pushed open doors while also struggling to make sure that they would not slam shut in the future.

But Black workers were not the only Americans fighting over who should have access to jobs during and after the war. In Baltimore, the bathrooms at the Western Electric Company became a battleground. When a Black woman was assigned to a previously all-white division, twenty-two white women walked out. Shortly thereafter, a secret petition circulated among white employees gathered fifteen hundred signatures demanding segregated toilets. The white workers' union fought with the company and FEPC officials over this issue for several months before going on strike. After the weeklong strike, President Roosevelt ordered the U.S. Army to seize the plant.

The local *Baltimore Sun* newspaper expressed sympathy and encouragement for the strikers, arguing that integrated toilets would upset the status quo of racial relations in the city. After two months under army supervision and with Western Electric back to full production, management resumed control of the plant and announced a "harmony" plan that called for the construction of more lockers and bathrooms to be used on a segregated basis. Ultimately, white workers got their wish: they could go to the bathroom with members of their own race.

Like the segregated restrooms at Tuskegee air base and other army camps, the organized white protests in Baltimore made a mockery of the idea that Americans were doing everything they could to win the war. Western Electric made radio- and wire-communications equipment for the army and navy. The factory produced fewer of these vital war materials for weeks because white workers would not use the same toilet as Black workers.

The protests, of course, were about more than toilets. Many white workers believed they had an inalienable right to the best jobs before, during, and after the war. From this perspective, even a single

Black employee was seen as dangerous, opening the door to integration and threatening to bring unwanted racial democracy and equality to the factory floor.

Western Electric was far from exceptional. During the war there were more than one hundred strikes over racial issues. Black economist and government official Robert Weaver feared that this "epidemic" of work stoppages would derail war production. These "hate strikes" cost war-production plants more than 2.5 million worker hours during a tense three-month period from March to May 1943.

The night crew of white women workers at a Detroit gear and axle factory walked out over having to use the same toilets as Black women. Several Chicago unions, such as the AFL Boilermakers, used the threat of wildcat strikes—strikes without the approval of their unions—to dissuade management from hiring Black workers. In Canton, Ohio, production at the Timken Roller Bearing and Axle Company ground to a halt when twelve hundred white workers protested the promotion of twenty-seven Black workers to skilled machine jobs. "I would rather lose the war than work with those Negroes," one striker said.

Tens of thousands of Black and white migrants flocked to Mobile, Alabama, for war work, making it the country's most congested shipyard. Surveying the overcrowded city, novelist John Dos Passos wrote, "The mouldering old Gulf seaport with its ancient dusty elegance of tall shuttered windows under mansard roofs and iron lace overgrown with vines . . . looks trampled and battered like a city that's been taken by storm." Black workers endured dismal housing conditions and segregated public transportation for the chance to secure a war job.

By 1943, more than seven thousand Black men and women

worked at the city's largest shipyard, Alabama Dry Dock and Shipbuilding Company, none in skilled positions. Only a handful of Black Americans found jobs at Gulf Shipbuilding Corporation, Mobile's second-largest war employer. Local NAACP president John LeFlore led a community campaign in support of Black war workers, eventually securing an FEPC order for Alabama Dry Dock and Shipbuilding Company to hire and promote more Black workers. Management and the AFL unions, which organized most of the skilled labor in the shipyard, balked and continued to deny Black Americans access to skilled jobs. "It is pitiful to see what we colored workers have to go through in Mobile," one Black shipyard worker said. "We are buying bonds, paying victory tax, income tax, and taking all kinds of chances with our lives."

In May 1943, labor shortages finally compelled Alabama Dry Dock to promote a dozen Black men to previously all-white welder positions. Although the men were assigned to a segregated night-shift unit and comprised a tiny fraction of the twenty-five hundred additional welders the shipyard needed to keep pace with demand, white workers violently protested the move. On the morning of May 25, after the Black welders had gone home from their shift, small groups of white workers gathered in the shipyard, growing angrier as they swapped rumors about Black workers assaulting white women.

Within a couple of hours, a mob of four thousand white shipyard workers and local citizens had formed, armed with pipes, hammers, clubs, and hunks of steel. They set on any Black workers they could find, shouting racial epithets and "This is our shipyard" as security guards looked on. White rioters threw two Black workers into the Mobile River and seriously injured more than four dozen more. "It was a great day for Hitler and the Emperor of Japan," said Charles Hanson, regional director of the CIO union that represented most of the Black workers at the shipyard. Black workers could not safely return to work for weeks, and some fled Mobile permanently. After a carful of white men threw rocks at his house, one Black shipyard worker moved his family to Richmond, California. "I didn't even wait for my check, I just decided to leave," he recalled.

As production at the shipyard fell by nearly half, federal officials were eager to find a solution. Three days after the violence, FEPC and War Manpower Commission representatives met with company and union leaders and hammered out a compromise. Alabama Dry Dock would create four all-Black shipways, where Black workers could hold welding and skilled craft jobs under the supervision of a white foreman. In the rest of the shipyard, Black Americans would continue to be relegated to work as laborers and helpers.

Although the separate shipways meant more skilled work and higher pay for some Black workers (welders earned twice as much as laborers), the segregated compromise after a harrowing outbreak of racial violence still stung. LeFlore called the plan an "emasculation" of the FEPC's mission, while *The Pittsburgh Courier* termed the "so-called compromise" a "surrender to the Nazi racial theory and . . . a defeat suffered by the United States." A year after the racial attacks, the Black shipway workers demonstrated their skill by completing the tanker SS *Tule Canyon* in seventy-nine days, setting an Alabama Dry Dock record.

The wave of hate strikes crested in Detroit in the summer of 1943. Like Mobile's, Detroit's population boomed during the war, as more than 50,000 Black and 450,000 white migrants made their way to the city. By 1943 there were more transplanted Southerners, both Black and white, in Detroit than in any city in the South. A number of these migrants found jobs at the Packard Motor Car Company, which during the war made Rolls-Royce engines for American fighters and marine diesels for PT boats.

In a city that was a tinderbox of racial antagonism, Packard stood out. An openly racist personnel manager blocked Black applicants at the hiring gate. The National Workers League, a local fascist group, spread anti-Semitic and anti-Black vitriol on the shop floor. A small but vocal band of white workers had ties to the Ku Klux Klan and pledged to run Black workers out of war jobs and out of the city. The United Auto Workers voiced official support for equal opportunity, but the sentiment was not widely embraced by the white rank and file. The plant witnessed more than a dozen hate strikes in the early years of the war, and whites regularly booed Black workers when they entered the building to begin their shifts.

Like at most war plants, the twenty-five hundred Black workers at Packard were blocked from skilled work. Relegated to hot and exhausting work in the foundry, they melted metal and poured it into molds to form engine parts. After pressure from Black union members and federal officials, management promoted three Black workers to the aircraft engine assembly line in May, prompting several hundred white workers to walk off the job. When white union leaders hesitated to support the Black workers, the Black union steward called a counterstrike.

Inspired by Randolph and the March on Washington Movement, many Black war workers in Detroit used wildcat strikes to demand equal rights in defense plants. The Black strike at Packard ended after the three men were returned to their assembly-line jobs.

Days later, on June 3, 1943, twenty-five thousand white workers (90 percent of the total workforce) retaliated by walking off the job, shutting down the entire plant. Many crowded the factory gates, cheering racist soapbox speakers. "I'd rather see Hitler and Hirohito win the war than work beside a nigger on the assembly line," one man screamed.

The War Department immediately condemned this massive hate strike. The Army Air Force desperately needed Packard to continue cranking out engines to keep pace with the ramp-up of bombing missions in Europe and the Pacific. Colonel George Strong, the War Department's Detroit representative, suspended the strike ringleaders and threatened to fire all the striking workers, which would have made them eligible for the draft. White strikers returned to work the following week, but conditions in Packard and across Detroit remained tense.

"White anger must be reckoned with," argued *The Christian Century* magazine, surveying the situation in Detroit. "It is clear that a large portion of the white population have been growing more belligerent from week to week." The *Baltimore Afro-American* called the white Packard strikers "Hitler's Helpers." Harry McAlpin, who in 1944 became the first Black reporter to cover a presidential news conference in the White House, worried that "the Axis has now found anew America's 'Achilles heel' . . . its unbridled race prejudice against the Negro."

NAACP chief Walter White was in Detroit during the Packard strike for the association's conference on the war. "American boys will die on some far off battle field for lack of engines which were not made in Detroit today," he declared. "Every man responsible for this strike and every other one like it is an ally and agent of Hitler and Hirohito and an enemy of America. . . . Tokio and Berlin will rejoice at this unexpected aid." As White surveyed the conference delegates gathered at the Second Baptist Church, he said Black people had been fighting for justice since the Civil War. The wartime battle on the home front was as difficult as it had ever been, he said, and things seemed to be getting worse by the day. "Let us drag out in the open what has been whispered throughout Detroit for months—that a race riot may break out here at any time." Less than three weeks later, these words would prove prophetic.

TEN

RIOT

What shall it profit us to cross the seas to destroy Hitler, if Hitlerism is to rise triumphant over our homes?

—JOHN ROBERT BADGER,
Chicago Defender COLUMNIST

It was just past midnight on June 21, 1943, when Thurgood Marshall's phone rang. Marshall was working late as usual, but he was not expecting any calls. He picked up the phone and heard Detroit NAACP leader Gloster Current's urgent voice. Current said a fight had broken out that evening between Blacks and whites on Belle Isle, a 980-acre island park where tens of thousands of Detroiters had flocked to enjoy a sweltering 90-degree Sunday afternoon. As the sun went down, the brawl spiraled out of control. Hundreds of white sailors from the nearby naval armory rushed in to join the fight, as did hundreds of Black and white parkgoers. By the time Current called New York, five thousand people were involved, and the racial clash was spreading across the Belle Isle bridge, which spanned the Detroit River, and into the east side of the city.

After Marshall and Current hung up, the situation in Detroit got worse. News from Belle Isle traveled quickly through white and Black neighborhoods. Whites heard that a gang of Black men had raped and killed a white woman on the bridge. Black Detroiters heard that white men had killed a Black woman and child and thrown their bodies into the river.

The rumors were false, but they stoked anger and calls for revenge all the same. Black people looted white-owned stores and attacked white factory workers who had just finished their shifts. Black teens killed John Holyak, a fifty-nine-year-old war worker whose son, an army private, had been captured by the Japanese on Bataan. White people stoned Black motorists and pedestrians and dragged Black passengers from streetcars and buses, then beat them in the streets. A white gang stabbed and hit Sam Mitchell, a Black World War I veteran. White teens shot and killed Moses Kiska, a fifty-eight-year-old who was waiting for the bus to his war job at the Detroit Arsenal Tank Plant. "We didn't know him. He wasn't bothering us," one of the teens confessed. "But other people were fighting and killing and we felt like it, too."

Police cruisers and wagons flooded into the densely populated Black neighborhood of Paradise Valley. Officers shouted racial epithets, beat pedestrians, and shot at both looters and war workers on their way to factories. *Michigan Chronicle* publisher Louis Martin said the police department's riot plan was to swarm into the Black part of the city, "disarm the residents and then proceed to outdo the Gestapo in killings and brutalities." A small group of Black soldiers at Fort Custer, two hours outside the city, secured guns and a truck in an attempt to drive to Detroit to aid their families, but they were quickly arrested by military police.

Officers largely turned a blind eye to the white violence and, after daybreak on Monday, the white mobs grew larger and bolder. They turned over dozens of cars and set them ablaze. With a leader carrying an American flag, thousands of whites marched downtown to city hall, chasing and beating Black people en route. Inside city hall, Mayor Edward Jeffries Jr. stayed sequestered in his office with the door locked and shades drawn. As racial violence engulfed the city, the mayor spent most of the day talking with Michigan governor Harry Kelly and regional army commanders, debating when to declare martial law.

Finally, as darkness fell over the city on Monday night, Mayor Jeffries recognized that the city police could not control the situation. Governor Kelly telephoned President Roosevelt to request federal troops, and FDR quickly issued a proclamation to use military forces to quell the "domestic violence" in Detroit. Twenty-five hundred army troops and military police arrived in armored cars and jeeps with automatic guns. They successfully pushed white and Black crowds off the main streets without firing a shot.

The devastation in Detroit was immense. In just over twenty-four hours, thirty-four people were killed. Twenty-five of the riot victims were Black, seventeen of them killed by police. Hundreds more were wounded, some maimed for life.

Marshall flew from New York to Detroit on Thursday alongside his NAACP associates Walter White, Lucille Black, and Daisy Lampkin. The city was still on edge, with police and soldiers patrolling the streets and enforcing a curfew. Black people were afraid to leave their homes or go to work in the war factories.

Marshall and his colleagues turned the basement of the St. Antoine YMCA into a relief and counseling headquarters, where they ministered to the physical and emotional wounds of Black Detroiters. "Men, women, and even children told their stories of violence inflicted upon them not only by members of the mob but also by Michigan state troops and the Detroit police," White said. They looked like "bombed-out victims of Nazi terror in Europe."

Marshall also conducted his own investigation of the riot. He hired two private detectives, one Black and one white, to suss out information in different neighborhoods. In the basement headquarters, he collected affidavits from people who suffered or witnessed attacks by white police and rioters. "I saw from my stoop a colored soldier walking up the street in full uniform attending to his own business, when suddenly a police officer grabbed him from behind and struck him in the head . . . leaving him bleeding profusely in the street," one woman said. The soldier himself testified that he was beaten so severely by a police officer that blood saturated his army uniform.

Even after federal troops had subdued the city, several people described how police rounded up all the Black residents from the St. Antoine YMCA and forced them to line up by a wall with their legs spread and hands in the air. The police had their revolvers drawn and shouted vile names at the residents. One officer shot a man who supposedly reached for his pocket.

At the nearby Vernor Highway Hotel, Marshall learned that police exchanged fire with a Black gunman in the parking lot and then blasted the building with thousands of bullets and dozens of tear-gas canisters. Once they cleared the building, police ransacked the apartments, stealing money, whiskey, and valuables, while other officers detained the Black residents on the sidewalk outside. "There was evidenced a desire [by] the supposed keepers of the peace and protectors of law and order to do all in their power to make said residents the victims of as much inhuman indignities as possible," said one Vernor resident whose apartment was looted by police. "These actions on their part strongly pointed to the fact that all the Hitlers are not in Germany." Marshall said the apartments "resembled part of a battlefield."

These community testimonies were ammunition for a grand-jury hearing that never came. Instead, the governor appointed a committee of the Michigan attorney general, the Wayne County prosecuting attorney, the state police commissioner, and the Detroit police commissioner to investigate the riot. Tasked with examining their own agencies, these city and state officials not surprisingly blamed the riot on Black Detroiters. "Perhaps most significant in precipitating racial tensions existing in Detroit is the positive exhortations by many Negro leaders to be 'militant' in the struggle for racial equality," the committee report argued. They described the NAACP as the "biggest instigator of the race riot" and complained that Black newspapers promoted violence when they called for Double Victory.

Marshall reached a very different conclusion. "Much of the blood spilled in the Detroit riot is on the hands of the Detroit police department," he wrote in a scathing report titled "The Gestapo in Detroit." Marshall saw the Motor City as part of a larger national pattern of police brutality that escalated in the summer of 1943. "Nearly all police departments limit their conception of checking racial disorders to surrounding, arresting, maltreating, and shooting Negroes," he said. Meanwhile, the police made little attempt to check violence by whites.

Walter White and Mary McLeod Bethune urged President Roosevelt to take to the radio to address the nation about the violence in Detroit and elsewhere. "Why are you silent, Mr. President, as your people die at the hands of mobs on the streets of Detroit and other cities?" White asked via telegram. *The New Republic* similarly wondered, "Why hasn't Mr. Roosevelt come to us with one of his greatest speeches, speaking to us as Americans, speaking to us as the great mongrel nation?"

Roosevelt demurred, fearful that speaking about domestic racial issues would irritate Southern congressmen whose votes he needed to pass future war bills. In his stead, Vice President Henry Wallace traveled to Detroit in late July, where he delivered a powerful speech to a crowd of union workers and civic groups. "We cannot fight to crush Nazi brutality abroad and condone race riots at home," Wallace said. "Those who fan the fires of racial clashes for the purpose of making political capital here at home are taking the first step toward Nazism."

DETROIT WAS JUST ONE of more than 240 cities, towns, and military bases that witnessed outbreaks of racial violence in the summer of 1943. In Los Angeles in June, thousands of white servicemen, police officers, and civilians attacked Mexican American, Filipino American, and Black American youth. Sailors beat teenagers with clubs and stripped zoot-suiters of their clothes, leaving them half-naked and bloodied on the street.

A week later in Beaumont, Texas, eighty miles east of Houston, two thousand white shipyard workers stormed off the job and marched into town after reports that a Black man had raped a white woman. The mob swelled in size and set upon the Black business district, burning down a jewelry store, three funeral homes, and a pharmacy owned by a Black man who had supported the war effort by purchasing several thousand dollars in war bonds. White gangs attacked fifty Black draftees waiting at the Greyhound bus station to travel to their military base.

The *Baltimore Afro-American* ran a photo, captioned "Star Spangled Banner in Beaumont," of a charred and tattered American flag that burned along with a Black-owned radio shop. Black troops, serving abroad or training stateside, who saw the image of the desecrated flag were left to wonder what kind of country they were being asked to defend. They were prepared to give their lives for a flag that many of their white countrymen seemed to treat with contempt when it was held in Black hands.

Some Black homeowners in Beaumont wielded shotguns to chase away raiders, but most were overwhelmed and watched as their homes were ransacked and set ablaze. The white chief of police said the mob was "the most unscrupulous and vicious" he had seen and that "they not only wanted to kill Negroes but also desired to loot and steal." Thousands were left homeless or were too scared to return to their homes, fleeing Beaumont for East Texas or Louisiana.

The racial violence that swept across the country forced many Americans to consider anew the relationship between white supremacy at home and abroad. The newspaper at Chicago's navy training station accused white rioters of "out Nazi-ing the Nazis," while a *Chicago Defender* columnist asked, "What shall it profit us to cross the seas to destroy Hitler, if Hitlerism is to rise triumphant over our homes?" While some politicians and city officials tried to blame the attacks on Axis-inspired propaganda or outside agitators,

Philadelphia Tribune columnist Eustace Gay argued that the riots were homegrown. "The blame must rest squarely on the shoulders of those Americans who love their country less than they hate thirteen million fellow citizens," he wrote. A. Philip Randolph likewise encouraged Black Americans not to blame Nazi propaganda for the riots in Detroit and elsewhere. "These riots," he continued, "are the result of our government's policy of segregating and discriminating against Negroes for decades, long before Hitler was ever heard of, and the riots will continue long after Hitler is dead and forgotten if our government does not stop practicing the segregation of Negro citizens and integrate the Negro into the government and war and peace time industry on a basis of equality with their white brothers and sisters."

Langston Hughes watched the summer's outpouring of racism from New York. The news inspired his poem "Beaumont to Detroit: 1943":

> Looky here, America
> What you done done—
> Let things drift
> Until the riots come [. . .]
> You tell me that hitler
> Is a mighty bad man
> I guess he took lessons from the ku klux klan [. . .]
>
> I ask you this question
> Cause I want to know
> How long I got to fight
> BOTH HITLER—AND JIM CROW.

On the first day of August, the violence came to Harlem, the neighborhood Hughes called home. Just before dusk, a Black soldier and white cop got into an altercation at the Braddock Hotel, a popular jazz spot on West 126th Street and Eighth Avenue. The soldier, Private Robert Bandy, was at the bar with his mother, and intervened when the officer, James Collins, struck a Black woman, Margie Polite. Collins hit Bandy with his blackjack, which the soldier then grabbed and wrestled away from the officer. As Bandy fled, Collins shot him in the shoulder. Bandy was treated and released from Harlem Hospital later that evening.

While Bandy was at the hospital, a rumor swept through Harlem that a white policeman had shot and killed a Black soldier in uniform as the soldier's mother looked on. Furious Black New Yorkers flowed into the streets, taking out their anger against businesses, mostly white owned, that they felt exploited their community.

By the next morning, six Black people had been killed by police, two hundred were injured, and several hundred more were arrested. Broken glass from store windows littered the sidewalks and property damage totaled nearly a million dollars. The NAACP, Urban League, and other moderate civil rights groups condemned the actions of those who looted and destroyed businesses, while also emphasizing that police brutality and housing discrimination were prevalent in Harlem.

The incident that sparked the uprising angered Harlemites because they were inundated with news about beatings and mistreatment of Black soldiers. The 369th Coast Artillery, a New York outfit that traced its military lineage to the famed "Harlem Hellfighters" (369th Infantry Regiment) in World War I, was stationed at Camp Stewart, Georgia. They wrote to friends, relatives, and

Black newspapers back home in New York to describe the insults and humiliations they suffered in the Jim Crow South. "The mistreatment of Negro soldiers, particularly in the South, is a terribly sore point with Negroes," Walter White contended. Why did Harlem revolt? author Richard Wright asked. "They had jobs, but they did not have respect, justice, freedom of living space. They had jobs, but their sons and daughters were being kicked and hounded in the Army and the Navy and they resented it."

Aspiring writer James Baldwin turned nineteen the night of the riot. Born and raised in Harlem, Baldwin worked early in the war at an army quartermaster depot near Princeton, New Jersey, laying railroad tracks. Preternaturally observant, Baldwin understood that nearly everyone in Harlem was shaken by the indignities and violence suffered by Black troops. They felt more at ease with their sons, cousins, nephews, and uncles serving in the Pacific, Europe, or North Africa than in the Jim Crow South. "It was, perhaps, like feeling that the most dangerous part of a dangerous journey had been passed and that now, even if death should come, it would come with honor and without the complicity of their countrymen," he wrote. Looking back on the war years, Baldwin later wrote, "the treatment accorded the Negro during the Second World War marks, for me, a turning point in the Negro's relation to America. To put it briefly, and somewhat too simply, a certain hope died, a certain respect for white Americans faded."

ARMY CAMPS COULD NOT ESCAPE this tide of racial violence. In the spring of 1943, Thurgood Marshall and his mentor William Henry Hastie, who had recently resigned his position as civilian aide to the secretary of war, visited a dozen army bases to investi-gate the treatment and morale of Black troops. What they found was disturbing.

Civilian violence against Black troops in uniform was a recur-rent phenomenon, Hastie told fellow attorneys in a speech at the National Lawyers Guild. "It may well be the greatest factor now oper-ating to make thirteen million Negroes bitter and resentful and to undermine the fighting spirit of three-quarters of a million Negros in arms," he said. It was commonplace for white officers and civil-ians to address Black soldiers by racial epithets.

Black troops could take segregated latrines and sitting in the back of the bus for only so long. It was only a matter of time before this bitterness and hatred boiled over into violence. Hastie empha-sized that the army "is aggressively engaged in teaching our soldiers how to treat the people of India, the South Sea Islanders, the Arabs, everyone but their fellow American soldiers." Hastie said that he and Marshall would submit their report to the War Department but warned that there was no reason to expect that the 1943 record would be any better.

The day after Hastie's speech, an incident at Camp Van Dorn, Mississippi, proved his point. Named after Confederate general Earl Van Dorn, the camp sprang up after Pearl Harbor in Centreville, a tiny town in an isolated area of southwest Mississippi. The camp was home to more than thirty thousand soldiers, including just over six thousand Black troops.

The Black units included the 364th Infantry Regiment, which followed a troubled road on their path to deployment. When the 364th was stationed at Camp Claiborne, Louisiana, in 1941, local police charged three soldiers with raping a white woman. They were court-martialed, convicted, and sentenced to be hanged. The sergeant and privates reached out to the NAACP, and Thurgood Marshall agreed to take their case. The soldiers said that they had paid the woman for sex and that they signed confessions only after the police roughed them up and threatened to allow a white gang to lynch them. Marshall successfully appealed the case and the soldiers' sentences were reduced.

Things got worse when the army then sent the 364th to Phoenix, Arizona. On Thanksgiving in 1942, members of the unit got into an altercation with Black military police officers. After the MPs shot and wounded two soldiers, other members of the 364th protested, eventually pulling guns and exchanging fire with the MPs. The soldiers fled downtown and took refuge in the homes of Black friends. Phoenix cops joined the MPs in cordoning off twenty-eight blocks and searching houses. When the soldiers refused to come out, MPs peppered houses with machine-gun fire. By daybreak, two Black soldiers and one civilian were dead. Nearly two hundred soldiers were arrested; fifteen were court-martialed and sentenced to as much as fifty years in prison.

When the 364th was shipped to Mississippi in May 1943, they saw it as punishment. Many members of the unit were starting to view their insubordination as a badge of honor, with some bragging about how they would take over Camp Van Dorn and Centreville. Conditions at Van Dorn were bad even by the standards of other army camps in the Jim Crow South. One Black unit was forced to work on the nearby farm of a local white politician.

On May 30, a week after the 364th arrived, a white MP was questioning Private William Walker, a thirty-year-old from Chicago, for having his uniform sleeves rolled up. A scuffle ensued, and when a local sheriff arrived, Walker started to run away. He made it only a few steps before the sheriff shot and killed him. The news that a Black soldier lay dead just outside of the camp gates spread quickly. A group of Black soldiers broke into the supply room, grabbed dozens of rifles, and threatened to get revenge. "I had seen white hatred many times, but that night at Van Dorn the Black mask was dropped and I saw stark Black hatred," said Clyde Blue, a private in a Black quartermaster unit also stationed at the camp. Only the intervention of the unit's chaplain persuaded the men to return to their barracks.

White Mississippians were already opposed to Black troops being stationed in the South and the 364th's threatened revolt fueled their fears and animosity. Whites in Centreville armed themselves to prepare for a race battle and wrote to their representatives to demand that the 364th be sent north. "The negro soldiers stationed in Mississippi have been raping our women and murdering our men," one white man wrote.

The War Department investigated the incident and promised to drum out the "troublemakers" in the 364th and make an example of the unit. The army wanted to show other Black units that unrest and mutinous conduct would be dealt with swiftly and severely. The unit was confined to base for the remainder of 1943 before being sent to the Aleutian Islands for garrison duty in early 1944. Walker's killing and the virulent racism they encountered at Camp Van Dorn left such a deep scar on the 364th that for decades rumors circulated that white troops and military police had massacred twelve hundred Black soldiers and buried them in trenches on the outskirts of the camp.

Two hundred miles north at Camp McCain, other Black troops

were also rebelling. On the Fourth of July 1943, a group of enlisted men from the 470th Quartermaster Truck Regiment got weekend passes to go to Starkville, Mississippi. As they tried to catch a bus back to camp, they were arrested and beaten by local police. When the men got back to base and told their story, their fellow troops were outraged. The next night, twenty fully armed Black soldiers decided to retaliate. They snuck out of camp and walked just up the road to Duck Hill.

The tiny village of Duck Hill was not just a convenient target. In 1937, two Black sharecroppers, Roosevelt Townes and Robert McDaniels, were accused of killing a white storekeeper. Moments after they were formally charged, a gang of white men snatched Townes and McDaniels from a Duck Hill courthouse, chained them to trees in the woods, tortured them with blowtorches, and finally shot them, as a mob of five hundred white townspeople, including women and children, watched. *Time* and *Life* published grisly photographs of the event, marking the first time a white national magazine published lynching images.

When soldiers from the 470th stopped on the railroad tracks outside of Duck Hill and started firing on the town, their reasons for revenge were myriad. Their rifles blazed for ten minutes, riddling homes and businesses with bullets, while white residents trembled inside. After expending their ammunition, the men returned to base.

The army court-martialed the shooters and sentenced them to a dozen years of hard labor. The War Department tried to keep the story quiet, but failed. The Mississippi revolt was covered both in the Black press and in the mainstream white press. "There were no casualties at the battle of Duck Hill," *Time* reported. "But the Army could not underestimate its significance, for there are many Duck Hills around the big Southern camps." A Black chaplain put the matter more bluntly: "The South was more vigorously engaged in fighting the Civil War than in training soldiers to resist Hitler."

Dozens of other army camps witnessed serious racial battles during the summer of 1943, and Black troops increasingly refused to accept subordination and humiliation while serving their country. "When [Black soldiers] tell you first hand what a Black man is up against in a white man's army, the look in their eyes scares the hell out of you," a *Chicago Defender* columnist observed. "Mainly, their bitterness adds up to—'I would just as soon die fightin' for democracy right here in Georgia, as go all the way to Africa or Australia. Kill a cracker in Mississippi or Germany, what's the difference!'"

After Black troops at Camp Stewart engaged in a three-hour-long shootout with military police, the *Baltimore Afro-American* called on the White House to end racial discrimination in army camps: "We say to Mr. Roosevelt that the war on the home front has lasted long enough. He can end it. He ought to do it now. We expect him to do it."

But President Roosevelt remained silent regarding the war at home, in large part because most white Americans endorsed racial segregation within and beyond the military. An Office of War Information survey in 1943 found that 96 percent of white Southerners and 85 percent of white northerners insisted on military segregation, while 90 percent of northern Blacks and 67 percent of Southern Blacks wanted integrated units. Within the army, 76 percent of white troops felt Black troops were treated fairly in the military, an opinion shared by only 35 percent of Black soldiers. Black newspapers argued that the military did not need to wait for public-opinion surveys to end racial segregation. "It ain't a question of sampling," a *Chicago Defender* columnist wrote. "All the Army has to do is say 'integration' and there it will be."

For their part, the War Department saw the battles at army camps and the anger of Black troops as a public relations problem. Assistant Secretary of War John McCloy led the effort to communicate more positive images of Black soldiers and the importance of their role in the war effort. The Bureau of Public Relations released *The Negro Soldier*, a forty-three-minute-long propaganda film produced by Frank Capra that all Black troops and many white soldiers watched as part of their army orientation. Langston Hughes called it "the most remarkable Negro film ever flashed on the American screen." The Bureau of Public Relations also sent out upbeat press releases about the work of Black troops overseas and welcomed more Black correspondents to cover the war theaters.

The War Department released a *Command of Negro Troops* pamphlet for white officers, with section titles such as "Know Your Men," "Good Soldiers Are Made, Not Born," and "Negro Soldiers Are Americans." By the following year, many white officer candidates took a ten-hour course on Leadership and the Negro Soldier. "The issue is not whether the Negro will be used in the War, it is how effectively he will be used," the course manual pointed out, nearly three years after America officially entered the war. Late in coming, these public relations efforts still walked a careful line to avoid offending those who clung tightly to white supremacy. "The Army has no authority or intention to participate in social reform as such but does view the problem as a matter of efficient troop utilization," the manual warned.

MOBILE, DETROIT, BEAUMONT, Harlem, Camp Van Dorn, Camp McCain, Camp Stewart. Everywhere Americans looked in the summer of 1943 there were ominous signs. While Allied troops successfully invaded Sicily in July, and Mussolini was overthrown shortly thereafter, America was in danger of winning the war abroad while losing the war at home.

Throughout all of this, nearly three hundred thousand more Black men joined the army through the draft or enlistment. By the end of 1943, more than three quarters of a million Black Americans were in the army, a 61 percent increase over the prior year, with tens of thousands more serving in the navy.

As a summer of bloodshed in America came to a close, Black troops were beginning to see overseas combat in more significant numbers. Many of these troops shared the frustration and rage that drove members of the 364th and 470th to fight back against white military police or seek revenge against white civilians. Fury was not unique to the soldiers the army court-martialed or labeled "troublemakers." "I was an angry young man," said Vernon Baker, a lieutenant in the 92nd Infantry Division who earned the Medal of Honor for his heroism in Italy. "We were all angry. But we had a job to do, and we did it."

ELEVEN

COMBAT

The Nazis have maintained that the art of
flying is the privilege of the Nordic "superior" race because it requires courage. Now
lo and behold a great many of their flaxen-
haired Aryans are being killed by bombs
dropped by Negroes who appear to have mas-
tered the exclusive art of aviation.

—*Stars and Stripes*

The Tuskegee Airmen were angry, too, but they had a job to
do. After what seemed like endless training flights in Alabama, the pilots finally deployed in spring 1943. As racial
battles raged on the home front, Lieutenant Colonel Benjamin O.
Davis Jr. and the 99th Fighter Squadron saw combat for the first
time in Pantelleria, a small Italian island in the Mediterranean Sea.
They were there as part of a plan devised by General Dwight D. Eisenhower, who had set his sights on Italy after Allied troops trounced
Axis forces in North Africa earlier in the year. This made Pantelleria, which sat halfway between Tunisia and Sicily, a key strategic

target. If the Allies secured the rocky forty-two-square-mile island, they would control crucial Mediterranean Sea lanes and air routes and open a clear path to invade the Italian mainland, what British prime minister Winston Churchill called the enemy's "soft underbelly."

Capturing Pantelleria, however, would not be easy. Aerial reconnaissance over the island found over one hundred gun emplacements and dozens of concrete-fortified pillboxes spread throughout the mountains. Two huge underground hangars, carved into a rocky hillside and protected by a thick layer of volcanic rock and earth, sheltered Axis combat aircraft. At least ten thousand Italian and German troops defended the island, and the jagged coastline prevented the Allies from staging a large-scale amphibious landing. Eisenhower believed that Pantelleria could be taken only with airpower, and he directed Lieutenant General Carl "Tooey" Spaatz to dedicate all of the Allied Northwest African Air Forces to the job, code-named Operation Corkscrew.

Of the hundreds of American pilots in the Allied Northwest African Air Forces tapped for the mission, Davis and the two dozen Tuskegee Airmen stood out. This would be the first time Black American pilots flew in combat in the U.S. Army. Flying two missions a day, the Black airmen took out enemy machine-gun sites, escorted bombers on raids, and patrolled the skies over the Mediterranean. They dropped bombs marked with 1941 (the year of the Pearl Harbor attack) and handwritten messages to Mussolini and Hitler.

During the first week, the Tuskegee fliers did not encounter any enemy aircraft, and Davis described the missions as similar to dropping bombs on the range. Soon, though, German Messerschmitt 109s counterattacked, hurtling from high altitudes to strike American bombers. "When I saw the swastikas, I knew this wasn't play anymore, those Nazi pilots' mission was to kill me," said Charles Dryden, a twenty-two-year-old airman from New York City. Axis ground troops fired hundreds of red tracers that looked like a stream of crimson sparkles. As the bright sun and its reflection off the sea blinded the pilots, Dryden jerked his head around to locate the attacking planes. Suddenly, the six Tuskegee fighters broke hard right, turning their P-40 Warhawks 180 degrees to chase off the Nazi planes.

The saturation bombing of Pantelleria lasted for four weeks. Allied aircraft flew more than fifty-two hundred bombing sorties and dropped over six thousand tons of bombs on Axis targets. Many of the explosions were so powerful that Allied troops in North Africa, including Black quartermaster and engineer units, could feel the impact.

On June 11, 1943, just as Allied infantry units were preparing their assault, Pantelleria's military governor surrendered the island and the 11,200 Italian and German troops there became prisoners of war. Eisenhower's airpower strategy proved more successful than he could have hoped. The Air Force's official history of the Pantelleria bombing campaign concluded that it "furnished a spectacular illustration of the intense and violent force that the Allies could bring to bear upon the enemy."

Three weeks after Pantelleria, the Tuskegee Airmen scored their first aerial victory over the Luftwaffe. First Lieutenant Charles Hall, a twenty-two-year-old who had paused his premedical coursework at Eastern Illinois State Teachers College to join the Army Air Corps, shot down a Nazi plane in a dogfight over Sicily on July 2. "It was my eighth mission, but the first time I had seen the enemy close enough to shoot at him," Hall said.

Hall's triumph was front-page news in Black newspapers across the country. *The Pittsburgh Courier* praised Hall as the "first American Negro pilot in world history to shoot down an enemy plane," and profiled his mother, Anna Hall, and sister, Victoria Littlejohn, who were both war workers in Fort Wayne, Indiana. *Stars and Stripes*, the official military newspaper, called the airmen the "Black Angels" and wrote that Hitler was "unable to bear the thought of negroes squashing Nazis like bugs." While the military paper saw this as a victory over Nazi racial ideology, the airmen knew the story was more complicated. The U.S. Army Air Corps, motivated by similar ideas about white superiority, had grudgingly admitted Black pilots only two years prior and segregated them into a separate unit. Still, the airmen appreciated the long-overdue acknowledgment of their capabilities.

"I would like to meet the pilot who shot down that Jerry!" exclaimed General Eisenhower when he greeted the 99th fliers upon their return to the air base that afternoon. Hall enjoyed the ice-cold bottle of Coca-Cola the unit had saved for the pilot who scored the first enemy kill. The celebration was bittersweet, however, because the 99th had also lost their first two pilots in combat. First Lieutenant Sherman White, a former University of Chicago student from Montgomery, Alabama, and Lieutenant James McCullin, a Kentucky State University graduate from St. Louis, did not return to base.

Ollie Stewart, a *Baltimore Afro-American* war correspondent embedded with the 99th, witnessed the mix of elation and sorrow. Stewart and his fellow Black war correspondents played an invaluable role in bringing the war to life for Black readers in the States. "If all Americans could see these boys taking off and landing day after day, as I have, and watch our ground crews patch and oil and check each ship for perfection after every trip over territory where death lies waiting, I feel there would be much less bitterness and prejudice in our native land," he wrote. Airman Charles Dryden struggled to reconcile the life-and-death nature of combat. "War is terrible, war is horrible," he said. "There is nothing glamorous about it; it looks like it, but it is not. . . . Even if I could see [enemy pilots], it was very impersonal because you're trying to shoot down a machine, you're not even thinking that there's a pilot in that machine. You're trying to down him before he downs you."

When the Allies launched Operation Husky, a major amphibious assault on Sicily on July 10, the Tuskegee Airmen provided cover for the 3rd Infantry Division landing at Licata, a city on the island's south coast. The Allies faced stiff resistance from Axis forces and suffered nearly twenty-five thousand casualties. The invasion contributed to the political instability in Italy, and on July 24, Mussolini was deposed and arrested. A new government led by General Pietro Badoglio withdrew Italian troops and began negotiating peace terms with the Allies. By August 17, the Allies had reached the port of Messina on the northeast tip of Sicily and prepared to cross the strait to reach the Italian peninsula.

Operation Husky was an important victory, but Ollie Stewart said there was no cheering from the pilots and ground troops who fought in Sicily. "Cheering is for those who have never seen starving women and children begging to eat from your garbage can, or roads choked with Sicilians trudging on foot with their belongings back to homes demolished by bombs," Stewart wrote. "Liberated people dig in ruins for signs of loved ones they cannot find. This is war—this is victory. Now, after Sicily, what? Already colored pilots from the fighter squadron are ranging far and wide, escorting bombers on missions that will soften up the point of the next attack."

While the horrors of battle were inescapable, Davis and the other 99th fighter pilots felt like they were finally helping win the war. After two years of training and countless nights when it seemed like they would never deploy overseas, the Tuskegee Airmen were proving themselves in combat. They were heroes to millions of Black Americans, approaching the stature of pioneers and icons like heavyweight champion Joe Louis, Olympic track star Jesse Owens, and contralto Marian Anderson.

With recognition came pressure. All the pilots and mechanics knew that the fate of Black Americans in the Air Corps depended on how well they executed each mission. Davis said the airmen and crew could take little pleasure in their daily achievement until their overall performance was deemed an unqualified success. The unit continued to toil, day in and day out, to prove that Black pilots deserved to be in the Air Corps.

Just weeks after Sicily, the Tuskegee Airmen faced a new threat. This time it was not the Luftwaffe but their own commander launching the attack. Colonel William Momyer led the 33rd Fighter Group, of which the 99th Squadron was a part. Other than the two dozen Black pilots in the 99th, all the pilots under Momyer's command were white. The Tuskegee Airmen felt that Momyer never wanted them attached to his unit. "Colonel Momyer was just plain prejudiced towards us," recalled Spann Watson, a Howard University alum from rural Johnston, South Carolina.

Momyer played petty tricks to embarrass and undermine the 99th. He scheduled briefings and then moved the time up an hour without notifying the Black pilots, so that they arrived when the meeting had ended. This particularly infuriated Davis, who understood from his stint as the lone Black cadet at West Point that if he was not early, he was late. After the Allies secured Sicily, Momyer assigned only the all-white squadrons for missions over the Italian peninsula, where they could notch additional combat triumphs. "We didn't get a chance to gain victories because we didn't go with the invasion force to Italy," Watson said. "We remained in Sicily, hundreds of miles from the battle zone."

In September, Momyer wrote to Major General Edwin House, the head of the 12th Air Support Command and the ranking U.S. Army Air Force officer in Italy, to recommend that the 99th be permanently removed from combat operations and assigned to coastal patrol duty. "It is my opinion that they are not of the fighting caliber of any squadron in the group," Momyer wrote. "They have failed to display the aggressiveness and desire for combat that are necessary to a first-class fighting organization."

Momyer's report made its way through Army Air Force leadership, receiving support at each level of the military hierarchy. One endorsement added, "The Negro type has not the proper reflexes to make a first-class fighter pilot." This comment harkened back to the racial pseudoscience in the 1925 War College report that suggested Black Americans lacked the intelligence, courage, and moral character to thrive as military leaders or soldiers. With the backing of his superiors, Momyer's report threatened to block Black pilots from combat for the rest of the war and potentially well beyond.

The situation escalated when someone leaked Momyer's report to *Time* magazine. In an article titled "Experiment Proved?" readers across America learned that "unofficial reports from the Mediterranean theater have suggested that the top air command was not altogether satisfied with the 99th's performance." Agatha Jo Scott Davis, who was doing war work at Sperry Gyroscope Company in Brooklyn, sent an angry letter to the editor defending her husband and his squadron. "By publishing an article based on 'unofficial reports' you have created unfavorable public opinion about an organization to which all Negroes point with pride," she wrote. "You should realize that these few printed words in *Time* . . . have struck at one of the strongest pillars upholding Negroes' morale in their effort to contribute to the winning of the war."

Davis got his opportunity to defend the 99th when he was called to the Pentagon to meet with the War Department Committee on Special Troop Policies chaired by Assistant Secretary of War John McCloy. Although Davis was privately furious at the Momyer report and the everyday hostility and racism his men encountered, he maintained his composure and offered a quiet, reasoned defense of the unit. None of the Tuskegee Airmen had combat experience before Pantelleria, he noted, and if they lacked an aggressive spirit at first, they quickly took to the fight. His squadron had fewer pilots than other units, so Black pilots had to fly more missions on more consecutive days than their white counterparts. And the 99th did everything that was asked of them in combat. "If given a mission to bomb a target, I went ahead and bombed it," he said. Davis concluded by saying that he respected Momyer as his commander and lamenting that "if his opinion is correct, there is no hope."

The Tuskegee Airmen were livid at having their combat performance disparaged. "I was proud of what I was doing, and I did it well," said James Wiley. "I resented that even the War Department considered us an 'experiment.' Here I was, fighting for my country, and I was just an 'experiment'!" This feeling of outrage was shared by the Black press, which rallied readers to support the 99th. Truman Gibson, a University of Chicago–trained lawyer who became civilian adviser to Secretary of War Stimson after William Hastie resigned, applied pressure on the War Department. After a summer of racial conflict in American cities and on military bases, Stimson was eager to avoid a highly publicized battle over the most prominent Black American military unit. The War Department commissioned an in-depth study of the 99th's combat performance from the July battle over Sicily through early 1944.

With the military establishment watching them closely, the Tuskegee Airmen delivered a combat performance at the Battle of Anzio to silence their critics. By January 1944, the Allies had successfully landed at Salerno and were pushing their way north toward Rome. They encountered heavy German resistance at the Gustav Line, which stretched from the Tyrrhenian Sea to the Adriatic Sea and was defended by fifteen Nazi divisions, artillery, machine-gun emplacements, minefields, and barbed wire. The Allies decided to outflank the Germans by invading the coastal city of Anzio, between Rome and the Gustav Line. Joining white pilots in the 79th Fighter Group, the 99th provided air cover for Operation Shingle, an amphibious landing that put tens of thousands of Allied troops and vehicles within striking distance of Rome. The Tuskegee Airmen shot down a dozen Nazi planes.

"Any outfit would have been proud of the record," *Time* reported, in an about-face from their article four months earlier. "These victories stamped the final seal of combat excellence on one of the most controversial outfits in the Army, the all-Negro 99th Fighter Squadron." A white pilot in the 79th praised the 99th as "a first-rate bunch, fighting the same war that we are," while airman Lemuel Custis told *The New York Times*, "When the 99th first went over the general impression was that it was an experiment. Now I think the record shows that it was a successful experiment." Looking back on Anzio years later, Custis said, "If we had failed, the whole history of Air Force integration would have changed. But we didn't go into it to fail."

WHEN THE TUSKEGEE AIRMEN patrolled the skies over the Mediterranean, many of the vessels they protected were Liberty ships manned by merchant mariners transporting cargo and troops. The Merchant Marine formed the supply line connecting troops fighting overseas and the home front's arsenal of democracy. Civilian volunteers, too young or too old to be drafted or otherwise ineligible for the armed services, joined career seamen from the United States and Allied nations in transporting tremendous quantities of ammunition and airplanes, boots and bombs, food and fuel. They carried thousands of soldiers to Europe and the Pacific and kept them supplied. This was no simple task, since each soldier needed an average of twelve tons of supplies per year. The Merchant Marine expanded from fifty-five thousand men at the beginning of the war to more than a quarter million by 1945. These volunteer sailors staffed what President Roosevelt called "a great bridge of ships" forming America's "Fourth Arm of Defense."

Wartime shipping was dangerous work. Although not officially in combat roles, the men who served on Merchant Marine ships suffered higher casualty rates than in any branch of the military. Ships faced constant threat from Axis submarines, warships, airplanes, and, in narrow shipping channels like the Mediterranean, land artillery. German U-boats sank hundreds of Liberty ships, including the SS *Frederick Douglass*, which was torpedoed in September 1943. Three months later, a German bomber raid on the port of Bari, Italy, sank seventeen Allied vessels, including five American merchant ships.

For Black Americans, the Merchant Marine was a powerful symbol of equality because unlike the army, Air Corps, navy, or Marines, merchant crews were racially integrated. "The men who man the ships that feed the world know no color lines," *Chicago Defender* war correspondent Ben Burns wrote. "They are a model of real democracy." Twenty-four thousand Black Americans served in the Merchant Marine during the war, delivering valuable cargo while under constant threat of attack. Many Black mariners saw more action during the war than Black servicemen in army or navy labor battalions. "Jim Crow breaks down on Liberty ships," Burns continued. "Here every hand—no matter what color—is needed to battle the enemy and every single Negro in the crew has a battle station where he can fight back when Hitlerites strike. There are no 'For Whites Only' signs on the guns."

No one symbolized the distinguished service of Black mariners more than Captain Hugh Mulzac, who led a racially mixed crew aboard the Liberty ship SS *Booker T. Washington*. Born on Saint Vincent island in the British West Indies, Mulzac served on American merchant ships during World War I and became a U.S. citizen in 1918. He earned his shipmaster license two years later and captained the SS *Yarmouth* on Marcus Garvey's Black Star Line between New York and West Indian and South American ports in the early 1920s. While he was qualified to command any merchant vessel, racial prejudice limited him to work as a steward or third mate for two decades. After Pearl Harbor, the CIO-affiliated National Maritime Union and National Negro Congress pressured the United States Maritime Commission to make Mulzac a shipmaster. Finally, in 1942, at the age of fifty-six, Mulzac was tapped to be a Merchant Marine captain.

Standing slightly stooped, with a thin face and soft voice, the bespectacled Mulzac looked more like a country schoolteacher than a seaman. But his appearance belied the ferocity with which he approached his work. He spurned the U.S. Maritime Commission when they initially offered him a ship with an all-Black crew, declaring that he would not command a Jim Crow ship under any circumstances.

He worked with the National Maritime Union to hire a racially integrated crew where Black and white Americans were joined by mariners from more than a dozen nationalities, including Filipinos, Hondurans, Irish, and West Indians. The Black press dubbed it a "United Nations" crew. "We West Indians and Negro Americans and Africans can prove today that for us Democracy is not merely an empty rotten name as the Nazis and Fascists have said," Mulzac said. "We are fighting so that our women and our children may enjoy more of that freedom which exists under democracy."

When the 10,500-ton *Booker T. Washington* launched in Los Angeles harbor in October 1942, with Mulzac at the helm and a portrait of its namesake, the so-called Wizard of Tuskegee, painted on the ship's immaculately clean boiler, it was national news. "The Booker T. will serve not only in the war of ocean transport but in the war against race discrimination," *Time* reported. As Marian Anderson sang the national anthem, Mulzac ruminated on all the years that the color line had prevented him from fulfilling his potential. "Everything I ever was, stood for, fought for, dreamed of, came into focus that day," he remembered. After being prevented from captaining a ship for more than two decades, he was finally able to use his training and capabilities fully. He said it was like being born anew.

When Mulzac and his crew returned from their first voyage, they were feted in New York City at a dinner with twelve hundred people. Singer Paul Robeson and pianist Hazel Scott performed, and Langston Hughes recited a poem he composed in Mulzac's honor that read in part,

> More than ship then,
> Captain Mulzac,
> Is the BOOKER T.,
> And more than captain
> You who guide it on its way.
> Your ship is mankind's deepest dream
> Daring the sea—
> Your ship is flagship
> Of a newer day.

Under Mulzac's command, the *Booker T. Washington* made nearly two dozen round trips to Europe and the Pacific, transporting hundreds of troops and thousands of tons of cargo. He opened the door for three other Black captains who commanded merchant vessels with mixed crews during the war—Adrian T. Richardson, John Godfrey, and Clifton Lastic—as well as hundreds of Black officers who held positions of authority they were denied in the navy.

After transporting bombs, repair parts, and other supplies to the Tuskegee Airmen and other troops in the Mediterranean theater, Mulzac joined Benjamin O. Davis Jr. for a tour of the airfields in Italy. The captain returned the favor by inviting Davis and the pilots, including his nephew Lieutenant John Mulzac for a shipboard reception. The aviators and mariners embodied Black excellence.

Like the Tuskegee Airmen's, Mulzac's successful contributions to the war effort did not insulate him from racism. He and his crew were harassed and insulted by white American soldiers when the *Booker T. Washington* dropped anchor in the Panama Canal Zone. "You talk about conditions in South Africa and down South, but the Panama Canal Zone under the American flag is a terrible crime," he said. At a Greyhound bus station in Richmond, Virginia, a white cop ordered Mulzac and his purser, white merchant officer John Beecher, both of whom were in uniform, to move from the main waiting room.

> "You'll have to get over in that little waiting room over there," the cop said.
>
> "This is all right here," Mulzac replied.

"I have got orders," the cop insisted. "You're colored, you'll have to go."

"I have orders, too," Mulzac shot back. "The government has given me orders to fight for democracy. It seems your State Government has given you orders to fight against democracy. I'm over there fighting for you fellows over here. We are carrying stuff in the ships, day and night, watching for submarines for draft dodgers like you fellows over here who tell us where to sit."

The police officer was livid and threatened to arrest the two men for violating Virginia's segregation laws.

Reluctantly, Mulzac and Beecher picked up their luggage and waited outside for their bus to Norfolk. They could not risk being stuck in a Richmond jail when they were scheduled to leave port days later to deliver supplies to troops in the Mediterranean. "Had Captain Mulzac wrapped himself in the American flag and seated himself in the Greyhound bus station of the one-time Confederate capital, the police would have torn away the flag first and ousted the captain second," the *Baltimore Afro-American* fumed. "We know now that patriotic service and heroism have no meaning for Dixie either. Jim crow is as much for the colored man who commands a ship . . . as for the humblest colored American who washes cuspidors. If he didn't know it before, Captain Mulzac, along with all others who risk their lives for us, knows now that in war or in peace, he can only be a second-class citizen at home."

This second-class status was punctuated when Mulzac returned from a successful round trip to North Africa and tried to buy a home in Brooklyn. Mulzac and his wife, Jamaican-born Miriam Aris, found a nice white-stone row house in Crown Heights that they thought would be perfect for them and their four children. Their real estate agent drew up the paperwork and negotiated a fair price. Everything seemed to be going smoothly until Mulzac and Aris arrived at the house to sign the papers and close the deal. The sellers reneged, explaining that they and the other white homeowners had agreed never to sell to Black people because they feared real estate values in the neighborhood would decline. Mulzac was angry but not surprised. "Here I am, in command of a ship which under me has just completed its seventh successful voyage to North Africa, zigzagging through submarine-infested waters and mine-laden areas to deliver the goods," he said, "and this is what confronts me . . . when my family and I . . . are barred from purchasing a home of our own because of our pigmentation."

The war at home could not keep him from the war abroad. Two months later, Mulzac and his crew were back on the Atlantic, en route to Naples. They delivered tons of supplies to fortify the Allied troops, who finally broke through the Nazis' Gustav Line in May 1944. In June, after months of contributions from the Tuskegee Airmen and the Merchant Marine, the Allies secured Rome.

WITH THEIR PERFORMANCE in the Mediterranean, the Tuskegee Airmen broke a significant barrier for Black Americans in the military. Another barrier fell in the Pacific theater in the spring of 1944, when the 24th Infantry Regiment and the 93rd Infantry Division became the first Black infantry troops to see combat in the war.

Earlier in the year, the Allies had largely seized control of the Pacific and began to pressure Japan from two directions. General Douglas MacArthur led an offensive in the southwest Pacific, while forces led by Admiral Chester Nimitz pushed through the central Pacific. Both campaigns fought from island to island, attempting to collapse Japan's defensive perimeter, sever enemy lines of supply and communication, and seize islands close enough for B-29 long-range bombers to reach the mainland.

Black infantry troops arrived as reinforcements on Bougainville Island, halfway between New Guinea and the Solomon Islands, after the majority of Japanese soldiers had been defeated. Fletcher P. Martin, *Louisville Defender* editor and war correspondent, embedded with the infantry and told Black Americans how their boys were doing in the Pacific. He painted a picture of a brutal conflict. Black soldiers on jungle patrols tripped over the twisted, bloated corpses of enemy dead. Flamethrowers, bayonets, and sniper fire became part of everyday life. A repulsive stench permeated the damp air.

In his dispatches, Martin eagerly touted the fighting skills of Black infantry in order to refute the army's belief that Black men lacked the courage necessary for combat. He accompanied a small band of troops led by a young lieutenant from Washington, D.C., as they scampered up a jungle crag in pursuit of retreating Japanese forces. "During the inky blackness of night and a pelting rain the enemy attacked the Negro troops with knives, grenades, and rifle fire," Martin wrote. "This correspondent . . . felt death's hot breath very close. Our troops fought with viciousness and valor, meeting steel with steel in hand-to-hand encounters." Black troops blew up enemy pillboxes with grenades and fired point-blank into enemy trenches. The Black infantry experienced "a baptism on Bougainville," Martin concluded.

Like his white counterpart, war correspondent Ernie Pyle, Martin laid bare the terrible human cost of war. After spending several months in Bougainville, he wrote, "In the days to come there will be more deaths . . . and still more deaths. They're inescapable. It's part of the price. We who have watched know the horror of the whole picture. And whether it is a Black body, white body, yellow body—the scene is no less horrible." Reading back over his dispatches, Martin worried that readers would see the Black infantry as hardened and emotionless. "Those of us here look upon the 24th Infantry not as an invincible bunch of professional killers, but as a small family which has been called to do an unpleasant job," he wrote. "They are average Americans who prior to the war were men doing varied things to earn a living. When the call came for duty, they answered."

Like all soldiers, Black infantrymen in the Pacific enjoyed getting mail from home. Mail call brought love letters from wives and girlfriends, clippings from Black newspapers and magazines, and pictures of children born or grown taller since their fathers deployed. Letters brought news that the USS *Liscome Bay* was hit by a torpedo from a Japanese submarine in the Battle of Makin near the Gilbert Islands, and sank in less than half an hour. Among the 644 sailors who lost their lives was Cook Third Class Doris Miller, the hero of Pearl Harbor.

Another letter the troops received was from the mother of a soldier in the 24th Infantry who had been killed in action. With a shaky hand she wrote that she had received the official telegram from the War Department notifying her of her son's death. She thanked his fellow troops for the nice things they said about him. "I am glad he was a good soldier," she wrote. "He was a good son."

It took more than two years of organized pressure on the military but, by the spring of 1944, Black Americans were in combat roles in multiple theaters. They were doing their part for the Double V campaign, fighting fascism abroad.

TWELVE

CIVIL RIGHTS BATTLEFRONTS AT HOME

Our boys, our bonds, our brothers are fighting for YOU. Why can't we eat here?

—HOWARD UNIVERSITY STUDENTS,
PICKET OF SEGREGATED RESTAURANT
IN WASHINGTON, D.C.

The other half of the Double V, victory over racism at home, continued apace. In April 1944, for example, Thurgood Marshall achieved the greatest civil rights victory of his career. Marshall represented Lonnie E. Smith, a Black dentist from Houston who, like other Black voters, was denied a ballot in Texas's Democratic primary in which candidates for Congress, governor, and state offices were being nominated. The NAACP saw Smith's case as an ideal opportunity to challenge the constitutionality of the all-white primary system. Working alongside William Hastie, Marshall argued before the U.S. Supreme Court that the Texas Democratic Party's policy of barring Black people from participating in primary elections violated the Fourteenth and Fifteenth Amendments. Similar voter disenfranchisement tactics across the South enabled whites to dominate a one-party political system for decades. In an 8–1 decision, the Supreme Court's *Smith v. Allwright* ruling overturned two lower-court decisions to find that all-white primaries were unconstitutional.

The *Smith* case was part of a larger fight to redefine democracy in the United States during the war. Marshall and grassroots civil rights activists including Ella Baker, Bayard Rustin, and Pauli Murray recognized that America was a democracy in name only. White supremacy was explicitly sanctioned in large swaths of the country and implicitly approved everywhere else. Black Americans were treated as second-class citizens, or half American, even as they were being asked to sacrifice their full lives in the war.

The *Smith* decision sent shock waves across the country because it potentially meant that hundreds of thousands of Black Southerners would gain access to the ballot. The NAACP's *Crisis* magazine called it "a giant milestone in the progress of Negro Americans toward full citizenship" and saw voter registration as the most important step taken toward erasing racial inequalities since Emancipation. *Time* called the *Smith* decision a "time bomb" and wrote that "the lid came off the race problem" when the court made its ruling.

White politicians across the South vowed to resist any attempts to extend democracy to Black Americans. "The South, at all costs, will maintain the rule of white supremacy," declared Louisiana senator John H. Overton. "Southerners will not allow matters peculiar to us to be determined by those who do not know and understand our problem," Florida senator Claude Pepper said. "The South will allow nothing to impair white supremacy." Senator Ellison "Cotton Ed" Smith of South Carolina challenged "all those who love South Carolina and the white man's rule [to] rally in this hour . . . to save her from a disastrous fate."

There was nothing subtle about these demands to maintain white supremacy. They were voiced by elected officials and published in prominent national newspapers and weeklies. One did not need a law degree to understand that the *Smith* decision struck at the core of American democracy. Much of the Double V fight against racism at home took place out in the open, for the world to see. If ordinary white Americans chose not to understand the depths of racism in their country, it was not for lack of knowledge or information. It was a willful decision to turn away from burgeoning Black freedom struggles and an intentional refusal to reckon with the realities of racism in America.

When Congress debated absentee voting for soldiers, Southerners insisted that federal rules should not supersede state election laws. In practice, this meant that Southern states could continue to disenfranchise Black troops, as they did other Black citizens. Mississippi senator James O. Eastland argued that white servicemen were "fighting to maintain white supremacy and the control of our election machinery." Senator William Lander, a Republican from North Dakota, pushed back, contending that Black servicemen and -women should be guaranteed the right to vote. "Bullets make no discrimination between Black and white, Jew and Gentile, Catholic and Protestant, rich and poor," he said. "Then why should ballots?"

With President Roosevelt up for reelection in the fall, many white Southerners saw the high court's *Smith* ruling as a further encroachment of New Deal politics into the South. Former Mississippi governor Mike Connor warned that Roosevelt and the national Democratic Party would continue to partner with Black voters in the north to "place the black heel of negro domination on our necks." "America is White, not Red, not Black," Connor argued, "and the time has come for the Democratic Party to tell the New Dealers, with all of the force at our command, that we propose to keep it White."

Former Louisiana governor Sam Jones saw the ruling against all-white primaries as an unwelcome step down the path toward ending white dominance in the South. "It is abundantly and increasingly clear that the New Deal high command hopes to use the war as an instrument for forcing the social 'equality' of the Negro upon the South," he argued. These racial fears manifested among whites across the South. In North Carolina, a businessman distributed pamphlets during the campaign declaring "I Can't Vote for Mr. Roosevelt in November" because he "has done more to give [Blacks] social equality than all men and political parties combined." As a warning of where these teachings would lead, the cover page featured a picture from a wedding in Connecticut with a Black groomsman escorting a white bridesmaid.

All of this vitriol meant Marshall was doing his job. He was still basking in the glow of his Supreme Court victory when he addressed eight hundred NAACP branch leaders and members in Chicago in July 1944. "We must not be delayed by people who say 'the time is not ripe,' nor should we proceed with caution for fear of destroying the status quo," he said. "Persons who deny us our civil rights should be brought to justice now. Many people believe the time is always 'ripe' to discriminate against Negroes. All right then— the time is always 'ripe' to bring them to justice."

Marshall understood all too well that Southern state governments and white citizens would do everything they could to circumvent the *Smith* decision and would use intimidation and deadly violence to keep Black people from the polls. Black Americans were undaunted in the face of these immense challenges. As Marshall and his NAACP Legal Defense Fund colleagues fought to ensure legal compliance with the court's ruling, grassroots activists, including a large number of Black veterans, demanded equal access to the ballot.

WHILE THURGOOD MARSHALL SECURED an important civil rights victory in *Smith v. Allwright*, Rosa Parks was employed at Maxwell Air Force Base in Montgomery, Alabama. She worked on the base as a civilian seamstress in the Army Air Corps. When the army issued a directive prohibiting segregation of post exchanges, transportation, and movie theaters in late summer 1944, Maxwell was among the first to implement the changes. Eating in the cafeteria and riding on the trolleys at Maxwell were Parks's first exposure to racial integration. "You might just say Maxwell opened my eyes up," she said. "It was an alternative reality to the ugly policies of Jim Crow." She could sit wherever she pleased and chat amiably with white passengers on buses at Maxwell, but when they reached the edge of base and transferred to the city bus, she had to sit in the back. The arbitrary nature of segregation was infuriating. In the simple act of transferring from one bus to another, Parks went from being treated equally to being regarded as a second-class citizen.

Despite the advances at Maxwell, Parks was troubled by the contradictions of the war. Her brother, Sylvester, served overseas in the Pacific and Europe as a member of the Medical Detachment Engineering Services Regiment, but when he returned to Montgomery he could not register to vote or find work. Her brother's experiences dovetailed with the stories she read in the Black press of Black troops catching hell in the military. "I had always been taught that this was America, the land of the free and the home of the brave," she said. "I felt that it should be actual, in action rather than just something we hear and talk about." Like thousands of other Black Americans during the war, Parks joined her local NAACP chapter to fight for civil rights. Her activism, which emerged on a national stage during the Montgomery Bus Boycott a decade later, grew in part from seeds planted during the war.

Much of the credit for the NAACP's membership gains during the war goes to Ella Baker, a fierce grassroots organizer. Growing up in Norfolk, Virginia, and Littleton, North Carolina, Baker was raised on her parents' stories of her ancestors defying slave masters and fighting for dignity during Reconstruction. Baker excelled as a debater at Shaw University in Raleigh, North Carolina, and cut her teeth as an organizer in 1930s Harlem, where she directed the Young Negroes' Cooperative League, a loosely affiliated national coalition of cooperatives and buying clubs. Her ability to inspire people as a speaker and her savvy management of the money produced by new memberships led the NAACP to hire her as an assistant field secretary in 1940 and promote her to director of branches three years later.

Baker recognized that the NAACP national office was detached from the experiences and concerns of the majority of Black Americans. Walter White and the New York staff were skilled at wooing white donors and lobbying politicians but focused largely on professional-class Black Americans. Baker, by contrast, wanted the NAACP to be a people's organization where working-class Black folks without much formal education would feel respected and heard. "We must have the 'nerve' to take the Association to people wherever they are," Baker told her colleagues. She recruited at churches and schools—the usual NAACP territory—but also in bars, poolrooms, and bootblack shops. Similar to the circuits Thurgood Marshall traveled to investigate legal cases, Baker's journeys took her tens of thousands of miles across the South and mid-Atlantic encouraging people to join their local NAACP branch and start branches where they did not already exist. "My desire [is] to place the NAACP and its program on the lips of all the people . . . the uncouth MASSES included," she said.

Baker was resoundingly successful as an organizer. With her leadership, the NAACP expanded from 350 branches and 50,000 members in 1940 to nearly 1,000 branches and 450,000 members by the end of the war. Baker called members "shareholders in a huge firm in the business of fighting for freedom."

A number of these new NAACP memberships came from active-duty Black soldiers and sailors. The 665th Port Company sent $80 from Iran. A chemical decontamination unit in Europe contributed $215. The 387th Engineer Battalion raised money to send flowers to the families of battalion members killed overseas and donated the remaining $197.25 to the NAACP. The 366th Infantry claimed to have the most NAACP members of any regiment, and while they were stationed in Italy their newsletter printed regular updates on which of their companies had donated the most money.

"We are making a sacrifice for victory abroad, but that does not ensure us of a victory in our own country," wrote a corporal in the 392nd Engineer Battalion from Normandy, along with a contribution from his unit. "We hope that the next coming generation will not have to endure the humiliation and suffering that we've gone through." Like the 392nd, the 41st Signal Construction Battalion landed in France shortly after the Allies' D-Day invasion. After they built communication lines from the beaches of Normandy throughout France, every man in the unit chipped in a few dollars to help fight for their civil rights at home. "We look upon the N.A.A.C.P. as one of the important elements in making America the America we are fighting for," Private Lennie Fuller wrote. "An America that will say, 'I'm your country,' to every man and woman who fought or worked for victory."

These donations were among the purest illustrations of the Double V campaign in action, with Black soldiers fighting fascism abroad and racism at home. The membership boom and donations gave the NAACP funds to fight legal cases, and the growing membership numbers enabled them to apply more pressure on politicians and the War Department.

Baker recruited and trained legions of activists who would battle for civil rights over the next several decades. Unlike the army and navy, which openly disparaged the leadership ability of Black troops and systematically blocked the small number of Black officers from leading men into combat, Baker believed in the leadership potential of all Black Americans. She organized a half dozen regional leadership conferences to cultivate grassroots leaders. In Atlanta, Baker taught aspiring organizers how to listen to the concerns of local people and connect these concerns to relevant programs of action. Thurgood Marshall ran an evening session on police brutality, bus and train segregation, job discrimination, the GI Bill, and veterans' rights. Rosa Parks and E. D. Nixon, who each became important civil rights leaders in Montgomery, Alabama, attended the Atlanta meeting and learned from Baker. "Instead of the leader as a person who was supposed to be a magic man, you could develop individuals who were bound together by a concept that benefited the larger number of individuals and provided an opportunity for them to grow into being responsible for carrying out a program," Baker later argued. "Strong people don't need strong leaders."

In military parlance, Baker's vision of leadership emphasized the potential of enlisted personnel and noncommissioned officers, rather than pedigreed graduates of the military academies in West Point and Annapolis. It was a vision that valued the common sense and teamwork of the ordinary Black soldiers and sailors who helped win the war abroad and returned to fight for civil rights at home. Baker had little interest in the type of hierarchical leadership practiced by military generals or their civilian equivalents in social movements, where a single person was in charge. Instead, she pioneered a model of leaderful community organizing that would influence groups ranging from the Student Nonviolent Coordinating Committee (SNCC) in the 1960s to Black Lives Matter (BLM) in the twenty-first century.

While Baker fostered militant grassroots organizing, many white Americans fell under the spell of Swedish social scientist Gunnar Myrdal's *An American Dilemma: The Negro Problem and Modern Democracy*, published in spring 1944. After a year when racial violence engulfed the country, Americans were eager to read and talk about race. Myrdal's 1,300-page book argued that racism contradicted America's democratic ideals and that the dogma that supported racial oppression could be uprooted through education. Following the directive of the Carnegie Corporation, the project's sponsor, Myrdal presented facts about racial violence and oppression in a way that would be palatable for the broadest possible audience.

An American Dilemma was wildly influential. In a matter of months, more than one hundred local, state, and national interracial commissions, human-relations committees, and fellowship groups formed. These committees debated race and published bookcases full of well-intentioned studies and educational materials. Like Myrdal, they emphasized a "hearts and minds" approach that prioritized education and moral persuasion rather than specific policies or legislation to challenge racial structures.

This way of discussing race was attractive to many white Americans because it allowed them to condemn individual prejudice without giving up their privileged access to better jobs, housing, and schools. White politicians, social scientists, and citizens came to define the "race problem" in terms of "race relations" rather than "racism." This race-relations model obscured potential frameworks for understanding that it was pervasive structural racism—legal barriers that doomed Black Americans to inferior housing and schools, less accumulated wealth, lower-paying jobs, and more—and not individual prejudiced attitudes that "curdled the morale" of Black Americans, as philosopher Alain Locke put it. *An American Dilemma* allowed average white Americans to denounce the explicit white supremacy advocated by Southern segregationist politicians and others without fully understanding or seeking to address the depths of racism Black Americans encountered not only in the South but in cities like New York, Detroit, and Los Angeles.

As Gunnar Myrdal tried to diagnose American race relations from a sociological perspective, Black Americans became increasingly assertive in demanding equality. Young civil rights activists pioneered strategies and tactics that would provide models for civil rights protests in the 1950s and 1960s.

James Farmer and Bayard Rustin were members of the Fellowship of Reconciliation, an interracial peace organization, and used nonviolent direct-action protests to fight segregation. Farmer, the son of Black teachers, cofounded the Congress of Racial Equality (later CORE) in 1942 with other Black and white pacifists and served as the national chairman during the war. In Detroit, he led groups of CORE and NAACP activists into restaurants that refused to serve Black people. The groups sat and occupied almost all of the available counter spaces and booths for hours at a time. These "sit-in" protests eventually persuaded management to desegregate the restaurants. During the war, CORE activists in other cities fought against segregation at skating rinks, theaters, and hotels, and began planning interracial "freedom rides" to force interstate buses to desegregate.

Rustin, a Quaker pacifist, worked with A. Philip Randolph on the March on Washington Movement and joined Farmer as an early leader of CORE. Like thousands of other Black conscientious objectors, he believed that conscription was morally unjust. "War is wrong," he wrote to the draft board. "For eight years I have believed war to be impractical and a denial of our Hebrew-Christian tradition. . . .

Today I feel that God motivates me to use my whole being to combat by non-violent means the ever-growing racial tension in the United States." For Rustin, both war and the military's policy of segregation were an affront to Christian brotherhood. "Such segregation is based on the moral error that racism (American) can overcome racism (Fascist), that evil can overcome evil, that men virtually in slavery can struggle for a freedom they are denied." For refusing to participate in the war effort, Rustin was sentenced in 1944 to serve three years in prison. He staged a hunger strike at the U.S. penitentiary in Lewisburg, Pennsylvania, to protest segregation in the facility.

Activist and lawyer Pauli Murray, a friend and collaborator of Ella Baker, Thurgood Marshall, and A. Philip Randolph, taught a class on nonviolent direct-action protests for the NAACP chapter at Howard and advised a group of undergraduate students who organized sit-in protests to challenge segregation at several restaurants in Washington, D.C. The students carried signs reading WE DIE TOGETHER—WHY CAN'T WE EAT TOGETHER? and ARE YOU FOR HITLER'S WAY OR THE AMERICAN WAY? Most of the protesters were Black women, fighting not only for their own rights but also for those of their classmates and relatives who had been drafted into the military. "Our boys, our bonds, our brothers are fighting for YOU," they declared. "Why can't we eat here?" On at least one occasion, Black soldiers in uniform saw the student picketers and entered the restaurant to join the sit-in.

Baker, Rustin, and Murray were at the vanguard of a civil rights revolution that would reshape America. Like their parents and grandparents before them, they refused to accept that Black lives were less valuable than white lives and demanded that democracy extend to Black Americans. Millions of Black citizens and their allies fought in the domestic theater of the Double Victory campaign, risking their lives to vanquish racism at home. These fights extended to the military, where Black men and women refused to be degraded. Their protests had severe consequences, including the largest mutiny trial in U.S. history.

THIRTEEN

MUTINY

The Navy has a slogan—"Remember Pearl Harbor"—a reminder of foreign treachery against democracy. There is another slogan the Navy should adopt. It is a reminder of what treachery to our own ideals within a democracy does to that democracy. The pointless, meaningless deaths of over 320 Americans must be given a point, must be given a meaning—for the living. Remember Port Chicago!

—*Mutiny?*, NAACP PAMPHLET

Shortly after ten p.m. on July 17, 1944, a blast with the force of five kilotons of TNT decimated the Port Chicago ammunition depot located thirty miles northeast of San Francisco. At Port Chicago, Black seamen worked in shifts around the clock loading naval ships bound for the Pacific. Every day they transferred hundreds of tons of bombs and shells from railroad boxcars to the ships. Sometimes the bombs were wedged so snugly in the boxcars that the sailors struggled to loosen them safely. It was dangerous work, and on this day, it proved deadly. It was the worst home-front disaster of the war and led to the largest mutiny trial in U.S. history. It would also prove to be Thurgood Marshall's most challenging military case of the war.

On that warm July night people throughout the Bay Area awoke to something that felt like an earthquake. Sailors sleeping in their barracks a mile and a half from the port thought they were under attack from Japanese bombers. "Everybody felt at that point that it was another Pearl Harbor," said Jack Crittenden, a nineteen-year-old seaman from Montgomery, Alabama. "People running and hollering . . . Finally they got the emergency light together. Then some guys came by in a truck and we went down to the dock, but when we got there we didn't see no dock, no ship, no nothing."

One ship, the *Quinault Victory*, was lifted out of the water, spun around, and shattered into pieces. Only tiny fragments of another ship, the *E. A. Bryan*, were ever recovered. All the people on the pier, aboard the two naval ships, and on a nearby Coast Guard fire barge were killed instantly. Three hundred and twenty people died, including 202 Black enlisted sailors. Only 51 bodies were recovered.

As at Pearl Harbor, surviving Black sailors raced to help injured crewmates and fought fires that could have triggered additional explosions. All of them were shaken by what they witnessed. "I was there the next morning," Crittenden recalled. "Man, it was awful. . . . You'd see a shoe with a foot in it . . . You'd see a head floating across the water—just the head or an arm . . . just awful . . . That thing kept you from sleeping at night." One of the seamen had been home in San Diego on leave after his wife gave birth to their son. When he returned to Port Chicago after the explosion and found all of his buddies had been killed, "something just snapped within him," he said.

The Black sailors at Port Chicago had voiced their safety concerns numerous times over the prior year. Despite handling tons of high explosives every day, the men were given no specific training. Men learned how to operate winches to move thousand-pound bombs by watching other sailors operate the machines. White officers pitted different divisions against each other, pushing the sailors to race to load the most tonnage during their shifts. Winners got access to recreational privileges, radios, and Black newspapers, but as the pace ratcheted up so did the risk of an accident.

Like other Black servicemen assigned to heavy, backbreaking labor in the cold of Alaska and the heat of New Guinea, the Black sailors at Port Chicago also chafed at working in segregated units under the supervision of white officers. They described themselves as a "chain gang," "mule team," and "slave outfit," and understood that they were cheap labor compared with civilian contract stevedores, who loaded and unloaded cargo from ships. A year before the explosion, a group of men had written to a local attorney warning that morale had dropped to "an alarming depth" and asked for help. "We, the Negro sailors of the Naval Enlisted Barracks of Port Chicago, California, are waiting for a new deal," they concluded. "Will we wait in vain?"

The navy began its investigation four days after the explosion. Three senior naval officers and a judge advocate interviewed 125 witnesses over a month, only five of whom were Black sailors. The white officers deflected blame for prioritizing output over safety and for the seamen's lack of training. Instead, they pointed their fingers at the Black enlisted men. "The consensus of opinion of the witnesses . . . is that the colored enlisted personnel are neither temperamentally or intellectually capable of handling high explosives," the judge advocate concluded. "It is an admitted fact, supported by the testimony of the witnesses, that there was rough and careless handling of the explosives being loaded aboard ships at Port Chicago." Much in the same way military leaders blamed Black troops for the violence they encountered at army camps in the South, now the navy blamed Black soldiers for the port's shoddy safety protocols. The enlisted Black sailors who were on the Port Chicago dock that July night were not alive to defend themselves from these accusations.

Most of the surviving Black sailors were eventually transferred to the naval barracks in Vallejo, California, near the Mare Island shipyard and ammunition depot. They were in shock and still mourning the deaths of so many of their friends. Men startled at every slammed door and dropped box. Without any information about what caused the first explosion, they were anxious and scared about returning to ship-loading duty. They already resented their day-to-day treatment as laborers, and now they worried that every bomb they moved could be their last. To make matters worse, the navy gave white officers thirty-day survivors' leave to visit their families before returning to regular duty but denied Black sailors the same benefit.

As the men worked at the barracks in Vallejo and it became clear they would soon resume duty under the same officers, they began to talk among themselves about refusing to load ammunition. In early August, when the officers tried to march the Black sailors to the Mare Island ammunition depot, the majority refused to go.

The men were told they would face severe penalties if they did not return to work, but the protests persisted. By the end of the afternoon, more than 250 Black sailors were imprisoned on a barge, where they were held for three days.

Joseph Small, a sturdily built Seaman First Class, emerged as a protest leader. The younger sailors respected the twenty-two-year-old Small like an older brother. As tempers flared on the cramped ship, Small urged the men to stick together, remain composed, and avoid getting in trouble with the guards. In the chow hall, he organized the men to cook, serve meals, and clean the kitchen. "We've got the officers by the balls—they can do nothing to us if we don't do anything to them," he told the men. "If we stick together, they can't do anything to us."

Small and others were optimistic that if they demonstrated they were not refusing to work, only refusing to load ammunition, they would be transferred to other duty. The men did not anticipate that what they saw as a work stoppage—akin to a wildcat strike—the navy saw as mutiny. "As far as we were concerned mutiny could only be committed on the high seas," Small recalled. "We didn't try to take over anything. We didn't try to take command of the base. We didn't try to replace any officers; we didn't try to assume an officer's position. How could they call it mutiny?" The sailors would pay dearly for this faulty assumption.

When the men were released from the ship, they were marched to a baseball field under armed guard. Admiral Carleton Wright, commander of the 12th Naval District headquartered at Mare Island, arrived in a jeep and proceeded to berate and threaten the Black sailors. "I want to remind you that mutinous conduct in the time of war carries a death sentence," Wright said, "and the hazards of facing a firing squad are far greater than the hazards of handling ammunition." Men not long removed from civilian life, who less than a month earlier had seen hundreds of their friends and fellow sailors blown up, were now being told they could be executed if they did not load explosives. When the admiral left, the officers ordered the men to go to one side if they would follow orders to load ammunition and to the other side if they refused.

It was a wrenching decision and men wept openly as they tried to balance their own lives against their bonds with other Black sailors. More than 200 men decided to return to work, and the admiral recommended they be charged with summary courts-martial for refusing to obey orders. When the navy notified President Roosevelt of the decision, he wrote, "It seems to me we should remember in the summary courts-martial of these 208 men that they were activated by mass fear and that this was understandable. Their punishment should be nominal." The other 50 men who refused to load ammunition were charged with conspiring to make a mutiny, transferred thirty miles south to the brig at Camp Shoemaker, and interrogated. The charges the men faced carried lengthy prison sentences and possibly death.

The trial began on September 14 before a seven-member court of senior naval officers appointed by Admiral Wright. They served as both judge and jury. Lieutenant Commander James F. Coakley led the prosecution. (More than two decades later, Coakley would prosecute antiwar activists and Black Panthers as Alameda County district attorney.) Lieutenant Gerald Veltmann, a thirty-three-year-old Houston lawyer, headed the defense, and the Judge Advocate's office assigned five lawyers to represent groups of ten men. All of the officers trying and deciding the case were white. In the courtroom the senior naval officers were seated directly across from the prosecution and defense, while the Black sailors lined the periphery, listening anxiously while their lives hung in the balance.

The court-martial of the Port Chicago seamen was the first U.S. mutiny trial of World War II and the largest mass trial in navy history. Unusually for military trials, the navy encouraged newspaper and wire-service reporters to cover the proceedings. They hoped the national publicity would show that the Black sailors were receiving a fair trial while also serving as a warning to other troops who might be tempted to disobey orders.

The prosecution argued that the sailors' fear was no excuse for their insubordination and that the meetings Joseph Small organized aboard the barge constituted a conspiracy to mutiny. The defense countered that the officers had asked the sailors if they were willing to load ammunition after the explosion, but had not ordered them to do so. The men refused to move explosives because they were fearful, the defense contended, not conspiring to mutiny. "Those men were no more guilty of mutiny than they were of flying to the moon," Veltmann later argued.

The families of the fifty men contacted the NAACP, and in October, Thurgood Marshall flew to San Francisco to attend the trial and contribute to the sailors' defense. "This is not an individual case," Marshall argued. "This is not fifty men on trial for mutiny. This is the Navy on trial for its whole vicious policy toward Negroes." Marshall demanded a formal government investigation of Port Chicago, including why Black seamen were assigned to segregated labor units and why they were given no safety training before being required to move dangerous explosives. "I want to know why the Navy disregarded official warnings by the San Francisco waterfront unions—before the Port Chicago disaster—that an explosion was inevitable if they persisted in using untrained seamen in the loading of ammunition," Marshall said. "I want to know why the Navy disregarded an offer by these same unions to send experienced men to train Navy personnel in the safe handling of explosives. . . . I want to know why the commissioned officers at Port Chicago were allowed to race their men. I want to know why bets ranging from five dollars up were made between division officers as to whose crew would load more ammunition."

After six weeks of hearings, the jury of senior naval officers adjourned to make their ruling. Their deliberations barely extended over the lunch hour before they reached a verdict and found all fifty Black sailors guilty of mutiny. The men were sentenced to between eight and fifteen years in prison. Marshall wryly noted that the officers deliberated for about a minute and a half for each defendant. He immediately started working on the appeal process, which carried into the following year.

The NAACP published *Mutiny?*, a pamphlet ghostwritten by Mary Lindsey, a white reporter for the leftist *People's World* newspaper, to call attention to the case and urge members to write protest letters to the navy. "The Navy has a slogan—'Remember Pearl Harbor'—a reminder of foreign treachery against democracy," the pamphlet concluded. "There is another slogan the Navy should adopt. It is a reminder of what treachery to our own ideals within a democracy does to that democracy. The pointless, meaningless deaths of over 320 Americans must be given a point, must be given a meaning—for the living. Remember Port Chicago!"

Marshall took the appeal to the navy's Judge Advocate General's office in Washington, D.C. He argued that the military was too quick to label any disobedience by Black sailors or soldiers a mutiny and that the navy was making scapegoats of the men to cover up the practices that led to the explosion. Marshall's appeal was unsuccessful, and the Black sailors spent the rest of the war in the Terminal Island military prison in San Pedro, south of Los Angeles. Amid growing pressure to desegregate the military, the navy eventually shortened the sentences and released the men from prison in 1946. Efforts to clear the sailors' names would continue for decades after the war.

PORT CHICAGO WAS JUST ONE of several cases of Black military personnel protesting discriminatory treatment. Like sailors loading ammunition, the 12,500 Black Seabees (Naval Construction Battalion personnel) did important work for the navy. They built advanced bases, constructed underwater slips for naval vessels, and off-loaded cargo. Like other Black military laborers, they worked under white officers. A thousand Black Seabees, who had served nearly two years overseas in Tulagi and Guadalcanal in the Pacific theater, staged a hunger strike at Camp Rousseau in Port Hueneme, California, after their commanding officer refused to promote Black Americans and assigned Black Seabees only to unskilled manual labor. "It is discouraging and destructive to the morale when they see white men with much less preparation than they have, and with no more apparent qualifications of leadership than they possess, being advanced beyond them," NAACP secretary Roy Wilkins said. Nineteen of the Seabees were discharged for seditious behavior.

At Freeman Army Airfield, in Indiana, over a hundred Tuskegee

Airmen officers were arrested when they attempted to integrate an all-white Officers' Club. "I'd flown sixty-seven combat missions in Europe," Lieutenant Colonel Clarence Jamison recalled. "As an officer of the United States Army Air Corps, who'd put his life on the line for this country, why couldn't I use a United States Army Officers club?" The Black pilots had endured racism at Tuskegee, from segregated bathrooms on base to violence at the hands of police in town. They had risked their lives and lost friends fighting for a country that treated them as less valuable than white citizens. Now they were fed up. Their protest happened to take place at an Officers' Club, but it was about much more than that. "It was a slap in the face," Jamison said. "It defiled the graves of [Black pilots] . . . who'd made the ultimate sacrifice for their country but couldn't get into a dive club because of their skin color."

At Fort Devens, in Massachusetts, over fifty Black women went on strike to protest racial discrimination in the Women's Army Corps. Many of the women were college graduates and were enticed to enlist in the WAC by promises of skilled jobs, only to be assigned cleaning duty. Alice Young, a twenty-three-year-old from Washington, D.C., who left nursing school to join the WAC, recalled that her hospital commander told her, "I do not have colored WACs as medical technicians. They are here to scrub and wash floors, wash dishes and do all the dirty work." The four strike leaders—Mary Green, Anna Morrison, Johnnie Murphy, and Young—were court-martialed. "If it will help my people by me taking a court-martial, I would be willing to take it," Morrison said in her court testimony.

Hundreds of other Black soldiers and sailors staged their own individual protests, refusing to obey racially unjust orders from officers, military police, and local sheriffs. Among them, Lieutenant

Jackie Robinson was court-martialed at Camp Hood, Texas, in the summer of 1944 when he refused to move to a seat in the back of an army bus. Robinson was with the light-skinned wife of another Black officer and the two picked seats in the middle of the bus. "The driver glanced into his rear-view mirror and saw what he thought was a white woman talking with a black second lieutenant," he remembered. "He became visibly upset, stopped the bus, and came back to order me to move to the rear. I didn't even stop talking, didn't even look at him. . . . I had no intention of being intimidated into moving to the back of the bus."

Although Robinson was four years away from breaking the color barrier in Major League Baseball, he was already a well-known athlete after starring in four sports at UCLA. He knew that word of his court-martial would garner national attention. Robinson wrote to Civil Advisor to the Secretary of War Truman Gibson after the arrest to ask his advice. "I don't want any unfavorable publicity for myself or the Army but I believe in fair play and I feel I have to let someone in on the case," he wrote. "I don't care what the outcome of the trial is because I know I am being framed and the charges aren't too bad." Under intense pressure from the Black press, the army acquitted Robinson, granted his request for exemption from active military service, and discharged him in the fall. The unit Robinson was attached to, the 761st Tank Battalion, nicknamed the "Black Panthers," went on to distinguish itself in the Battle of the Bulge as part of General George Patton's 3rd Army.

"Why do Negro soldiers and sailors mutiny?" the *Chicago Defender* asked, after seventy-four soldiers in the 1320th Engineer General Service Regiment in Hawaii were court-martialed and convicted of mutiny. The men worked in a labor battalion, clearing airfields and moving tons of earth. They refused to show up for work after their Black officers were transferred. The *Defender* argued that the men's defiance was deeply rooted in histories of Black resistance. "From slavery to slave labor has been the fate of the Negro who becomes a soldier or sailor. As a slave, the Negro revolted—fought, bled and died to break the chains that bound him. As slave labor in the Army and Navy, he is doing no less."

Thurgood Marshall and the NAACP were involved in almost all these court-martial and mutiny cases and saw a clear pattern emerging. "It is apparent that most of these incidents arose from a final break in the spirit of the Negro soldiers due to continued mistreatment," he said. "The tendency in 'military circles' seems to be that any concerted display of resentment against ill-treatment among Negro soldiers is called 'mutiny.'" The common thread that connected the Black sailors at Port Chicago, Seabees at Camp Rousseau, Tuskegee Airmen at Freeman Airfield, WACs at Fort Devens, and thousands of other Black troops was their desire to serve their country without being discriminated against or degraded. "The Negro will give his life for his country—but he will not be a slave," as the *Defender* put it.

When Black troops deployed to war zones around the world, they knew they might die fighting for freedom wearing the uniform of a country in which they were not free. Nowhere was this truer than on the shores of Normandy, where tens of thousands of Black troops played a crucial role in the liberation of France on and after the D-Day invasion.

FOURTEEN

D-DAY AND THE MIRACLE OF SUPPLY

Although port battalions and work troops are not generally regarded on par with front-line combat troops by casual newspaper readers at home, it is a matter of record that no group of soldiers in this theatre has done more to make possible Allied victory. They liberate no towns, see no flags, drink no champagne nor kiss happy girls. Yet, when things become critical, the first cry of the high command is, "Give us more supplies."

—OLLIE STEWART, *Baltimore Afro-American*

B y the time the sun rose over the English Channel on D-Day, June 6, 1944, most of the men in the 582nd Engineer Dump Truck Company were already seasick. Salt water sprayed their faces as the ship bobbed and swayed in the chop. Overhead, B-17 Flying Fortresses, B-24 Liberators, and B-26 Marauders raced toward the shore. The engineers heard and felt the Allied bombs and battleship guns pounding Hitler's "Atlantic Wall" of trenches, pill-boxes, and bunkers that fortified the French coast. Each blast felt like a concussive punch.

Looking to either side of their transport ship the engineers saw hundreds of vessels, many with large silver antiaircraft balloons floating above them. The balloons were tethered to the ships and manned by the 320th Barrage Balloon Battalion, a Black unit whose men were assigned to protect more than 150 vessels during the Channel crossing. The engineers learned about the 320th earlier in the year when both units were stationed in England. Amid the drone of airplane engines and thump of explosions, seeing those silver balloons buoyed the engineers' spirits. It was a clear sign that other Black troops were in the largest armada ever assembled.

When the 582nd landed at Utah Beach midmorning on D-Day, they immediately set to work. Their job was to destroy the steel and log obstacles the Nazis installed along the beach, carry ashore and install bridge equipment, and haul away land mines. Nazi bullets did not discriminate, and engineers faced heavy machine-gun fire as they prepared the landing zone. The engineers enabled thou-sands of infantry troops to safely reach the beach and then pushed up the steep coast to open an exit for Allied troops to move inland.

Other Black units landed at Normandy on D-Day, including the 385th Quartermaster Truck Company, the 490th Port Battal-ion, and the 327th Quartermaster Service Company, about seven-teen hundred Black troops in all. That these troops were not classified as combat soldiers made no difference to enemy machine gunners or snipers. Amphibious truck drivers faced enemy fire while bringing troops and supplies ashore (the amphibious trucks were called DUKWs, or "ducks," because of General Motors' nomenclature).

"I remember watching one colored man in a DUKW loaded with supplies," recalled Hollywood filmmaker John Ford, who directed a Coast Guard camera crew on D-Day. "He dropped them on the beach, unloaded, went back for more. I watched, fascinated. Shells landed around him. The Germans were really after him. He avoided every obstacle and just kept going back and forth, back and forth, completely calm. I thought, 'By God, if anybody deserves a medal that man does.'" Ford considered leaving his relatively safe place to get a photograph of the soldier but thought better of it. "I was willing to admit he was braver than I was."

Landing in different zones on both Utah and Omaha beaches, members of the 320th Barrage Balloon Battalion searched for each other amid the chaos of battle. After nightfall they worked in groups of three and four to launch a dozen of their hydrogen-filled balloons over the beaches. The balloons hovered at low altitudes, making it more challenging for the Luftwaffe to strafe the coast or accurately drop their bombs. Enemy planes that dared to fly low risked hitting the thin steel cables, armed with explosives, that dangled from the balloons. These floating mines formed a silver curtain of defense along the coast.

"Flying balloons looks like kids' play, but it is a scientific and intricate art," said the unit's commanding officer, Colonel Leon Reed, a white Southerner who earned the respect of his troops. The men had to be able to anticipate how balloons would fly in variable weather and recognize different aircraft, so they did not accidentally snag Allied planes. While they might not have been as glamorous as the Tuskegee pilots, *Baltimore Afro-American* correspondent

Francis Yancey told readers, it took great skill to "jockey elephantine monstrosities of destruction thousands of feet high in the sky." "If a Nazi bird nestles in my lines, he won't nestle nowhere else," said Private Cleveland Hayes of Okolona, Mississippi.

Waverly Woodson Jr., a premed student at Philadelphia's Lincoln University and medic with the 320th, performed heroically on D-Day. En route to Omaha Beach, his landing craft hit a mine and was torn apart by a Nazi shell. The man next to him was blown up, and Woodson feared that his own shrapnel wounds would kill him. Another medic bandaged Woodson's gashes as the ship drifted to shore. Woodson waded through chest-high water and scrambled for shelter on the beach. "The beach was covered with dead soldiers and you were stepping over them to get to dry ground," said Floyd Siler, another member of the balloon battalion. Woodson set up a medical aid station and over the next thirty hours he tended to more than two hundred injured men. He patched wounds, removed bullets, and dispensed blood plasma. He amputated a soldier's foot and saved three men from drowning.

Black newspapers hailed Woodson as the "No. 1 Invasion hero," and the military newspaper *Stars and Stripes* said Woodson and his fellow medics "covered themselves with glory on D-Day." The army awarded Woodson and four other 320th medics the Bronze Star, the service's fourth-highest award. Woodson's commanding officer recommended that he receive the Distinguished Service Cross, the army's second-highest decoration for heroism, and U.S. General John C. H. Lee felt that he deserved the Medal of Honor, the army's highest honor. These recommendations were ignored. None of the more than four hundred Medals of Honor awarded during the war were bestowed on Black troops.

In the White House, President Roosevelt closely followed news from the front. He understood that the invasion of northwest Europe, code-named Operation Overlord, would be the turning point in the war on the western front. If the Allies prevailed, they could push through France and threaten the Rhine-Ruhr region, Germany's industrial hub. With Hitler's army engaged in destructive battles on the eastern front with the Soviet Union's Red Army, opening a second front would further drain the Nazis' supplies of ships, planes, guns, tanks, and soldiers, and bring the war to an end more quickly. Churchill, who had long opposed the cross-Channel invasion in favor of fighting in the Mediterranean, called it "the most difficult and complicated operation ever to take place." Nearly 160,000 Allied troops (including 73,000 Americans and 83,000 British and Canadian forces) landed by sea and air on D-Day, and nearly 7,000 Allied ships and 3,000 aircraft took part in the invasion. If this immense assault failed, the path to defeating the Nazis in Western Europe would be deeply in doubt.

When Roosevelt settled before a microphone in the Diplomatic Reception Room just before ten p.m. to speak to the nation, his address took the form of a prayer. "Almighty God: Our sons, pride of our Nation, this day have set upon a mighty endeavor, a struggle to preserve our Republic, our religion, and our civilization, and to set free a suffering humanity," Roosevelt said. "They fight not for the lust of conquest. They fight to end conquest. They fight to liberate. . . . They yearn but for the end of battle, for their return to the haven of home."

Roosevelt paused, then continued in his deliberate cadence. "Some will never return. Embrace these, Father, and receive them, Thy heroic servants, into Thy kingdom. . . . With Thy blessing, we shall prevail over the unholy forces of our enemy. Help us to conquer the apostles of greed and racial arrogancies. Lead us to the saving of our country, and with our sister Nations into a world of unity that will spell a sure peace, a peace invulnerable to the schemings of unworthy men. And a peace that will let all of men live in freedom, reaping the just rewards of their honest toil. Thy will be done, Almighty God. Amen."

Huddled in foxholes and bivouacs, Allied troops said their own prayers for the buddies they watched die and for the fight that remained ahead of them.

LANDING THOUSANDS OF TROOPS on D-Day was an amazing feat, but it was only the first part of the battle. Reinforcing and supplying these soldiers as they pushed across the countryside and hedgerows was the second and larger phase. By the end of June, the Allies had landed 850,000 troops and 150,000 vehicles at Normandy. "D-Day" simply stood for the day of the invasion. Thousands of troops landed on the French coast on D-Day plus one, D-Day plus two, and for weeks thereafter. All of these men required food, ammunition, and replacement parts for airplanes, tanks, and trucks.

Black troops were even more important in this phase, because they were the backbone of the army's service and supply units. As American combat forces pushed into Nazi-occupied France, they could go only as far as their supply lines could take them. Which meant they could go only as far as Black supply troops could take them.

Black troops were everywhere after D-Day. General service engineers removed thousands of mines and repaired railroad tracks. DUKW drivers zipped back and forth across the Channel, ferrying materials from port to coast, then carrying supplies inland. The 320th manned their silver curtain of barrage balloons, preventing the Luftwaffe from descending to strafing altitude. The balloons, one newspaper correspondent wrote, "keep the front door to the front lines open." They were joined by antiaircraft gunners, on a hilltop above the beaches, who watched the skies for enemy planes. "They are all hoping and praying that some hapless Jerry who does not know the wrath of these boys from Forty-seventh and South Parkway, Lenox avenue, Beale street, Auburn avenue, and Hastings street, will just please come flying into range," wrote *Defender* war correspondent Edward Toles.

After helping secure Utah Beach, the 582nd used their dump trucks to carry troops fifty miles west to the important port of Cherbourg and evacuate wounded soldiers and prisoners, dodging mines and machine-gun fire on the roads. The engineers carried members of the 82nd Airborne Division to the front, and the paratroopers dubbed the truck drivers "the Paradumpers." Just miles behind the front, quartermasters baked and transported bread every day using mobile mixers, ovens, and toasters.

Black service troops buried many of the nearly twenty-three thousand Americans who died in and around Normandy. When they landed, the invasion beaches were littered with corpses washed in with the tides. Burying the dead was important for both morale and sanitation. It was backbreaking and emotionally devastating work. Neat rows of crosses belied the gruesome tasks of battlefield cleanup and interring fellow soldiers. "Not many of us were killed, but we died in different ways," a grave registration troop recalled. "The work was nightmarish, and it ate at our hearts . . . cracked some of us, darkened the spirits of others, and numbed the rest."

Although the D-Day contributions of Black troops would be obscured over time, contemporary American officials, military leaders, and journalists praised their efforts. "Negro combat engineers and other Negro troops, among those unloading the ships and handling supplies on shore, did their duty excellently under fire in this zone of heavy combat and suffered many casualties," said Secretary of War Henry Stimson. General Eisenhower, who planned the invasion, told a quartermaster truck company, "I want you to know that I appreciate your splendid work. Your accomplishments are a source of gratification to me and to your army commander."

Visiting France in August, *New York Times* war correspondent Raymond Daniell compared witnessing the work of Black service and supply troops to going backstage in the theater. "I got a glimpse of the scene shifters, stage hands and electricians who contributed their unseen parts of the drama unfolding before the eyes of those in front of the footlights," he wrote. "Here were the men and machinery behind the lines, whose toil and sweat had made possible the victorious lightning thrusts of our armies toward Paris and the Seine."

By October, Allied troops led by General George Patton, General Bernard Montgomery, and Lieutenant General Omar Bradley had advanced more than four hundred miles, liberating Paris and Brussels and entering western Germany. Eisenhower praised supply troops for fueling these victories. "My hat is off to the boys following through on the beaches and at Cherbourg," Ike said. "I mean the ordinary GI who's working ten hours a day on the most sweaty, unromantic job in the war—no glamour, no adventure, just long, hard days of long, hard labor at soldiers' pay. Without these lads sweating it out there, General Patton and others who have been in the headlines would never have done the things they have done."

Time said it was the "miracle of supply" that put the Nazis on their heels. "Although port battalions and work troops are not generally regarded on par with front-line combat troops by casual newspaper readers at home, it is a matter of record that no group of soldiers in this theatre has done more to make possible Allied victory," *Afro-American* war correspondent Ollie Stewart wrote. "They liberate no towns, see no flags, drink no champagne nor kiss happy girls. Yet, when things become critical, the first cry of the high command is, 'Give us more supplies.'"

The heart of the Allies' supply effort in Western Europe was a truck convoy, driven mostly by Black quartermaster troops, called the Red Ball Express (the name came from a railway tradition where railmen marked priority cars with a red dot). As three dozen divisions fought their way across France and Belgium, the Allies had to move twenty thousand tons of supplies every day from the invasion beaches and Cherbourg port to the front. "Logistics—this was the dullest subject in the world," General Bradley wrote. "But logistics were the lifeblood of the Allied armies in France." Without the Black truck drivers and the supplies they delivered, Allied forces could not move, shoot, or eat. With most of the French rail system in ruins, the Allies turned to a fleet of thousands of six-by-six, two-and-a-half-ton General Motors cargo trucks, nicknamed the "Jimmy" or "Deuce and a Half."

These trucks and the Black men who drove them made the U.S. Army the most mobile and mechanized force in the war and gave the Allies a decided strategic advantage over the German infantry divisions, which were overly reliant on rail, wagon trains, and horses to move troops and supplies. From August through November 1944, twenty-three thousand American truck drivers and cargo loaders, 70 percent of whom were Black, moved more than four hundred thousand tons of ammunition, gasoline, medical supplies, and rations to battlefronts in France, Belgium, and Germany. A typical German division during the same period had nearly ten times as many horses as motor vehicles; the German army ran on oats as much as oil. This limited the range of the vaunted *Blitzkrieg*, or lighting attacks, because German tank and motorized units could not move far ahead of their infantry divisions and supplies. In contrast, when the Allies reached the Seine River nearly two weeks earlier than expected, the truck convoy allowed the Allies to chase the retreating German armies without outrunning their supply lines. General Patton concluded that "the 2½ truck is our most valuable weapon," and Colonel John D. Eisenhower, the supreme commander's son, argued that without the Red Ball truck drivers "the advance across France could not have been made."

Driving day and night, the Red Ball truckers earned a reputation as tireless and fearless troops. They steered their loud, rough-driving Jimmies down pitch-black country roads and through narrow lanes in French towns. They drove fast and adopted the French phrase *tout de suite*—immediately, right now—as their motto. "Patton wanted us to eat, sleep, and drive, but mostly drive," one trucker recalled. An armored division commander credited the Red Ball drivers with allowing tankers to refuel and rearm while fighting. "Our Negro outfits delivered gas under constant fire," he said. "Damned if I'd want their job. They have what it takes." A 5th Armored Division tank driver said, "If it wasn't for the Red Ball we couldn't have moved.

They all were Black drivers and they delivered in the heat of combat. We'd be in our tanks praying for them to come up."

The quartermaster and port battalion troops who drove and loaded Red Ball trucks were from Detroit and Dallas, Birmingham and Baltimore, and small towns across the country. James Rookard, a nineteen-year-old truck driver from Maple Heights, Ohio, saw trucks get blown up and feared for his life. "There were dead bodies and dead horses on the highways after bombs dropped. I was scared, but I did my job, hoping for the best. Being young and about 4,000 miles away from home, anybody would be scared."

Like Rookard, Medgar Evers was nineteen when he arrived in Normandy and contributed to the Red Ball Express as a cargo checker in a port company. The European theater was a long way from his hometown of Decatur, Mississippi, and while stationed in France he became close friends with a French family. It was the first time in his life that white people had treated him like a full human being, and he questioned if he could ever return to Mississippi.

Ultimately, he did go home, and his service in France and Belgium steeled his resolve to fight white supremacy in America. After the war, Evers became the NAACP field secretary for Mississippi and fought for voting rights and to end Jim Crow segregation.

As they did for mess attendants on navy ships in the Pacific, the boundaries between combat roles and service roles blurred in war zones. Trucks often had to scrap their way through enemy pockets and sometimes required armored escorts to get valuable cargo to the front. Colonel Charles Lanham, an infantry commander whom Ernest Hemingway called "the finest and bravest and most intelligent military commander I have known," praised the nerve of truckers in a battle south of Saint-Lô. "As daylight broke, we were literally cheek by jowl with the Germans—in the same villages, in the same fields, in the same hedgerows, in the same farm yards," Lanham said. Dozens of firefights broke out, to the front and rear of Lanham's position and along the flanks. "It was early that morning that I first became aware of the fact that our Negro truck drivers were leaving their trucks and [fighting] German soldiers all over the landscape. . . . Many reports reached me throughout the day of the voluntary participation of these troops in battle and their gallant conduct."

Back across the Channel, the ports in and around London continued to hum with war activity. In the six months after D-Day, the port of Southampton was the busiest in the world. More than 6,400 vessels left Southampton bound for France carrying nearly 2 million military personnel, 170,000 vehicles, and over 1.7 million tons of supplies. Black troops made up twenty-five of the twenty-seven port companies at Southampton, more than half of the truck companies, and almost all of its quartermaster and engineer general service regiments. "Over on this side of the Channel are thousands of our boys toiling day and night loading those important war materials, never letting up that feverish inflow of goods, war gear, bombs, guns, jeeps, tanks, lumber, steel, and Spam," *Defender* war correspondent Edward Toles told readers at home.

Almost everything the Allies transported to the front passed through the hands of at least one Black American. The Allies' push toward Germany would have sputtered to a halt without these Black port troops working day and night.

In Birmingham, England, the women of the all-Black 6888th Central Postal Directory Battalion made sure troops in the European theater received mail from home. Black American nurses had already served in Australia, Africa, and England, but with more than eight hundred WACs, the Six Triple Eight, as the battalion was known, was by far the largest unit of Black women to serve overseas during the war.

In unheated warehouses with windows blacked out to prevent light showing during nighttime air raids, the women worked in shifts around the clock. Adopting the motto "No mail, low morale," they processed an average of sixty-five thousand pieces of mail per shift and developed systems to get letters to their intended recipients. This was no simple task, with units moving constantly and thousands of soldiers having common names like "Robert Smith." When the Red Cross suggested that the Six Triple Eight should stay in a segregated hotel when they were on leave in London to limit their mingling with white soldiers and civilians, servicewomen protested until they were finally placed in integrated hotels. "What we had was a large group of adult Negro women who had been victimized, in one way or another, by racial bias," said Major Charity Adams, who led the 6888th. "This was one opportunity for us to stand together for a common cause."

APPRECIATING THE VITAL PART Black supply troops played required counting up what military planners called a "division slice," the total number of troops in a combat division plus their support units. If an average American infantry division had fourteen thousand soldiers, they were supported by twenty-one thousand supply and service troops, for a division slice of thirty-five thousand. With an average of three supply troops to support every two combat troops, American divisions were better supported than their German counterparts, which were closer to a 1:1 ratio of service to combat troops. "Global war generated a need for service troops far greater than anyone visualized before Pearl Harbor," wrote Brigadier General Hal Pattison, who served in Europe with the 4th Armored Division and supervised the army's official history of the war as the chief of military history. The full strength of the American and Allied forces, and the important roles Black troops played therein, came into clear view only when viewed from this macro perspective.

Black journalists were among the earliest to appreciate the importance of counting the division slice because they witnessed firsthand the important supply and service work Black troops performed. "If you could see our boys handing out food to hungry regiments; see them pouring gas into empty tanks, rolling in mile-long convoys into danger zones singing, 'Take My Hand Precious Lord, Take My Hand,' you wouldn't care whether any of them ever fired a gun from a trench or not," Ollie Stewart wrote. "This is certainly a war of supplies, and colored boys keep our army in motion. I'll never stop writing about these quartermaster lads until they get the credit they deserve."

Despite the importance of supply, combat troops still received the accolades. The army continued to block most Black troops from these roles, believing they lacked the courage and discipline to excel in frontline combat. For those who wanted to see Black Americans earn a share of this glory, hope hinged on the fewer than fifty thousand Black combat troops, including the 92nd Infantry Division and the 761st "Black Panther" Tank Battalion. Fighting valiantly, they did their part to defeat the Nazis and secure victory in Europe.

FIFTEEN

VICTORY IN EUROPE

Whites treated us like boys or animals and
then expected us to make Leonidas at Thermopylae Pass.

—DAVID CASON JR., STAFF SERGEANT IN
THE 92ND INFANTRY DIVISION

The 92nd Infantry Division spent D-Day, June 6, 1944, at
Fort Huachuca, an expansive training camp for Black soldiers seventy-five miles southeast of Tucson, Arizona, near
the U.S.–Mexico border. Over the next year they became the only
Black infantry division to fight in Europe. Every move the division
made was tracked closely by military officials and the press, and
their battlefield performance was both celebrated and maligned. As
they pushed Nazi troops out of Italy, the 92nd was seen as a litmus
test for Black Americans serving in combat roles.

The 92nd had been closely scrutinized since they were activated
in 1942. At Fort Huachuca the division endured both infantry training in the hot Sonoran Desert sun and their white officers' racist attitudes. The division commander, Major General Edward Almond,

a Virginian and World War I veteran, maintained separate Officers' Clubs and opposed the integration of the military until his death in 1975. He never believed Black Americans could be good soldiers.

"The white man is willing to die for patriotic reasons, the Negro is not," Almond asserted. "No white man wants to be accused of leaving the battle line. The Negro doesn't care." The 92nd had Black officers at the platoon level, whom Almond regularly referred to by first name rather than rank. He argued that Black officers lacked "pride, aggressiveness, and a sense of responsibility." Army brass regularly tapped white Southerners like Almond to lead Black units because, the thinking went, they knew how to control Black troops. "People think that being from the South we don't like Negroes," Almond said. "Not at all. But we understand his capabilities. And we don't want to sit at the table with them."

Almond set the tone for how other white officers and enlisted men treated the 92nd. "I believe that the Negro generally cannot overcome or escape his background of no property ownership, irresponsibility, and subservience," argued Colonel William McCaffrey, the division's chief of staff. "The Negro is panicky and his environment hasn't conditioned him to accept responsibilities." He believed Black soldiers "learn slowly and forget quickly," while another white officer said simply, "I don't trust Negroes." These officers were not only expressing their individual prejudices, they were also reiterating racist assumptions about Black troops that were deeply entrenched in the army's culture. They could have been reciting verbatim the 1925 Army War College study "The Use of Negro Manpower in War," which was used to justify shunting Black men into service and supply units rather than combat battalions.

When the 92nd trained in the California–Arizona Maneuver Area, a Black officer reprimanded a white private from another unit for not saluting. The private replied, "If you would take your clothes off and lay them on the ground I would salute them but I wouldn't salute anything that looks like you." The utter disrespect the 92nd encountered fed resentment, bitterness, and low morale among the men. When Almond rose to address the division at a dedication for a new baseball field at Fort Huachuca, ten thousand Black GIs greeted him with boos and catcalls.

When the 92nd disembarked in Naples, Italy, in late July 1944, they were happy to be rid of Fort Huachuca and eager to prove themselves. They received a warm welcome from Black soldiers in service units. "Most times you would see a Black soldier, he was carrying ammunition, cans of fuel, or chow for the food line," said quartermaster Private Edward Winn. "These guys were carrying rifles. A Black GI carrying a rifle was not a normal sight to see every day in Europe in 1944."

Like the Tuskegee Airmen, the 92nd knew that as one of only two Black infantry divisions and the first Black American combat troops in the European theater their successes and failures would be magnified. Nearly a dozen Black newspaper correspondents were in Italy to cover the 92nd, and Black papers across the country carried regular dispatches and photos as the division went into battle in August.

Almond, true to form, blocked Black troops from the Officers' Club at the division's headquarters in the coastal city of Viareggio. When the 366th Infantry, a Black unit attached to the 92nd, arrived in Italy, he greeted them by saying, "I did not send for you. Your Negro newspapers, Negro politicians and white friends have insisted on you seeing combat and I shall see that you get combat and your share of the casualties."

Assigned to the U.S. 5th Army under the command of Lieutenant General Mark Clark, the 92nd was part of the larger Allied campaign to drive Hitler's army out of Italy. The success of this campaign came down to the Gothic Line, a two-hundred-mile-long defensive barrier in northern Italy stretching from the Ligurian Sea to the Adriatic Sea. The Nazis fortified the imposing terrain in the Apennine Mountains with artillery, casements, machine-gun nests, and bunkers. After the Allies captured Rome in June, Hitler ordered his troops to retreat north and defend the Gothic Line, Germany's new southern border, at all costs.

In August, the 92nd crossed the Arno River, destroying enemy machine-gun positions and capturing their first Nazi prisoners. Through the fall of 1944, the soldiers fought their way north toward the Gothic Line over rugged terrain and through cold, wet, and muddy conditions. Their operations began to take on a familiar pattern. Facing experienced German troops, the 92nd pushed up steep mountains only to be driven back by enemy fire. During a one-week stretch the division suffered over four hundred casualties while advancing only eight thousand yards. "I wish you could have seen those boys fighting and clawing their way up that hill," a Black platoon leader told war correspondent John "Rover" Jordan. "Every German up there had automatic weapons. They had grenades and mortars. They threw all of the artillery they had at us. But that didn't stop those kids. I wish you could have seen them. I wish everybody in America could have seen them."

While Black press reports remained upbeat, the initial excitement of combat waned, and unit morale suffered. Nazi propaganda featuring pictures of wartime racial violence in Detroit urged Black soldiers to surrender. White officers blamed Black troops for the division's failure to seize and hold key enemy strongholds and transferred officers among platoons, companies, and battalions to try to achieve better results. The reshufflings were so frequent that at times soldiers barely knew who their current commander was.

As the 92nd fought in Italy, the 761st Tank Battalion, the "Black Panthers," joined General Patton's 3rd Army in France. While Patton privately expressed reservations about the fighting ability of Black troops, he gave the unit a characteristically rousing welcome to the front that took on mythic status among the soldiers. "Men, you are the first Negro tankers to ever fight in the American Army," Patton shouted from atop a half-track vehicle. "I would never have asked for you if you weren't good. I don't care what color you are so long as you go up there and kill those Kraut sons of bitches. Everyone has their eyes on you and is expecting great things from you. . . . Don't let them down, and damn you, don't let me down!"

Unlike the 92nd, the Black Panthers benefited from strong leadership. Lieutenant Colonel Paul Bates, a white officer from Los Angeles, earned the respect and trust of his Black enlisted men and officers as they endured training in the Jim Crow South. "Bates gave us the dignity, honor, and pride that America wouldn't," said one tanker.

The 761st repaid this trust by fighting as tenaciously as any unit in the war. Taking up the slogan "Come Out Fighting," they served for 183 consecutive days, fighting in six countries and four major Allied campaigns. They earned hundreds of decorations for heroism.

Ruben Rivers, a twenty-three-year-old tank platoon sergeant from Oklahoma, who posthumously earned the Medal of Honor for fighting through combat wounds, led several tank advances against German positions in northeastern France. "These men were such terrific fighters," Bates said. "They hated the Germans so much, I think they had a lot of hatred in their hearts when they left Camp Hood, Texas."

At the Battle of the Bulge, in the frigid, thickly forested Ardennes region of Belgium, the 761st beat back a Nazi Panzer battalion. In six weeks of brutal fighting from December 1944 to January 1945, they helped the Allies thwart Hitler's last major offensive on the western front. Trezzvant Anderson, a *Baltimore Afro-American* war correspondent who was embedded with the 761st, wrote dozens of dispatches during the war as well as a book afterward extolling the bravery of the Black Panthers. After the 761st successfully broke through the German Siegfried Line and suffered heavy casualties, Anderson wrote, "The 761st was winning, but it was paying for its victories with lives that could never be replaced. That was the price of war, and it made the men fight more viciously . . . [The Panthers were] fighting for revenge, and it was also 'COME OUT FIGHTING' or be killed! It was stark, it was grim, it was real!"

Farther south in Italy, the 92nd was also engaged in a grueling struggle. Axis forces staged a devastating offensive the day after Christmas 1944 against the 92nd and other American forces in the Serchio Valley, on the western edge of the Gothic Line. By morning, the small town of Sommocolonia was the site of bloody hand-to-hand combat. A company of Black troops kept fighting until two thirds of them were wounded or killed. German infantrymen set fire to houses sheltering wounded GIs and shot them when they tried to escape through the windows.

The American troops were led by Black first lieutenants Graham Jenkins and John Fox. As enemy troops surrounded their positions, Jenkins radioed his final message to his captain, "They're coming after us. Please, when you get back to the States, tell my wife and my kid and my mother that I love them." A German soldier shot and killed Jenkins as he comforted a wounded GI.

Fox called for a smoke screen to provide cover for his remaining men to withdraw and then called in coordinates for artillery fire that moved closer and closer to his own observation post.

"That round was just where I wanted it, bring it in 60 more yards," he called.

"Fox, that will be right on you, I can't do that," came the reply from the artillery officer at headquarters.

"Fire it!" Fox yelled back.

By calling in an artillery strike on his own enemy-surrounded position, Fox bought time for his remaining troops to withdraw and for American forces to organize a counterattack to retake the village. Allied troops found his body in the rubble of his observation post days later. The 92nd Division's artillery commander endorsed Fox for the Distinguished Service Cross, the army's second-highest military honor, but Almond declined to forward the recommendation. Decades later, Fox's fellow soldiers pushed for the army to officially recognize Fox and his gallantry in combat. In 1982, the army posthumously awarded Fox the Distinguished Service Cross. His award was upgraded to the Medal of Honor in 1997.

DESPITE EVIDENCE OF HEROISM and resolve, army officials worried that the 92nd was not cut out for combat. Similar to the criticisms that sought to undermine the Tuskegee Airmen, these concerns quickly found their way into the national press. *Newsweek* told readers that the army's efforts to use Black troops in combat had "so far been more productive of disappointment and failure than of anything else." *The New York Times* chided the "super-sensitive Negro press" for exaggerating the unit's accomplishments and the racism they faced. "There has been one helluva smear job going on as far as the 92nd is concerned," said Robert Millender, a Black warrant officer in the division.

When white troops suffered combat defeats, like the 36th Infantry Division at the Battle of Rapido River near Cassino, Italy, they were not attacked as cowards or regarded as failures. In some cases, journalists put a positive spin on their shortcomings. *The Saturday Evening Post*, for example, ran a multipage article, "The Glorious Collapse of the 106th," praising the pluck of a novice white infantry division that was thrashed at the Battle of the Bulge.

Black combat soldiers were afforded no such leeway. Black troops serving thousands of miles from home were furious and dejected to read attacks on the 92nd in the white press. "Let us make mistakes and the papers play them up, but let us do a good job and they never report it," said a Black truck driver who transported supplies along the Ledo Road in the China-Burma-India theater.

The army dispatched Civilian Advisor to the Secretary of War Truman Gibson, a Black lawyer, to Italy to investigate the combat performance of the 92nd. After speaking to more than a thousand officers and enlisted men, he presented his findings in a March 1945 press conference. Upon entering the room, a *New York Times* correspondent sarcastically shouted, "Now we're going to hear about the glorious 92nd." Gibson acknowledged that the division's performance fell short of expectations and that some soldiers did panic and retreat, but he also outlined how the army had undercut the 92nd since their days at Fort Huachuca in Arizona. "You can't train a man to be a fighting soldier for eight hours a day, then slap him in the face with his race when he leaves camp at night," he said. "There is no question in my mind about the courage of Negro officers or soldiers and any generalization on the basis of race is entirely unfounded."

The *New York Herald Tribune* misquoted Gibson as saying that Black troops "often 'melt away' in the face of the enemy." This was language military officials used to refer to the 92nd, but papers across the country picked up the story, attributing "melt away" to Gibson. The Black press was livid at Gibson, who was supposed to be an advocate for Black Americans within the War Department. "It is enough our boys have to fight Nazis and Dixie race haters without having to face the venom and scorn of 'Uncle Toms,'" *Chicago Defender* editors wrote in calling for Gibson's resignation.

For many Black soldiers in the 92nd, it was hard to perform at their best as warriors when white officers routinely used racial epithets and regarded them as less than human. "Whites treated us like boys or animals and then expected us to make Leonidas at Thermopylae Pass," said Staff Sergeant David Cason Jr. "I will say if the 92nd, in the same geographical position, had been told those were southern crackers up in those mountains, 'get 'em,' they would have, myself included, clawed their way up if necessary. We would

have waded in our own blood up to our elbows to take them because we would have had a reason: an enemy we knew, despised, and
would have enjoyed destroying. The German, what could he mean
to us? Nobody bothered to make him our real enemy."

Lieutenant Colonel Marcus Ray, who commanded an artillery
battalion in the 92nd, shared his views with Gibson. "In white officered units, those men who fit the Southern pattern are pushed
and promoted regardless of capabilities and those Negroes who ex-
hibit the manliness, self-reliance, and self-respect which are the
'sine qua non' in white units, are humiliated and discouraged," Ray
wrote. "I do not believe the 92nd a complete failure as a combat
unit but when I think of what it might have been, I am heart-sick."

Even while the 92nd was being denigrated publicly, Black troops
responded to the army's need for infantry replacements. In the six
months after D-Day, nearly 350,000 American troops in Europe
were killed, wounded, or missing. Facing shortages of combat soldiers, the army broke with their strict policy of segregation and
called for volunteers, regardless of race, to become infantrymen.

By February 1945, nearly five thousand Black service troops answered the call, including many noncommissioned officers who
were willing to give up their stripes and take a reduction in rank for
a chance at combat duty. The men were formed into more than
forty all-Black rifle platoons and assigned to previously all-white
infantry divisions. It was the first time Black soldiers had officially
fought shoulder to shoulder with whites in an American infantry
unit since the Revolutionary War.

The Black soldiers' combat performance helped pave the way for
the desegregation of the military after the war. Eighty-four percent
of white officers said the Black volunteers did "very well," and the

remainder answered "fairly well." No commanders rated the soldiers' performance as "poor." "They were the best platoon in the regiment," one white company commander said. "They are very aggressive as fighters—really good at fighting in woods and at close quarters work. The only trouble is getting them to stop: they just keep pushing."

Sergeant Edward A. Carter Jr. was among the Black volunteers who distinguished themselves. Born to missionary parents in Los Angeles, Carter was raised in Calcutta, India, and Shanghai, China. At fifteen, as a student in a Chinese military school, he enlisted in the Chinese National Army to fight against Japanese incursions in Shanghai in 1932. At eighteen, he tried to join the U.S. Army but was turned away. Instead, he traveled to Europe to fight fascists in the Spanish Civil War alongside the Abraham Lincoln Brigade. He entered the U.S. Army three months before Pearl Harbor. Despite his combat experience and his fluency in Hindi, Mandarin, and German, Carter was assigned to a quartermaster truck company as a cook. As was true of other Black volunteers and draftees, the army cared more about Carter's skin color than about how his skills could help the war effort. His unit shipped out to Europe in November 1944 and transported important supplies to frontline soldiers.

Carter, a warrior through and through, was among the first to volunteer for infantry duty even though it meant he would revert from staff sergeant to private. He quickly impressed his company commanders, who gave Carter back his sergeant stripes and made him a squad leader in the infantry. On March 23, 1945, as the 12th Armored Division surged into Speyer, Germany, Carter's unit encountered heavy bazooka and small-arms fire. Leading a sparse detachment across an open field, he was wounded several times. When enemy riflemen tried to capture him, he killed six of them and captured the remaining two. He was awarded the Distinguished Service Cross, and posthumously awarded the Medal of Honor in 1997.

Despite everything they endured, the men of the 92nd fought on in Italy, taking more than ten thousand German POWs. The *Chicago Defender* said the unit was "writing in blood their resounding reply to slanders of their fighting ability." On April 29, 1945, the 92nd liberated the Italian cities of La Spezia and Genoa. Within eight days, Hitler committed suicide in an underground bunker and Mussolini was arrested and executed by Italian partisans. German commanders in Italy surrendered, ending the war in Italy on May 2. On May 7, in Reims, France, German High Command surrendered unconditionally to the Allies. The war in Europe was over.

NEGRO AMERICA HAILS V-E DAY! read the *Chicago Defender*'s banner headline, above a full-page "V." "In far-off foxholes in the Pacific and in Europe's Nazi-ravaged towns, Negro GIs went wild with enthusiasm as the final long-awaited curtain was brought down on the European war. . . . Along 47th street in Chicago, Lenox avenue in Harlem, Central avenue in Los Angeles and along U street here in the nation's capital, happy Negro mothers and fathers anxious to see their sons home again grabbed at the first newspaper extras announcing surrender of the Nazis."

In Europe, victory brought a flood of different emotions for Black troops. Guarding German prisoners of war gave Black soldiers the particular gratification of refuting myths of Aryan superiority. The

761st Black Panthers participated in the liberation of Gunskirchen, a subcamp of the Mauthausen concentration camp in Austria, and other Black troops witnessed evidence of Nazi atrocities and documented the mass murder and inhuman brutality they saw. "The crematory was a large room filled with immense furnaces that were used by the German SS troops, 24 hours a day, to burn dying inmates," a Chicago private told the *Defender*. "The place had a horrible odor of burned human flesh. The troops that captured the camp put out the flames that were burning bodies, and we could see the remains of those that had not been completely destroyed." If Black soldiers harbored any doubts about why the Third Reich needed to be crushed, those uncertainties vanished when the horror of the Holocaust became clear.

Black soldiers still harbored doubts about their own country, however. The racism they experienced during the war and the occupation of Europe made many of the victory celebrations ring hollow. Black troops were called racial epithets by white officers and enlisted men before D-Day, after VE-Day, and every day in between. White soldiers taunted members of the 92nd in Italy by chanting "We want Bilbo," in reference to U.S. senator and Ku Klux Klan member Theodore Bilbo of Mississippi.

As the Allies liberated towns and cities from Nazi control, Black troops saw white Southern soldiers raise the Confederate flag alongside or instead of the U.S. flag to celebrate their victory. Seeing a symbol of American slavery and racism flying above Normandy, Naples, Rome, Berlin, and dozens of small European villages made it clear that too many white troops did not intend to see freedom and democracy extend back across the Atlantic to the home front. They were fighting to maintain the status quo of race relations in

America, including Jim Crow segregation and white supremacy, rather than democracy and equality for all Americans. This infuriated Black soldiers and steeled their resolve to come home fighting for civil rights.

When English and French citizens welcomed Black troops into their pubs, restaurants, and homes, white military personnel did everything they could to enforce American segregation in Europe. "Everywhere our Armed forces go they carry their color hate and prejudice and disseminate them among the people," *The Pittsburgh Courier* argued. "In Australia, England, Hawaii and France, American soldiers and sailors have carried the torch of color hate and intolerance." War correspondent Roi Ottley reported that "the American race problem is being transplanted to British soil—sometimes with a venom unknown in the United States."

Seeing Black troops socialize with white women and more generally be treated as fully human enraged many white soldiers. Racial clashes among American troops were commonplace. Things got so bad in England as American forces prepared for D-Day that one military observer argued, "If the invasion doesn't occur soon, trouble will."

When D-Day hero Waverly Woodson Jr. and his fellow 320th Barrage Balloon Battalion members returned to Camp Stewart, Georgia, after serving 140 days in France, they immediately encountered racial discrimination and hostility. "The first words we heard was, 'Here comes that nigger group. Got all them medals over there in France. We're gonna make sure that we take care of them while they're down here,'" Woodson recalled.

In Michigan, squadrons of Tuskegee Airmen trained at Selfridge Field near Detroit after Black pilots flew nearly two thousand missions over North Africa and Europe. Photographer Gordon Parks said the treatment Black airmen received from white residents in the area was "by far, worse than what they would have received in the countries of America's enemies." When a Black pilot crashed during training, a local undertaker refused to embalm his body.

Black troops returned to Fort Lawton, Washington, where the mess halls remained segregated. To make matters worse, German POWs now joined white American troops in the "whites only" section of the mess hall. Fort Lawton was hardly an exception. Across the country, and especially in the South, where the majority of Nazi prisoners were held, Black troops reported that these Germans were allowed to ride buses and trains, use latrines, and eat in the cafeteria alongside white Americans. In a war full of humiliations, this treatment was particularly outrageous. White soldiers and civilians treated Nazis, who only weeks earlier had been fighting against the Allies and trying to kill Americans, with more respect than Black troops who served their country. Seeing white Americans being so friendly with German POWs was perhaps the clearest evidence that Jim Crow segregation and the Nazis' master-race theory were two sides of the same coin, and that many white Americans preferred racial apartheid over actual democracy. It was, one Black soldier said, as if white America favored the tyrant over the liberator, so long as the tyrant's skin was also white.

For Black troops it was clear that military victories on the battlefields of Europe were not the end of the war. Victory in the Pacific remained a summer away, but the scope of the war was greater than that too. Black troops understood that the most important fight awaited them at home, continuing battles that their parents and grandparents had been waging for decades.

SIXTEEN

VICTORY IN THE PACIFIC

I can truthfully report that the record of the American Negro in World War II matches, if not surpasses that of any white man. . . . They sent Black boys out in front, facing continuous enemy shelling and strafing to build the bridges, clear the swamps, fell the forests, build the roads, and the vital airfields. And then when the regular combat troops moved in, these Black boys dropped their picks and shovels, picked up guns and proved their worth in actual combat. And they died bravely. Many with songs on their lips and defiance in their hearts. But did they die in vain?

—DAN BURLEY, *New York Amsterdam News*
WAR CORRESPONDENT

While Allied forces fought on the beaches of Normandy and hedgerows of France, U.S. Marines, sailors, soldiers, and airmen were fighting seven thousand miles away in the Pacific against Japanese troops on the island of Saipan. In the early morning hours of June 15, 1944, amphibious landing craft delivered eight thousand Marines to the coast of the narrow, fourteen-mile-long island. Saipan was the most heavily defended of the Mariana Islands, and Japanese artillery, machine guns, and mortars raked the beaches. The fighting was chaotic, and many of the Marines and officers became separated from their units. A steady stream of landing vehicles dodged enemy fire to bring artillery, ammunition, and reserve regiments to shore. By nightfall, twenty thousand troops had established a beachhead and steeled themselves for brutal fighting in the days ahead. Among the American forces on Saipan were eight hundred Black Marines, eager to prove themselves in combat.

While racism was pervasive in all branches of the military, the Marine Corps stood out for its hostility to Black Americans. From 1798 until 1942, the Marines refused Black Americans the opportunity to serve. After President Roosevelt issued Executive Order 8802 in June 1941, banning discriminatory employment practices by federal agencies, he and U.S. Navy secretary Frank Knox directed Marine Corps commandant Thomas Holcomb to accept Black recruits. Holcomb, who had notably complained that he would rather have a Marine Corps of five thousand white men than twenty-five thousand Black men, insisted that integration would destroy the Corps's efficiency, and that if Black people wanted to serve, they could join the army instead.

Reluctantly, the Corps began accepting Black recruits in June 1942 and sent them to train at Montford Point, a segregated training facility adjoining Camp Lejeune in coastal southeastern North Carolina. White officers who had served in the Philippines, Nicaragua, the Caribbean, and other sites of U.S. occupation were assigned to train Black Marines, with the reasoning that they had experience managing "colored" populations. Albert Bryant, an eighteen-year-old from Greenville, Mississippi, who went on to become a brigadier general in the U.S. Army, recalled that a white officer sized up the Black recruits and said, "When I saw you people in uniforms, I knew we were at war."

In town, the white police were determined to put the Black recruits in their place. "We were mistreated in every way possible," remembered Edgar Cole, a young Marine from Dallas. "What bothered us was, they tried to pretend that we weren't Americans too. But we were young, courageous, and loved our country." Despite the racism they encountered on and off the base during their training, more than nineteen thousand Black Marines graduated from Montford Point during the war, with two thirds serving overseas.

The Black Marines who came ashore among the first waves in Saipan were in depot and ammunition companies. Their primary job was to unload ships, distribute ammunition, and keep the 2nd and 4th Marine Divisions supplied, but under heavy fire they quickly took on combat roles. "We got caught in the early part of Saipan in the Japanese counterattack," remembered Kenneth Rollock, a nineteen-year-old Marine from Harlem. "About a quarter mile from the beach, they came out screaming, and we just opened up. Anything moving we shot at." The Marines dug foxholes on the beach and scurried forward from position to position. "I watched those Negro boys carefully," said Lieutenant Joe Grimes, a white Texan. "They were under intense mortar and artillery fire as well as rifle and machine-gun fire. They all kept on advancing until the counterattack was stopped."

Private First Class Kenneth Jewel Tibbs, a nineteen-year-old from Ohio, was among the Black Marines who fought at Saipan. Like Rollock, Tibbs had enlisted the prior year, and after he shipped out, he wrote regularly to his girlfriend, Katherine Howell, who was pregnant. Their daughter, Helen, was born a month after an enemy bullet passed behind Tibbs's ear, felling him on the beach. He was the first Black Marine to be killed in action in the war. Private Vincent Long from Hempstead, New York, was fighting alongside Tibbs. "Until then, I'd never had anyone's blood on me before," he said. "It was tough going and everything was coming down on us. I picked up a Browning Automatic Rifle and started shooting like everyone else."

Unlike the 92nd Infantry in Europe, the Montford Point Marines were heralded for their combat performance. "Negro marines, under fire for the first time, have rated a universal 4.0 [U.S. Naval Academy mark of perfection] on Saipan," reported *Time* war correspondent Robert Sherrod. "Credited with being the workingest men on Saipan, they performed prodigious feats of labor both while under fire and after beachheads were well secured." Lieutenant James Wilson said the Black Marines were "damn good jungle fighters" and praised their "patience" and "combat efficiency." "When the battle of Saipan is recorded for history it will not be complete unless these Negro marines are given full credit for their contribution to the victory," argued the *Chicago Defender*. "The erroneous statement that 'they cannot master the intricacies of modern warfare,' has been disproved by the heroic deeds of untrained Negro messmen in the navy, shattered by the unparalleled success of the Negro flyers in Europe and buried by the fighting quality of the Negro marines on Saipan."

The Black press described the Montford Point Marines as ordinary young men who had volunteered to take on extraordinary roles in the war effort. The *Journal and Guide* profiled Private First Class William Wyatt and Private Sylvanius Everett, two recent graduates of Norfolk's Booker T. Washington High School, who fought at Saipan. War correspondent Fletcher P. Martin wrote that these men were typical of the Black Marines in the Pacific. "Former clerks and cooks, teachers and mechanics, carpenters and farmers, and the 'kid' who used to lay around the corner in Michigan and Mississippi, New York and Alabama, Ohio and Pennsylvania, Illinois and Arkansas, Virginia and California, they now operate as a potent unit and are unanimous in wanting to get to Tokyo first and fast."

The most important praise for the Montford Point Marines came from Lieutenant General Alexander Vandegrift, who succeeded Holcomb as Marine Corps commandant. After their performance at Saipan, Vandegrift declared, "The Negro Marines are no longer on trial. They are Marines, period." Still, no sooner was the island secured than the military built segregated camps for white and Black troops.

Saipan was a bloody turning point in the Pacific war. After just over three weeks of fighting, more than three thousand American troops were killed and thirteen thousand wounded. At least twenty-seven thousand Japanese soldiers died, and more than a thousand civilians committed suicide out of fear, stoked by Japanese propaganda, that they would be slaughtered by American troops. American invasions on the nearby Mariana Islands of Guam and Tinian claimed another twenty thousand Japanese soldiers. During these invasions, the U.S. Navy dealt the Imperial Japanese Navy a decisive defeat at the Battle of the Philippine Sea. General Hideki Tojo,

Japan's prime minister, had declared that the United States would never take Saipan. The Marines proved him wrong. Tojo resigned after the defeat and General Koiso Kuniaki was appointed prime minister to carry on the war effort.

Victory on Saipan gave the Allies control of the central basin of the Pacific and access to the eastern edge of the Philippine archipelago. It also moved the battlefront farther north toward the Japanese mainland. From the Mariana Islands, B-29 Superfortress bombers could reach the capital city of Tokyo, as well as Hiroshima and Nagasaki. While some Montford Point Marines stayed in the Mariana Islands to guard ports, airstrips, and supply depots, almost nine hundred others ventured seven hundred miles north to Iwo Jima.

"IWO JIMA PROBABLY is the world's most heavily defended island," wrote *Time*'s Robert Sherrod in February, as he prepared to go ashore with a combat team. "There is little over-optimism to be found among admirals, generals or their troops." Iwo Jima, an eight-square-mile volcanic piece of rock about half the size of Manhattan, was strategically important because its airstrips would either allow Japanese planes to intercept American bombers, or they would provide the Allies with a site to refuel and repair planes halfway between the Marianas and Japan.

By the time the invasion started on February 19, 1945, Black Marines had experienced combat, but the fighting on Iwo Jima was still shockingly ferocious. Sergeant Thomas McPhatter, a former student at Charlotte's Johnson C. Smith University, landed on the beach on the first day of the battle. As his landing craft approached the coast, he saw dead bodies bobbing in the water all around him. His unit crawled on their bellies, moving slowly up the beach. "I jumped in a foxhole and there was a young white marine holding his family pictures," McPhatter said. "He had been hit by shrapnel, he was bleeding from the ears, nose and mouth. It frightened me. The only thing I could do was lie there and repeat the Lord's Prayer, over and over and over." Scrambling out of his foxhole, McPhatter joined other Black Marines unloading ships and moving supplies ashore under heavy fire. "From the time we landed on the beach, the tempo of activity was high," said Archibald Mosley, a twenty-year-old from Carbondale, Illinois. Mosley and his unit supplied assault troops with weapons, food, water, and other supplies, enabling the Marines to push forward. "We were also doing everything else we could do to stay alive," Mosley remembered.

Black troops from army port companies and amphibious truck companies, attached to the Marines for the assault, ran circuits between ship and shore, delivering hundreds of tons of ammunition and supplies. Black DUKW drivers landed with 105mm howitzers to bolster the Marines' firepower. "Our job was not only to land the first artillery, but to move it inland to predesignated positions," said First Sergeant Houston Austin of Detroit. The ducks had a hell of a time making it to shore. Mortar fire filled many ships full of holes, while the high surf swamped others. Some drivers made a half dozen attempts to scale the beach's steep incline, under fire all the while. "We had drivers who had ducks shot from under them then came back for more," Austin said. "I had to order several men off their ducks after they had worked 48 hours unloading ammunition where one hit would have blown everything nearby sky-high."

A white platoon leader said Black amphibious truck drivers "made the difference between taking the island and handing it back to the Japanese." The island was so small that there was no space to safely withdraw and get out of range of enemy fire. "This whole island is a front," as one veteran put it. The courage American troops displayed led Admiral Chester Nimitz to say, "Among the men who fought on Iwo Jima, uncommon valor was a common virtue."

As in the Normandy invasion, Black troops played critical logistical roles on Iwo Jima. Military leaders expected the attack to last only a few days; instead it took more than a month. Food, ammunition, and medical support were all positioned offshore on naval ships. "There is no supermarket down the street in a warzone," recalled Joseph LaNier, a Black Seabee who handled cargo during the Iwo Jima attack. "Everything comes by ships, everything, and somebody has to unload those ships." Black Marines and supply troops kept combat forces armed and fed, and transported wounded men away from the island for care.

Also as in Normandy, Black troops buried those who were killed in action. "There were holes, and that was where you put the remains," McPhatter said, describing the makeshift cemetery on Iwo Jima. "There was never really a whole body. Then they'd put one layer of dirt on it and you'd put on another, like a cake. They'd put up these little crosses with dog tags, but no one really knows who was under the grave."

Corporal Archibald Mosley and other Black Marines saw the flag raised on Iwo Jima, a scene immortalized by Associated Press photographer Joe Rosenthal. It made the exhausted, battle-weary troops feel like the Marines were making some headway, but there was no time for rest. "We were still in the heat of battle," Mosley said. "After the flag was raised, we just went back to work." Albert Bryant continued to supply combat troops with ammunition after the flag was hoisted up. As shells shook the earth, his unit burrowed for cover, but the island's sand, a silty volcanic ash, filled in the small trenches as quickly as they dug. Some men suffocated in the collapsed foxholes. As the days of combat stretched into weeks, Black and white Marines fought side by side. "We were all Americans once the chips were down," Bryant recalled.

While Black Marines witnessed the Stars and Stripes go up, many felt like they were written out of the history of the battle and the war. "The Marines who climbed Mt. Suribachi and raised the flag, along with many others who served on the front lines, went home to ticker tape parades everywhere, and were celebrated with parades and commendations, may not have climbed that mountain or won the war without the efforts of support personnel," Mosley argued. Black Marines in the Pacific, as well as Black Americans in other theaters, described white photographers and newsreel cameramen turning their lenses away when Black troops were in view. Black newspapers and civil rights leaders railed against this erasure. "The seeming enthusiasm with which the major newsreel companies delete any and all scenes showing the Negro, they are giving . . . movie audiences the impression that there are no Negroes in this war," the *Norfolk Journal and Guide* declared. "The major weekly and monthly white magazines are guilty of the same tragic omission. Were it not for the Negro press, and especially those who at tremendous expense are maintaining their own war correspondents in the various theaters of war, the American public would be unaware of the contribution and sacrifices of our people in this global war."

The NAACP's Walter White saw the erasure of Black troops as having dire postwar consequences. "All of us are deeply concerned at the appalling lack of information among white Americans regarding the enormous part the Negro is playing in the fighting of the war despite the handicaps he encounters," he said. "It is our measured belief that when the war ends there will be a great deal of opposition to the Negro sharing the benefits of the victory unless every possible means is utilized to publicize what the Negro is doing."

White had reason to worry. The campaign to discredit Black troops, which stung the Tuskegee Airmen and 92nd Infantry, intensified as the Allies secured victory. United States senators disparaged the performance and character of Black soldiers, while photographic histories of the war overlooked Black American contributions almost entirely.

THIS SENSE OF URGENCY to publicize the unsung work of Black troops led three Black war correspondents to the China-Burma-India theater. Deton Brooks volunteered to be a *Chicago Defender* correspondent after an injury kept him from the military. Dan Burley, a skilled "boogie-woogie" piano player who chronicled Harlem nightlife for the *New York Amsterdam News* and used his sports column to argue for the integration of Major League Baseball, wrote about Black service troops and performed for them in the United Service Organizations (USO) unit he led. *The Pittsburgh Courier*'s Frank Bolden wrote about Black troops because he thought white correspondents would ignore their stories. "White America was convinced that Negro soldiers under fire would be cowards and turn and run, that is why I went over," he said. These journalists traveled to the war's forgotten theater to write about the Black engineer troops who helped build the Ledo Road.

When Japan seized Burma in early 1942 it cut off the Burma Road, the only overland supply route to China. Desperate to get supplies to an Allied nation, war planners mapped a new route, called the Ledo Road. This new road snaked more than a thousand miles from Ledo, a small town amid the tea plantations of Assam in western India, to northern Burma. There it connected with the old Burma Road, which builders upgraded so that trucks could continue safely on to Kunming, the capital city of China's Yunnan Province. Work started on the Ledo Road in late 1942 and continued through the end of the war. Fifteen thousand American troops worked on the road, and more than 60 percent of them were Black. They joined thirty-five thousand local Indian, Burmese, and Chinese civilian workers carving the supply route through jungle, mud, and swamps, and over mountains, gorges, and rivers.

Much as they had on the Alaska Highway, Black troops on the Ledo Road carried out a Herculean engineering project in challenging terrain and climate. They woke up at dawn and worked until sundown in sweltering heat, seven days a week. Monsoon season brought torrential rains that washed out portions of road that had only recently been completed. More than a thousand American troops died from malaria, typhus, equipment accidents, or enemy fire in sporadic fighting.

Still, the road builders pushed on. "The spirit of Negro troops in the Army Engineering units in the China-Burma-India theater of

war is excellent," said General Joseph Stilwell, the theater commander after whom the road was later renamed. "Before these troops
arrived no one ever thought of working during the monsoon season,
but I have seen these men continue on the job when there was 10
inches of rainfall in one day." War service looked different when
viewed from the Ledo Road. "They have fought not with guns but
with giant bull-dozers and clam shovels, preventing landslides and
throwing bridges in order that the men with guns could reach the
enemy," a sergeant wrote in the *Baltimore Afro-American*.

Dan Burley compared Ledo Road to the bustling Seventh Avenue in Harlem, and told readers of the *New York Amsterdam News*
that the men building the combat highway resembled men they
would recognize from their own hometowns. Sergeant Harland
Dunlap was a high school football and track star from New Jersey
who attended Florida A&M College. Paul Lee Jr., from a tiny town
near Jackson, Mississippi, earned a Purple Heart after being struck
by enemy gunfire on the road. Sergeant Joseph Strickland was a
tenor in the Knoxville College chorus, while Private James Williams was a Golden Gloves boxer from Chicago. Corporal Alvie
City of San Antonio coached tennis at Prairie View State College.
Private First Class Leroy Huff was an accomplished pianist from St.
Petersburg, Florida. While Ernie Pyle penned paeans to ordinary
white soldiers, Burley and his fellow Black war correspondents did
the same for Black GIs who performed backbreaking, critical, and
unheralded war labor thousands of miles from home.

Twenty-six thousand trucks traversed the Ledo Road from January to August 1945, carrying 129,000 tons of supplies from India
to China. "That road is the key to grand strategy in the China-
Burma-India theater," Deton Brooks wrote. "And unless this is un-

VICTORY IN THE PACIFIC 257

derstood, it is impossible to appreciate how great a contribution colored boys from the streets of Harlem or Bronzeville or the plantations of the deep south are making to successful operations in this area." Frank Bolden told readers that Black troops performed an engineering miracle to build this lifeline to China. "I hope when they return home they will not be passed over as they have been here on the forgotten front," he said.

DAYS RAN TOGETHER on the Ledo Road in the spring of 1945. The engineers worked on April 12, the day President Roosevelt collapsed and died of a cerebral hemorrhage at his retreat in Warm Springs, Georgia. Vice President Harry Truman took the oath of office later that day. The engineers worked on May 7, when German general Alfred Jodl signed the unconditional surrender of all German forces at General Eisenhower's headquarters in Reims, France, marking the end of the war in Europe. And the engineers worked on August 6 and August 9, when American warplanes dropped atomic bombs on Hiroshima and Nagasaki, killing well over one hundred thousand people, mostly Japanese civilians.

Like all U.S. citizens, Black Americans wrestled with the almost unfathomable loss of human life caused by America's decision to unleash what President Truman called "a new and revolutionary increase in destruction." Joel A. Rogers, a prolific Jamaican American historian and *Pittsburgh Courier* columnist, reflected the views of those hardened by four brutal years of war, writing, "I regret the loss of civilian lives by this bomb, but it was our lives against theirs." His *Courier* colleague, conservative columnist George Schuyler, expressed a more critical opinion. "Not satisfied with being able to kill people by the thousand, we have now achieved the supreme triumph of being able to slaughter whole cities at a time," he lamented. A *Defender* editorial a month after the blast noted, "The atomic bomb dropped on Nagasaki turned that town into a desert of rubble. Houses ten miles away were crushed. All persons not killed were either badly burned or blinded. At this late date the former residents of Nagasaki are still dying from the effects of the blast."

Speculating about whether the United States would have used the bomb against Germany, the *Defender* asked a question that was on the minds of many Black Americans: "Was this destructive missile reserved for use on the Japanese, a dark race?" In his *Defender* column "Simple and the Atom Bomb," Langston Hughes used his Black everyman character to cut to the chase. When Hughes suggests to Simple that perhaps the United States had not perfected the bomb before VE-Day, Simple retorts, "Uh-umm! No. buddy-o, you know better than that. They just did not want to use them on white folks. Germans is white. So they wait until the war is all over in Europe to try them out on colored folks."

While surveys found that a majority of Black Americans opposed the bombing of Hiroshima and Nagasaki, many lauded the Black scientists and war workers who contributed to the design and manufacturing of atomic weapons. William Knox, a Harvard- and MIT-trained chemist, went to work in 1943 on the highly classified Manhattan Project at Columbia University, the research and development enterprise that produced the first nuclear weapons. His research focused on the separation of uranium isotopes by using corrosive uranium hexafluoride gas. Like Knox, about a dozen Black scientists worked at different Manhattan Project research sites, including William's younger brother Lawrence Knox and Howard University graduate George Reed. Math prodigy J. Ernest Wilkins Jr., who earned his PhD from the University of Chicago at the age of nineteen and taught mathematics at Tuskegee Institute, returned to Chicago's Metallurgical Laboratory in 1944 to research methods for producing fissionable nuclear materials. Wilkins only learned about the purpose and product of his research when he heard the radio report about Hiroshima.

Few of the seven thousand Black workers at Clinton Engineer Works, hidden in the oaks and pines of Tennessee's Smoky Mountains, knew that the facility was producing enriched uranium to bomb Japan. These were good war jobs, even if the plant's dormitories, cafeteria, and shop floor were segregated. The nurses, maintenance, and construction workers were told the facility was working on something critical and that Germany was doing the same. "If we succeed first, we will win the war and rule the world," supervisors told them. "If the enemy beats us to it, they will do the same." The *Courier* argued that the Manhattan Project opened up new opportunities for Black scientists, but readers surveying the profiles of Black atomic workers were left to wonder about what it meant for Black Americans to make inroads in a field that wrought such tremendous devastation.

Back on the Ledo Road, Black troops, too, debated the use of the atomic bomb. More than anything, though, they wanted the war to be over. That day finally arrived on August 15, 1945, when Imperial Japan surrendered. Representatives of the Empire of Japan signed the official instrument of surrender on September 2 aboard the USS *Missouri*, as sixty Black navy stewards and four Black war correspondents looked on.

"As I sat above the surrender stage, where generals and admirals stood jammed at erect attention while brightly uniformed delegates of many nations enacted this simple scene, my thoughts flashed back to millions of ordinary soldiers—both Black and white—who had made this ceremony possible," Deton Brooks wrote in the *Defender*. "I saw clearly the picture of glistening, barebacked engineers ploughing through the steaming jungles of Burma and other Negro troops, either sweltering or drenching in equally dense jungles of Bougainville, Leyte, New Guinea, and Iwo Jima—building roads, hauling supplies, or like the 93rd Infantry Division or the 24th Infantry Division, fighting their way ever eastward, helping to tighten the knot making today's formalities possible."

The news spread quickly on the Ledo Road. Troops set off firecrackers, cried, played music, and painted jeeps to read HOMEWARD-BOUND TASK FORCE, HARLEM HERE WE COME, and LET MY PEOPLE GO. Sergeant Frank Sterling, a truck driver from Philadelphia, could not quite believe the news. "I hope these rumors of Japan's surrender are true," he said. "I won't celebrate, not when I think of the scores of War Department telegrams being sent to the next of kin of my buddies who died building this road."

Dan Burley was not on board the USS *Missouri* to witness Japan's surrender, but as Brooks's had, his thoughts immediately turned to the ordinary Black troops who helped win the war. Burley was deeply concerned that men who built the Ledo Road, and Black Americans more broadly, were already being written out of the war's history. "The Saga of Supply is perhaps the most dramatic story of the China-Burma-India theater of war, and also the most neglected," he wrote. "The titanic efforts of the American Negro who did most of the work . . . stand in danger of being forgotten in what will go down in the history books. Already the cover-up procedure is being put into operation and the recognition the Black sons of America so richly deserve stands perilously close to a Blackout."

On VJ-Day, Burley took to the pages of the *New York Amsterdam News* to fight the battle over how the war would be remembered. "I can truthfully report that the record of the American Negro in World War II matches, if not surpasses that of any white man," he argued. "To him belongs the credit for winning the battle of supply." Black Americans had to fight to be included in the draft and to be given a chance to take up combat roles. And yet, Black troops proved their mettle at Pearl Harbor, Bougainville, Normandy, the Battle of the Bulge, Saipan, Iwo Jima, and elsewhere. "They sent Black boys out in front, facing continuous enemy shelling and strafing to build the bridges, clear the swamps, fell the forests, build the roads, and the vital airfields," Burley reminded readers, "and then when the regular combat troops moved in, these Black boys dropped their picks and shovels, picked up guns and proved their worth in actual combat. And they died bravely. Many with songs on their lips and defiance in their hearts. But did they die in vain?" The answer to Burley's question would come on the home front in the years after the war.

SEVENTEEN

HOMECOMING

I had been on Omaha Beach. All we [Black soldiers] wanted to be was ordinary citizens. We fought during the war for America, Mississippi included. Now, after the Germans and Japanese hadn't killed us, it looked as though the white Mississippians would.

—MEDGAR EVERS, U.S. ARMY VETERAN
AND CIVIL RIGHTS ACTIVIST

As many Americans celebrated the end of the war, Black veterans returned to a country that disrespected their service and was openly hostile to them and their communities. On June 29, 1945, Mississippi senator James O. Eastland rose to speak on the floor of the Senate. "The Negro soldier was an utter and dismal failure in combat in Europe," Eastland charged. Citing conversations he had with American generals, the senator claimed Black troops refused to work or fight, that they sexually assaulted dozens of French women after the Normandy invasion, and that they were guilty of more than half the crime in the army. "The officers told us the soldiers had no initiative, no sense of responsibility, very low intelligence, and were a failure," Eastland said, flailing his arms as he spoke. "Negro soldiers have disgraced the flag of their country."

Mississippi's junior senator launched his attack on Black soldiers as part of a filibuster to block funding for the FEPC, which was established four years earlier to implement President Roosevelt's Executive Order 8802, banning employment discrimination in war work. The anti-FEPC filibuster succeeded, with the Senate providing the committee only $250,000, less than half of the amount President Truman had requested and just enough for the FEPC to struggle along in skeletal form for a final year. "The beating which FEPC has taken in Congress is evidence that the believers in the status quo will stop at nothing in their effort to prevent any basic change in the situation of the Negro," argued the NAACP's Roy Wilkins.

While the FEPC was the immediate target of Eastland's filibuster, his condemnation of Black troops served a larger and more sinister goal. Eastland and his ilk understood that Black Americans greeted victory abroad by redoubling their fight for civil rights at home, and that Black veterans were important leaders in this battle for freedom and equality. For Americans committed to upholding Jim Crow segregation and white supremacy, Black veterans and their military service were extremely dangerous.

So it was that Eastland, less than two months after the Allies defeated Hitler and the Nazis in Europe, declared in the nation's capital, "The Negro race is an inferior race." He continued in his Southern drawl, "I say frankly that I am proud of the white race. I am proud that the purest form of white blood flows in my veins. I know that the white race is the superior race. It has ruled the world.

It has given us civilization. It is responsible for all the progress on earth."

Only a handful of Eastland's Senate colleagues were on the floor during his filibuster, but his disparaging claims about Black troops were reprinted in newspapers across the country. He saw himself speaking for white America, not only for the South. "Thank God, the white soldier from Pennsylvania, the white soldier from New York, feels about the racial question today just as does the veteran from Mississippi or Georgia or South Carolina or Tennessee," he claimed.

Eastland was a racist, but he was right about this last point: most white Americans shared his views on postwar race relations. One poll found that white Americans by a 2–1 margin wanted "the country pretty much the way it was before the war," without any significant change or reform. The average white GI didn't "want a new America," *Fortune* magazine argued, "he wants the old one—only more of it."

The desire to return to the status quo permeated advertising during the war. Nash-Kelvinator, a defense contractor and kitchen appliance manufacturer, ran advertisements in *Life* magazine imagining the good life white servicemen and their families would enjoy after the war. In one ad, a young blonde promises her GI husband that he'll return to "the same America we have always known and loved" and that they won't "let anyone tamper with a way of living that works so well."

After four years of brutal war, returning to the way things used to be was obviously appealing to millions of white citizens, but it was exactly the opposite of what Black Americans were demanding. For Black Americans, returning to normal meant going back to a system of legalized racial apartheid in the South, where racial hierarchies were enforced through lynching and voter disenfranchisement. It meant riding in the back of the bus, stepping off the sidewalk to let a white person pass, and being denied access to lunch counters and swimming pools, all in order to remind you that you were a second-class citizen. In all regions of the country, returning to normal for Black Americans meant being harassed and beaten by police, not being able to get a mortgage to live in most neighborhoods, attending segregated and underresourced schools, and being the last hired and first fired in the workplace. The last thing Black people wanted was a return to a country that treated them as half American. They saw the war as part of a much larger "struggle to take democracy off of parchment and give it life," as *Crisis* magazine put it.

BLACK VETERANS BORE the brunt of these contradictory and irreconcilable visions of postwar America. When Black veterans tried to access the GI Bill of Rights, the signature government program that was designed to support returning veterans, they were often turned away or given the runaround. This discrimination was by design. Mississippi congressman John Rankin chaired the House Veterans Committee, and when the GI Bill legislation was being drafted he and other Southern Democrats ensured that the program would be administered by individual states rather than the federal government. This gave state and local officials the ability to determine who would and would not receive GI benefits. The offices that administered the program refused to hire more than a handful of Black employees. While the GI Bill legislation was nominally race neutral and did not require segregation or discrimination, in practice the decentralized structure allowed white administrators to exclude Black veterans.

At their local United States Employment Service (USES) job centers, Black veterans encountered white counselors who shunted them into unskilled and service-sector jobs, even if they had military training as carpenters, electricians, mechanics, or welders. In Mississippi, for example, white veterans received 86 percent of skilled and semiskilled positions, while Black vets took up 92 percent of the unskilled jobs. In Birmingham, Alabama, the USES job counselor told Willie May, who had gained experience stringing and repairing communication lines in the Army Signal Corps, that there were no suitable jobs available. The counselor then proceeded to place several white Signal Corps vets in jobs at the Birmingham Power Company. May settled for work as a Pullman porter, where he earned far less.

Like their white peers, Black veterans aspired to get low-interest mortgages and loans, guaranteed by the Veterans Administration (VA), to buy homes and start businesses. Some succeeded, but too many were turned away by banks that refused to approve loans for Black Americans, veterans or not. "Loans to Negro veterans are almost out of the question," the National Urban League observed. The GI Bill exacerbated housing segregation that was produced and maintained by federal mortgage redlining and housing covenants. In 1947, Black borrowers received only two of more than thirty-two hundred Veterans Administration–guaranteed home loans in Mississippi. The story was similar outside of the South. Of the sixty-seven thousand mortgages insured by the VA in New York and northern New Jersey suburbs, fewer than a hundred went to Black veterans.

Black veterans also had to contend with organized resistance and violence by white homeowners who saw Black Americans as a threat to their segregated neighborhoods and property values. Just south of San Francisco, white neighbors threatened and harassed army veteran John T. Walker before burning down his newly built home. Across the country, Black veterans who wanted to buy homes ran up against housing covenants that explicitly blocked them from many neighborhoods. In Albuquerque, New Mexico, a new housing subdivision for veterans was limited to white vets. One housing covenant from Seattle restricted the sale of property to "persons of the Aryan race." This was in 1946, a year after the Allies had defeated the Nazis on the battlefield.

With federal policies and private white citizens aligned against them, the dream of homeownership remained out of reach for many Black vets. Black veterans could afford the monthly mortgage payments, but the VA channeled resources through banks and real estate interests that discriminated on the basis of race. They were almost completely locked out of the postwar suburban housing boom and the ability to accrue equity from these investments. And since homeownership is the primary way average Americans generate and pass down wealth, Black vets were denied the opportunity to ensure financial stability and prosperity for their children and future generations. By funneling resources to white veterans and denying loans to Black veterans, the GI Bill intensified the racial wealth gap and shaped the terrain of opportunity in America for decades after the war.

The GI Bill enabled millions of veterans to attend college, but here again the extent of these opportunities differed dramatically along racial lines. Colleges in the north and west had de facto quotas and admitted only a token number of Black students. Even veterans who qualified academically and secured admission to these institutions encountered hostile VA counselors. When Tuskegee Airman Monte Posey went to the VA office in midtown Chicago to get approval to attend the University of Illinois at its new Chicago campus, the counselor told him that there were no professional opportunities for college-educated Black people. Rather than wasting his time at a university he should sign up for a trade, the counselor advised.

In the South, higher education was legally segregated and white colleges outnumbered Black colleges by more than five to one, even though Black Southerners made up a quarter of the region's population. Black veterans rushed to historically Black colleges, which, while dedicated and resilient, were chronically underfunded and unable to serve the postwar influx of students. As many as fifty thousand Black veterans each year did not attend college because there were not enough classrooms or dormitories to accommodate them.

While 28 percent of white veterans attended college on the GI Bill, only 12 percent of Black veterans were able to use this benefit. Even though thousands of Black vets would graduate from college due to the GI Bill, and many became part of the rising postwar middle class, the legislation actually widened educational and economic gaps between Black and white Americans. *The Pittsburgh Courier* argued that "the veterans' program had completely failed veterans of minority races."

To make matters worse, more than ten thousand Black soldiers were given "blue discharges" from the army, which made them ineligible for GI benefits (the name came from the blue paper on which they were printed). While they had many of the practical effects of a dishonorable discharge, blue discharges could be issued without a court-martial or legal proceeding. Gay troops and Black soldiers who were deemed "troublemakers" were disproportionately pressured into taking blue tickets out of the army. *The Pittsburgh Courier* called the policy a "vicious instrument that should not be perpetuated against the American soldier" and warned that "there is a widespread conspiracy to give blue discharges to as many colored soldiers and sailors as possible." In the fall of 1945, the *Courier* cautioned Black servicemen not to accept blue tickets and published instructions on how to appeal such discharges.

SUPPLY SERGEANT HENRY MURPHY hoped to take advantage of the GI Bill when he returned to Hattiesburg, Mississippi, after earning a Purple Heart for wounds he suffered in Germany. He also faced more immediate safety concerns. When Murphy arrived at Camp Shelby, his father, a local minister, brought him a change of civilian clothes in order to avoid trouble from white police and civilians. "He told me not to wear my uniform home," Murphy said. "Because the police was beating up Black GIs and searching them. If they had a white woman's picture in his pocket, they'd kill him." The young sergeant had no such pictures, but he did what his father said. As his dad drove the family Chevrolet, Murphy changed out of his olive drab army uniform and pulled on overalls, a field hand's uniform.

Murphy had good reason to be cautious. Black veterans were disrespected, harassed, attacked, and killed in the months and years after the war ended. Wearing a uniform, the same military attire in which they risked their lives during the war, made them a target. Sergeant James Tilman, who fought in Italy as part of the 92nd Infantry, remembered that when his unit crossed the Atlantic they were forced to wait on the dock in Norfolk, Virginia, because local officials did not want Black soldiers marching through town. After two hours, the officers finally persuaded two officials to allow the troops to walk the five miles to camp. "As we walked, people were giving us strange looks, as if we were convicts," Tilman remembered. "We were the first troops home, but no one clapped or cheered. . . . The few Black people we saw looked scared; maybe they thought they would get lynched or something if they cheered for us." Tilman was undeterred by this rude welcome home. "I was a dedicated man," he said. "I was a sergeant and I had one hundred men in my charge. I told them we were not going to walk through town like convicts with our heads down. I said we were going to march with our heads up and shout out in cadence."

Tuskegee Airman Alexander Jefferson flew more than a dozen missions with Benjamin O. Davis Jr. in Italy before being shot down and captured by the Germans. He spent the last eight months of the war in a Nazi prisoner of war camp. After being freed, he boarded a troop transport ship to return to America. As the ship steamed into New York Harbor, he was understandably thrilled to see the city skyline and the Statue of Liberty. When Jefferson, a lieutenant, walked down the gangplank, a white private shouted, "Whites to the right, niggers to the left." His jubilation was dashed before he even touched land.

Navy messman and Guadalcanal veteran Wallace Baptiste was proudly wearing his uniform, with ribbons and battle stars, when he boarded a ferry in New Orleans just after the war ended. "I sat down on one of the benches, and this old rebel who was down about sixty feet away at the other end of the bench demands to the operator that I be removed from *his* bench," he said. "I didn't need any trouble. I went ahead and moved, I just wanted to get home— I was lucky to be home at all after the Solomons—but that really dampened my spirits." *Pittsburgh Courier* war correspondent Ollie Harrington wrote that Black soldiers fought to "tear down the sign 'No Jews Allowed' in Germany," only to find signs reading NO NE-GROES ALLOWED were still commonplace in America.

Black veterans also found WHITES ONLY signs at many American Legion and Veterans of Foreign Wars (VFW) posts. These organizations left the question of racial integration up to state leaders and local posts, and as a result, Black vets were excluded in many places. In 1946, Black veterans protesting segregation outside of the American Legion annual convention in San Francisco were attacked by white Legionnaires. Some Black veterans established their own Legion and VFW posts, while others joined the progressive United Negro and Allied Veterans of America or American Veterans Committee.

Across the South, Black veterans faced deadly violence not by German or Japanese soldiers, but from their own countrymen. "Every Negro with his country's uniform on is a refutation of the Southern racial caste system," the *New York Amsterdam News* argued. Black newspapers carried grim news of the campaign of terror against Black veterans and said the names of the victims:

Eugene Bell, a father of two young children, was abducted and killed by a band of white men in Liberty, Mississippi. The attack was retaliation because when Bell was honorably discharged from the army he went to work for his father-in-law, rather than returning to work as a share-cropper on a white-owned farm (August 1945).

Sam McFadden was taken into custody by a white sheriff in Suwannee County, Florida. The sheriff, who thought McFadden was acting disrespectfully, forced the army veteran to jump at gunpoint into the Suwannee River, where he drowned (September 1945).

Timothy Hood, an honorably discharged Marine, was shot and wounded by a white streetcar conductor after he removed a Jim Crow sign from a trolley in Bessemer, Alabama. The white chief of police arrested Hood and then shot him in the head, claiming that the unarmed Hood "reached toward his hip pocket as if to draw a gun." The white coroner ruled the murder a "justified homicide" and the police chief was cleared (February 1946).

Isaac Woodard Jr., a Pacific theater veteran, was still wearing his army uniform when he was beaten by white police in Batesburg, South Carolina, while en route to rejoin his family. His eyes were gouged out by the sheriff's nightstick, blinding him for life. Woodard traveled the country speaking about his experience and calling for the Truman administration to protect Black Americans and desegregate the military. "Negro veterans that fought in this war don't realize that the real battle has just begun in

America," Woodard argued. "They went overseas and did their duty and now they're home and have to fight another struggle, that I think outweighs the war" (February 1946).

Kenneth Long was shot and killed by a white highway patrolman in El Campo, Texas, after the navy veteran refused to obey an order to tuck in his shirt (March 1946).

Etoy Fletcher, an army veteran, was abducted by four white men, forced to strip, and then flogged with a cable wire when he tried to register to vote in Rankin County, Mississippi (June 1946).

George Dorsey, who served several years in the Pacific, had been home for less than a year when he, his wife, Mae Murray, and their friends Dorothy and Roger Malcolm, were shot sixty times at close range by a white mob in Walton County, Georgia. Dorothy Malcolm was seven months pregnant when she was lynched (July 1946).

Maceo Snipes, an army veteran, was confronted by four KKK members who came to his farmhouse the day after Snipes became the first Black person to vote in a Democratic primary in Taylor County, Georgia. Snipes was shot and killed by Edward Williamson, who was also a World War II veteran. The *New York Amsterdam News* called Snipes "a new martyr in the cause of Democracy and freedom in America." The murder led young Morehouse College student Martin Luther King Jr. to write a letter to the editor of *The Atlanta Constitution*. "We want and are entitled to the basic rights and opportunities of American citizens," King argued (August 1946).

John C. Jones, an honorably discharged army corporal, was lynched by a white gang in Minden, Louisiana, for allegedly sneaking into a white family's backyard and looking through a window at a young white woman. "The veteran . . . had answered Uncle Sam's call for red-blooded men to fight for democracy abroad, even though he had never experienced democracy at home," *The Pittsburgh Courier* observed. "So, another veteran of World War II who emerged unscathed from the holocaust has been done to death on his native soil and has gone unavenged" (August 1946).

Alonza Brooks and Richard Gordon were murdered in Marshall, Texas, after voting. The veterans were killed by white mobs in separate incidents; Brooks was strangled, while Gordon's throat was slashed before his body was dragged behind an automobile (August 1946).

Joe Nathan Roberts, a navy veteran pursuing a degree at Temple University through the GI Bill, was visiting his parents in Sardis, Georgia, when he was abducted and shot to death by a group of white men who were outraged that he refused to call them "sir" earlier that day (June 1947).

Roland Price, a twenty-year-old veteran, was shot twenty-five times by a white police officer after an argument with a bartender in Rochester, New York (November 1947).

Herman Burns, a veteran and father of two, was beaten to death by Los Angeles police outside of the La Veda Ballroom (August 1948).

Isaiah Nixon, an army veteran, was shot and killed by two white men in Alston, Georgia, after he voted in the state primary. An all-white jury acquitted the killers (September 1948).

And on. And on.

"They're exterminating us," a shaken Black veteran from Georgia told Ollie Harrington, who investigated lynchings for the NAACP after serving as a war correspondent. "They're killing negro veterans. . . . In Italy and Germany we knew which way they were coming, but not here." *New York Amsterdam News* war correspondent Dan Burley told readers that even though Black troops established an impressive record in every theater of the war, the bigger battle began when they returned home. "The veteran from Okinawa may well be lynched on the streets of a Georgia town if he does not step off the sidewalk when a white woman or man passes," Burley wrote. "He had better not wear his uniform or battle ribbons in certain towns in Mississippi. He will be patted on the back in large cities in the North by victory-flushed white Americans and then knifed for the job of his desire by the same whites who are seeking to continue the age-old policy of 'last to be hired, first to be fired' where the Negro is concerned."

For Black Americans, this postwar reign of terror against veterans made victory parades and talk of American democracy ring hollow. Racial violence against Black people was not new, but seeing lives taken so regularly, so casually, and so carelessly made it clear that these were not isolated examples of bad cops or racist citizens, but rather a pattern of violence that demonstrated that the country did not equally value Black lives.

EIGHTEEN

WE RETURN FIGHTING

No nation is so great that the world can afford to let it continue to be deliberately unjust, cruel and unfair toward its own citizens.

—W. E. B. DU BOIS

On August 12, 1946, three Black amputee veterans with
mourning wreaths adorning their wheelchairs led an interracial march of fifteen thousand protesters to the Lincoln Memorial in Washington, D.C. The demonstrators condemned
mob rule in the South and demanded that President Truman call a
special session of Congress to enact antilynching legislation. "Our
lives are in jeopardy," the United Negro and Allied Veterans wrote
to President Truman.

Civil rights advocates pointed out that while the U.S. government
was vigorously prosecuting Nazi war criminals, the Justice Department was unable or unwilling to bring the killers of Black Americans
to justice. "Negro veterans . . . have been done to death or muti-

lated with savagery equaled only at Buchenwald," NAACP secretary Walter White wrote in an appeal to Eleanor Roosevelt, a United Nations delegate. The UN was less than a year old and the former first lady was soon to begin a five-year term leading the UN's newly created Commission on Human Rights.

W. E. B. Du Bois urged the NAACP to bring the inhumane treatment of Black Americans to the UN. An esteemed intellectual and activist, Du Bois had been organizing efforts for universal Black liberation across the African diaspora for more than four decades. He cofounded the NAACP in 1909 and served until 1934 as the director of publicity and research, a member of the board of directors, and editor of *The Crisis*, the association's monthly magazine. Between the world wars, he helped coordinate a series of Pan-African Congresses to push for an end to colonialism and white imperial dominion. Du Bois advocated for Black communities to become self-dependent, a position that put him at odds with the moderate, integrationist vision of Walter White and other national NAACP leaders. Du Bois resigned from the association in 1934, but rejoined in 1944, as the organization became more aggressive in fighting for legal and economic rights during the war.

Both Du Bois and White regarded the UN with suspicion. When the UN's basic structure was outlined at the Dumbarton Oaks Conference in October 1944, they saw how the Allies disenfranchised nonwhite countries in Africa, Asia, and Latin America and sought to ensure that the UN's human rights policies would not force the Allied powers to provide full citizenship and autonomy to the 750 million people living in the colonial world. When delegates from the forty-six nations at war with Germany and Japan met in San Francisco in the spring of 1945 to hammer out the UN

Charter, Du Bois and White were dismayed that the U.S. delegation refused to take up the concerns of Black Americans. The United States also supported a clause in the charter that prevented the international body from intervening in "matters which are essentially within the domestic jurisdiction of any state." As a result, America's system of racial apartheid would remain a domestic issue beyond the purview of the UN.

Despite these misgivings, White was encouraged that Eleanor Roosevelt, an NAACP board member, was leading the UN's human rights effort. For his part, Du Bois felt that the emerging Cold War between the United States and the Soviet Union made American political leaders more susceptible to international pressure if the plight of Black citizens could be laid bare for the world to see. Months after the Allies signed the UN Charter, Du Bois traveled to Manchester, England, for the Fifth Pan-African Congress. There he strategized with anticolonial activists such as Jamaican Pan-Africanist Amy Ashwood Garvey, future Kenyan president Jomo Kenyatta, future Ghanaian prime minister Kwame Nkrumah, and Trinidadian intellectual George Padmore.

In October 1947, the NAACP published *An Appeal to the World!*, a 150-page treatise on human rights abuses against Black Americans penned by Du Bois and a team of scholars and attorneys. "Peoples of the World, we American Negroes appeal to you," Du Bois wrote in his introduction. "Our treatment in America is not merely an internal question of the United States. It is a basic problem of humanity; of democracy; of discrimination because of race and color; and as such it demands your attention and action. No nation is so great that the world can afford to let it continue to be deliberately unjust, cruel and unfair toward its own citizens."

Du Bois took aim at the duplicity of Allied nations, who prosecuted human rights violations in Germany but looked the other way at colonial cruelties carried out by South Africa, Australia, and Belgium. "As long as Great Britain and the United States profess democracy with one hand and deny it to millions with the other, they convince none of their sincerity, least of all themselves," he argued. While the president offered support for nations threatened by totalitarian regimes—the so-called Truman Doctrine—Du Bois pointed out that the population of Black people in the United States was larger than the total population of Greece and Hungary, and nearly as large as that of Romania and Yugoslavia. If these nations deserved protection by the UN, so, too, did Black Americans, Du Bois argued.

As American Cold War foreign policy focused on containing Soviet expansion, Du Bois made it clear that Black Americans understood these threats differently. "It is not Russia that threatens the United States so much as Mississippi; not Stalin and Molotov but Bilbo and Rankin," he contended, referring to the archsegregationist members of Congress from Mississippi. "Internal injustice done to one's brothers is far more dangerous than the aggression of strangers from abroad." Du Bois arranged for the report to be leaked to *The New York Times* and other influential newspapers to turn up the heat on American officials.

The appeal did not sit well with Walter White or Eleanor Roosevelt, who felt that the tone was too radical and would provide the Soviet Union with propaganda to shame the U.S. Roosevelt worked in concert with U.S. State Department officials to ensure that the NAACP's petition would not appear on the UN agenda. She then submitted her resignation from the NAACP, though White persuaded her to reconsider and stay on the board.

The fallout from the NAACP's appeal to the UN shaped the association's trajectory for decades. White guided the NAACP national office on a moderate path, focusing largely on domestic civil rights issues including school segregation, voting rights, and housing discrimination, while distancing the association from Communists and fellow travelers. The organization's support for decolonization in Africa took place largely through approved UN channels. Du Bois resigned from the NAACP again in 1948, this time for good.

Du Bois and other Black internationalists saw the Black freedom struggle in America as inexorably tied to decolonization and independence movements in Africa, Asia, and Latin America. "The greatest question before the world today is this: can we have Democracy in America and Europe so long as the majority of people of the world are in colonial status?" Du Bois argued. "What was true of the United States in the past is true of world civilization today—we cannot exist half slave and half free." The global vision that had led Black Americans to oppose Italy's invasion of Ethiopia and travel to Spain to fight fascism also led generations of Black activists and many veterans to see Georgia and Ghana, Mississippi and Mozambique, St. Louis and Senegal, as intertwined.

As a proud veteran who served in France during the Great War, President Truman was dismayed by the attacks against Black vets. "When the mob gangs can take four people out and shoot them in the back, and everybody in the country is acquainted with who did the shooting and nothing is done about it, that country is in a pretty bad fix from a law enforcement standpoint," Truman confided in a letter to a friend. "When a Mayor and City Marshal can take a negro Sergeant off a bus in South Carolina, beat him up and put out one of his eyes, and nothing is done about it by the State authorities, something is radically wrong with the system."

At the same time, Black leaders wondered and worried about how far the new president would go on civil rights. Truman grew up in a segregated town in Missouri, his grandparents on both sides owned Black people as slaves, and he used racial epithets casually in personal letters. In the funeral procession carrying FDR's casket, Democratic senator from South Carolina Burnet Maybank assured a Southern friend that Truman could be trusted not to disturb segregation in the South. "Everything's going to be all right," Maybank said, "the new President knows how to handle the niggers."

Despite Truman's personal prejudices, civil rights leaders believed that the president could be persuaded to take action on violence against veterans. Walter White led a National Emergency Committee Against Mob Violence, a coalition of civil rights advocates, labor activists, and religious leaders, that met with Truman in September 1946. White read a list of lynchings that had taken place across the country, including the killings of John C. Jones, Maceo Snipes, George Dorsey, and other veterans. "My God!" Truman exclaimed. "I had no idea it was as terrible as that! We've got to do something." Three months later, Truman created the President's Committee on Civil Rights, a fifteen-person group that included two Black members, Philadelphia lawyer Sadie Alexander and Channing Heggie Tobias, who led race-relations efforts at the YMCA.

The president charged the committee with investigating the status of civil rights nationally and proposing measures to strengthen them. On June 29, 1947, Truman became the first U.S. president to address the NAACP. "As Americans, we believe that every man should be free to live his life as he wishes," Truman said from the steps of the Lincoln Memorial, before a crowd of more than three thousand people. "He should be limited only by his responsibility to his fellow countrymen. If this freedom is to be more than a dream, each man must be guaranteed equality of opportunity. The only limit to an American's achievement should be his ability, his industry and his character." Truman understood that speaking before the NAACP and advocating for civil rights would upset the white Southern members of the Democratic Party, but he clearly emphasized, "When I say all Americans, I mean all Americans."

When the President's Committee on Civil Rights submitted its report, *To Secure These Rights*, it was enthusiastically received by civil rights activists and the Black press. The 178-page report detailed how widespread discrimination harmed the nation, while infographics tried to make poll-tax legislation, Jim Crow segregation, fair-employment policies, and the shortcomings of federal civil rights enforcement understandable for average Americans. *To Secure These Rights* called on the White House, Congress, and state legislatures to adopt nearly three dozen wide-ranging proposals, including ending poll taxes, passing voting rights and federal antilynching legislation, outlawing racial housing covenants, establishing the federal Fair Employment Practice Act, and ending military segregation to "protect the dignity of the uniform of its armed services." The *Chicago Defender* saw the report as "a new blueprint for freedom," while the *Baltimore Afro-American* hailed it as "one of the most significant documents of all time." *The Washington Post* called the committee's recommendations "social dynamite," an opinion shared by Walter White, who deemed the report "explosive." More than a million copies of the report were distributed, and it was serialized in Black newspapers and liberal magazines.

As he weighed these recommendations, Truman felt pressure from two directions. White Southern constituents and politicians saw *To Secure These Rights* as a frontal attack on Jim Crow and racial hierarchies. "If you do away with segregation, allow negro children in white schools, churches, etc. you might as well drop a few bombs on us and not prolong the agony," one irate Virginian wrote to the president.

Southern Democratic congressmen had more than just rhetorical vitriol in their arsenal. With their numbers, seniority, and positions on key committees, they had the ability to block attempts to pass civil rights legislation and they did so repeatedly and ruthlessly. With the 1948 election fast approaching, Truman was calculating how many white votes he would lose and how many Black votes he would gain by supporting civil rights.

A. Philip Randolph, meanwhile, was pressuring Truman from another direction. As Congress debated a new peacetime draft bill, which would require all men eighteen years and older to register with the Selective Service and be eligible for military service, Randolph saw an opportunity to finish the campaign to desegregate the military that he had started seven years earlier with the March on Washington Movement. Testifying before the Senate Armed Services Committee in the spring of 1948, Randolph said, "Negroes are in no mood to shoulder a gun for democracy abroad so long as they are denied democracy here at home. In particular, they resent the idea of fighting or being drafted into another Jim Crow Army."

Giving voice to the anger of generations of Black veterans, soldiers, and their families, Randolph vowed to openly counsel and assist young men, both Black and white, to oppose the racially segregated draft system. Randolph had already formed the Committee Against Jim Crow in Military Service and Training along with Mary McLeod Bethune, the National Urban League's Lester Granger, and the NAACP's Walter White and Charles Hamilton Houston. "From coast to coast in my travels I shall call upon all Negro veterans to join this civil disobedience movement and to recruit their younger brothers in an organized refusal to register and be drafted," he vowed. "Many veterans, bitter over Army Jim Crow, have indicated that they will act spontaneously in this fashion regardless of any organized movement. 'Never again,' they say with finality." When a senator reminded Randolph that advocating draft evasion would amount to treason, Randolph shot back, "We have to face this thing sooner or later and we might as well face it now." Where he once threatened President Roosevelt to bring tens of thousands of Black protesters to march in the nation's capital, he now threatened Truman that a larger number of Black people would refuse to be drafted into a Jim Crow military.

After Congress passed the Selective Service Act in June 1948 and Truman signed it into law, Randolph renamed his committee the League for Nonviolent Civil Disobedience Against Military Segregation and began counseling young Black men not to sign up for military service. He was joined by Bayard Rustin, a Quaker and civil rights activist, who spent two years in prison because he refused to serve in the war or take alternative service to contribute to the war effort. While moderate Black leaders and newspapers criticized Randolph as an extremist and worried that his efforts would undercut the patriotism Black people demonstrated during the war, his campaign tapped into a feeling shared by many Black Americans that the times demanded more militant action. A poll of draft-eligible men in New York City found that more than 70 percent favored civil disobedience against military segregation.

Truman resented Randolph's pressure campaign, but he also understood that Black voters outside of the South could not be considered sure votes for the Democratic Party. The president's advisers warned him that Black voters were looking for action, not talk. A Black voting bloc could determine the election in Illinois, New York, and Ohio, they cautioned. Empty political gestures could swing Black voters and the election to the Republicans.

Congressional opposition meant that all of the major recommendations in *To Secure These Rights* were either off the table or years away from being implemented. All except one. As commander in chief of the army and navy, Truman had the authority to order the desegregation of the armed forces.

On July 26, 1948, Truman signed Executive Order 9981, committing the government to desegregating the military. A month later, white Southern delegates walked out of the Democratic National Convention, formed the States' Rights Democratic Party convention—the so-called Dixiecrats—and nominated South Carolina governor Strom Thurmond for the 1948 presidential election. "The Southerners want the State right to continue to deny Negro citizens the right to vote," the Black journalist P. L. Prattis remarked. While many white military officers and enlisted men also dug in their heels and resisted the order, by the end of the Korean War in 1953, the military was almost fully desegregated.

The desegregation of the armed forces was both late and early. Black troops suffered incalculable harm because government officials and military leaders refused to heed calls to end military discrimination before the war. Going to war with a segregated army, navy, and Marine Corps not only demeaned Black Americans, it was also inefficient and made the Allies less successful in combat. It was only a lack of political will to confront racism and white supremacy that prevented the military from desegregating in 1938 rather than 1948.

At the same time, Executive Order 9981 was an important civil rights milestone because it marked the first time any part of the federal government officially desegregated. Supreme Court justices read the draft manuscript of journalist Lee Nichols's *Breakthrough on the Color Front*, the first book-length study of military integration, before hearing arguments in *Brown v. Board of Education*, the landmark 1954 school segregation case. Black Americans still experienced racism in the desegregated military, but generations of Black enlistees and officers after World War II found the armed forces to be a relatively equitable institution that offered education, skills training, professional advancement, and a pathway to the middle class.

In May 1946, *Ebony* magazine declared that veterans were "not the same Negroes who put on uniforms after Pearl Harbor. The war has been an education. . . . Travel, better health and living conditions, even higher income has made the Negro younger generation the most aware, most articulate, and the most militant in all U.S. history." Black veterans swelled the ranks of the NAACP, CORE, and other civil rights organizations and became key players in Black freedom struggles across the country. "It had to change because we're not going to have it this way anymore," said Women's Army Corps veteran Luella Newsome. "I got through fighting in the ETO (European Theater of Operations) and now I am fighting in the STO (Southern Theater of Operations)," one veteran noted.

For decades after World War II, Black veterans fought for the principles of democracy in America. Reverend Hosea Williams, who earned a Purple Heart in France serving as an infantryman under General Patton, was beaten almost to death when he tried to drink from a "white" water fountain in Savannah, Georgia, after the war. He worked alongside Dr. Martin Luther King Jr. in the Southern Christian Leadership Conference (SCLC) to lead Black voter-registration drives in the South.

In Birmingham, Alabama, more than one hundred Black veterans marched in double file to the courthouse in Jefferson County and demanded the right to vote. Army veteran Amzie Moore served in the China-Burma-India theater before becoming a leader in the Mississippi Freedom Movement. Robert F. Williams, who served in the army during World War II and later in the Marines, led a militant local chapter of the NAACP in Monroe, North Carolina. He got a charter from the National Rifle Association and organized a rifle club to protect Black people from the KKK and other white vigilantes. He recruited veterans for his local NAACP chapter because they "don't scare easy," he said.

WAC veteran Dovey Johnson Roundtree used the GI Bill to attend Howard University Law School. She established a law firm in Washington, D.C., and, in the landmark civil rights case *Sarah Keys v. Carolina Coach Company* (1955), helped secure a ban on racial segregation in interstate bus travel.

Veteran Oliver Brown protested school segregation in Topeka, Kansas. His daughter Linda Brown was one of the students at the center of the historic *Brown v. Board of Education* decision. In *Brown*, Thurgood Marshall successfully persuaded the justices that segregated schools were inherently unequal and that the "separate but equal" doctrine, which had formed the legal basis for Jim Crow segregation since *Plessy v. Ferguson* in 1896, was unconstitutional.

Medgar Evers stood proudly among the generation of Black veterans who risked their lives fighting for democracy overseas and in America. After earning two Bronze Stars on the beachhead of Normandy and in northern France as part of the Red Ball Express, Evers returned to Mississippi. He celebrated his twenty-first birthday in 1946 by leading a group of Black veterans who attempted to register to vote in Decatur, Georgia, only to be turned away by a white mob with guns. Evers attended Alcorn A&M College on the GI Bill and earned a degree in business administration. He briefly sold insurance before becoming the NAACP's first field secretary in Mississippi in 1954. Evers, along with fellow World War II veteran Amzie Moore and NAACP southeast regional director Ruby Hurley, investigated the murder of fourteen-year-old Emmett Till in 1955. They had to persuade potential Black witnesses to testify, keep them in protective custody during the trial, and then secretly shepherd them out of town when the all-white jury found Till's killers not guilty.

In 1962, Evers helped U.S. Air Force veteran James Meredith integrate the University of Mississippi. When Meredith tried to register for classes, a white mob harassed and threatened him. "I had been on Omaha Beach," Evers told reporters after the protests over the integration of Ole Miss. "All we [Black soldiers] wanted to be was ordinary citizens. We fought during the war for America, Mississippi included. Now, after the Germans and Japanese hadn't killed us, it looked as though the white Mississippians would."

As it did for other civil rights activists, standing up against white supremacy made Evers a target, and he and his family received death threats regularly. In the summer of 1963, someone threw a Molotov cocktail through a window of the Evers family home in Jackson, Mississippi, and Evers was injured when someone tried to run him over outside his NAACP office. "If I die, it will be for a good cause," he said. "I've been fighting for America just as much as the soldiers in Vietnam."

On the night of June 11, 1963, Evers was attending a meeting at a local church. His wife, Myrlie, and children were waiting up for him, watching President John F. Kennedy on television telling the nation that civil rights was "primarily a moral issue" and that it should be possible "for every American to enjoy the privileges of being American without regard to his race or his color." Just after midnight, when Evers pulled into the driveway, he was struck by a bullet from a high-powered rifle fired by a gunman hiding in the honeysuckle bushes. When Myrlie and the children heard the gunshot, they rushed outside to find Medgar slumped in a pool of blood. Within an hour he was gone.

His killer, Byron De La Beckwith, a member of the Ku Klux Klan and Mississippi White Citizens' Council, and a Pacific theater veteran, was arrested several days later. The FBI connected a fingerprint on the rifle scope to De La Beckwith's military service prints, collected when he enlisted in the Marines in 1942. De La Beckwith was tried twice in 1964 before all-white juries, but both trials ended with hung juries.

Myrlie Evers refused to let her husband's murderer walk free, and she pushed for decades for authorities to reopen the case and look for new evidence. Finally, in a 1994 state trial, a jury convicted De La Beckwith of first-degree murder and sentenced him to life in prison.

Four thousand mourners gathered at the Masonic Hall in Jackson, Mississippi, on June 15, 1963, to honor Evers. "The Southern political system put him (Mr. Evers' slayer) behind that rifle," Roy Wilkins said. "The killer must have felt that he had, if not immunity, then certainly a protection for whatever he chose to do, no matter how dastardly." Little Rock NAACP leader Daisy Bates, NAACP southeast regional director Ruby Hurley, Rev. Martin Luther King Jr., and Rev. Ralph Abernathy joined the funeral march through the streets of Jackson in the sweltering summer heat. After the service, Myrlie Evers told the *Chicago Defender* that she feared for her family's safety after her husband's assassination. "It still isn't too late for them to harm us," she said. "I've lived here all my life. I know these people."

As an honorably discharged veteran, Evers was entitled to be buried at Arlington National Cemetery, across the Potomac River from Washington, D.C. The American Veterans Committee, an interracial veterans' organization that supported civil rights when the American Legion and the VFW did not, suggested and then arranged for the slain activist to be buried with full military honors at Arlington. Myrlie Evers had initially planned to bury her husband in Mississippi, but she welcomed the suggestion. "Since I felt Medgar belonged to everybody, I consider it a great honor to bury him in Arlington," she said. "I know he would have liked to be buried there." Hundreds of Black Mississippians prayed over the flag-draped casket at the train station in Meridian, Mississippi, before it made the trip north.

When Evers's casket arrived in the nation's capital, hundreds more people lined the route from Union Station to the McGuire funeral home, a thriving Black business and fixture of the district's Shaw neighborhood since the 1920s. Mourners passed out handbills with pictures of Evers that read "He sacrificed his life for you."

President John F. Kennedy arranged for Myrlie Evers and her two older children to visit the White House. The president gave nine-year-old Darrell Kenyatta a tie clasp and eight-year-old Reena Denise a bracelet, both engraved with a PT boat insignia. Kennedy earned two medals as a navy PT boat commander in the Pacific and he offered the gifts as symbols of his and Evers's shared service in World War II.

On June 19, Juneteenth, the funeral procession drove past the Lincoln Memorial, where more than 250,000 demonstrators would gather later that summer for the March on Washington for Jobs and Freedom, fulfilling a call that A. Philip Randolph had made more than two decades earlier. The procession arrived at Arlington and moved slowly past the thousands of white marble headstones that marked the final resting place for generations of American veterans.

"No soldier in this field ever fought more courageously, more heroically, than Medgar Evers," American Veterans Committee leader and Pacific theater army vet Mickey Levine told the graveside mourners. "We pledge that his fight is not ended. We shall go to Congress; we shall go to the people. We will not forget Medgar Evers and he shall not have died in vain."

Bishop Stephen Gill Spottswood of Washington's African Methodist Episcopal Church spoke next, evoking Evers's war service. "He is not dead, the soldier fallen here. His spirit walks throughout the world today," the bishop said. "I hope Medgar Evers will be the last Black American to give his life in the struggle to make the Constitution come alive. He laid down his life for Negroes that they might be freed from segregation and discrimination, that we might share in the full fruits of democracy. Now, he rests from his labors."

After a bugler sounded taps and an honor guard fired three volleys over the flag-draped coffin, the mourners softly sang "We Shall Overcome." Charles Evers, who took over his younger brother's job as NAACP field secretary for Mississippi and was also a World War II veteran, wept unabashedly. "Medgar Evers believed in his country; it now remains to be seen whether his country believes in him," Roy Wilkins said.

Before Evers's body was lowered into the grave, on a gentle slope surrounded by a grove of oak and sycamore trees, six white soldiers lifted the flag from the casket, folded it carefully, and presented it to Myrlie Evers. "The taps played, a salute and the flag was presented," Myrlie Evers-Williams remembered years later. "It felt as if we were truly being treated as Americans."

CONCLUSION

Thus we lived through a major war. The
question in the ghettos was, Can we make it
through a minor peace?

—MAYA ANGELOU

History, as nearly no one seems to know, is not
merely something to be read. And it does not
refer merely, or even principally, to the past.
On the contrary, the great force of history
comes from the fact that we carry it within us,
are unconsciously controlled by it in many
ways, and history is literally present in all that
we do. It could scarcely be otherwise, since it is
to history that we owe our frames of reference,
our identities, and our aspirations.

—JAMES BALDWIN

Wars seldom end on the battlefield. Since ancient times
people have fought over the meaning and memory of
combat, and the Second World War was no differ-
ent. More so than any twentieth-century conflict, World War II
has been seen in America as a good war, a noble fight against a

uniquely wicked regime. But while the evil of Adolf Hitler and the Nazi government was unquestionable, Americans went into and came out of the war with starkly different ideas about why the war was fought, whose service was valued, and who should enjoy freedom after the war. In telling the story of World War II from the Black American perspective, *Half American* continues a struggle over the war's memory that started more than seventy years ago and continues into the present day.

After the Allies secured victory, historian Lawrence Reddick was dismayed at what he saw as the coordinated effort among white military leaders, politicians, media, and social scientists to disparage the combat record of Black troops and to write Black Americans out of the history of the war. Not only did Mississippi senator James O. Eastland slander Black soldiers on the floor of the Senate as "failures in combat" who had "disgraced the flag of their country," but academic publications such as *The American Journal of Sociology*, *The American Journal of Psychiatry*, and *The Annals of the American Academy of Political and Social Science* released articles criticizing the performance of Black soldiers and sailors. *Life* magazine's pictorial history of World War II, a handsomely bound 368-page book, featured more than a thousand pictures of the war and only one Black American, a U.S. Navy musician weeping at President Franklin D. Roosevelt's funeral. *Collier's Photographic History of World War II* found space for one picture of a Black medic, among more than eight hundred photos. *Harper's Magazine* published a story by a white company commander in the 92nd Infantry Division who attacked the Black soldiers who fought and died under his command in Italy.

"If this campaign is not nipped in the bud, many more anti-Negro officers will write their memoirs, anti-Negro congressmen will quote the memoirs for the Congressional Record," Reddick argued. Before the war, Reddick thoroughly researched American history textbooks and was troubled by what he found. In addition to justifying slavery and the tactics of the Ku Klux Klan, the textbooks completely overlooked Black contributions to America, including military service. He was convinced the same thing would happen after World War II, with dire consequences. "Textbook writers will then quote the Congressional Record and we will have a generation growing up believing that Negroes are inferior fighters and therefore deserve inferior citizenship rights," he argued.

Reddick decided that he needed to fight back against these historical distortions and erasures. As curator of the Schomburg Collection of Negro Literature, History and Prints at the Harlem branch of the New York Public Library, he interviewed dozens of Black servicemen and servicewomen, and he placed advertisements in Black newspapers across the country, encouraging veterans and their families to donate war letters to the Schomburg Collection. Initially, dozens of letters arrived at the Harlem library each month, then hundreds.

For Negro History Week in February 1947, Reddick organized an exhibition at the library, *The Negro Warrior: His Record and His Future*, to tell a more accurate story about World War II. At the accompanying forum, a crowd of hundreds listened to Colonel Howard Queen, commanding officer of the 366th Infantry; Major Harriet West of the Women's Army Corps (WAC); Lieutenant Harriet Pickens of the Navy Women's Reserve (WAVES); and Captain James Bernard Knighten, who flew with Benjamin O. Davis Jr.

in the 99th Fighter Squadron, describe their war experiences. They spoke truths that did not appear in the Congressional Record or white magazines: *The Allies would not have won the war without Black servicemen and servicewomen, and the war against racism and white supremacy in America started before Pearl Harbor and continued even after the Nazis and Axis powers were conquered on the battlefield.*

Similar truths were spoken when a group of Black veterans met in the basement of the Phillis Wheatley Community Center in Greenville, South Carolina, in late 1945. The following spring, some four dozen of these veterans inaugurated the Captain Charles F. Gandy Jr. VFW Post 6734 off a dusty two-lane dirt road in Piedmont. Gandy was the F Company commander, 370th Combat Team, in the decorated and maligned 92nd "Buffalo Soldier" Infantry Division. He led his men across the Gothic Line in Italy, beating back Nazi troops and freeing Mount Pisano. He was killed by a German sniper's bullet during a three-day battle in the city of Lucca and was posthumously awarded the Silver Star for his gallantry in combat. The veterans who named the VFW post after Gandy wanted to ensure that his name and story, and their stories, too, would endure as part of the history of the war.

In the decades after the war, Black veterans gathered in living rooms, parks, hotel ballrooms, and elsewhere to share their memories of the war. More than a dozen Black veterans of the 93rd Infantry and their families met in Pasadena in 1969 to reminisce about their service. The first chapter of the Tuskegee Airmen veterans met in Alexander Jefferson's Detroit home in the summer of 1972 and hosted their first convention later that year. In 1979, Mary Rozier organized a reunion for the 6888th Central Postal Directory

Battalion, and two years later a group of Black women veterans organized the first of many gatherings of Black WACs. Across the country, Black veterans found community together, reflecting on what they endured and accomplished in the military and the battles against racism they continued to face. Each of these gatherings was a rebuke to those who sought to erase Black Americans from the history of the war.

Official recognition came slowly for Black World War II veterans. Of the 433 Medals of Honor awarded during the war, for example, none went to a Black American. In 1993, the army commissioned a study to investigate racial discrimination in the awarding of medals during and after the war. After a team of historians and military officers extensively reviewed service files and battle reports, they recommended that several Distinguished Service Cross recipients be upgraded to the Medal of Honor. In 1997, seven Black World War II veterans were awarded the Medal of Honor in a ceremony at the White House. First Lieutenant John Fox (92nd Infantry Division), Private First Class Willy James Jr. (104th Infantry Division), Staff Sergeant Ruben Rivers (761st Tank Battalion), and Private George Watson (29th Quartermaster Regiment) had been killed in action, while Staff Sergeant Edward A. Carter Jr. (56th Armored Infantry Battalion) and Lieutenant Charles Thomas (103rd Infantry Division) died in the decades after the war. Vernon Baker, then seventy-seven years old, was the only one who lived to receive the honor in person. As a first lieutenant in the 92nd Infantry, Baker took out three machine-gun positions and led a battalion charge through heavy fire and enemy minefields to help the Allies capture Castle Aghinolfi, a German mountain stronghold near Viareggio, Italy, in April 1945. He demonstrated extraordinary heroism during the war, although it took the army more than five decades to recognize this fact.

Only a few of the men who built the Ledo Road were still alive when the army finally acknowledged their important service sixty years later at a modest African American History Month event at Florida A&M University. Mose Davie was one of the Black engineers who received his long-overdue accolades. After serving as a battalion sergeant major in the 382nd Engineers Construction Battalion, he returned home to Nashville. He founded and graduated from Tennessee Evening Law School because he and other Black faculty members at Tennessee A&I State University were denied admission to the Nashville YMCA's Night Law School.

"I thought we'd accomplished something when we finished that road," Davie said in 2004. "I felt at that time the United States had let us down. They hadn't done anything to reward us for the patriotism we'd shown." Davie said he felt that an injustice was done to his fellow engineers who died before they were honored. "I felt we'd been let down, but I feel elated a little bit now, because they have subsequently recognized their mistakes."

After leading the Tuskegee Airmen during World War II, Benjamin O. Davis Jr. transferred to the newly created U.S. Air Force, where he served until 1970, earning the rank of lieutenant general. In 1998, President Bill Clinton awarded Davis a fourth star, raising the distinguished veteran to the rank of full general. Agatha Jo Scott Davis, his wife of more than sixty years, urged the taciturn Davis to write about everything he had accomplished and endured during his long career. Davis's autobiography, *Benjamin O. Davis, Jr., American* (1991), is frank both about the depth of racism Black Americans faced in the segregated military and about his pride in having served his country during and after World War II. Davis died on July 4, 2002, just four months after his beloved Agatha passed away. They are both buried at Arlington National Cemetery.

In 2007, more than three hundred surviving Tuskegee Airmen, as well as widows and relatives, received the Congressional Gold Medal from President George W. Bush in a ceremony at the Capitol Rotunda. Dr. Roscoe Brown, who shot down a German jet during the war and went on to serve as president of Bronx Community College for more than a decade after the war, spoke on behalf of the airmen. "We were flying in the skies over Europe defending our country, and at the same time fighting the battle against racial segregation," he said. Retired general Colin Powell counted himself among those who were inspired by the Tuskegee Airmen. "I know in the depth of my heart that the only reason I'm able to stand proudly before you today is because you stood proudly for America sixty years ago," Powell said.

Black veterans and their advocates understood that the stories we tell about the past matter. Stories that exclude Black Americans from the history of World War II go hand in hand with organized resistance to civil rights by white politicians and citizens. Stories that minimize or denigrate the vital contributions Black troops and defense workers made to the war effort are drawn from the same playbook that media and social scientists used after the war to brand Black Americans as lazy, prone to crime, and mired in a culture of poverty. Stories that overlook the racially discriminatory outcomes of the GI Bill obscure the root causes of the racial wealth gap and give the impression that white veterans thrived thanks solely to hard work rather than also benefiting from government assistance. Stories that downplay the intense violence Black veterans and civilians faced during and after the war make present-day police brutality and racial violence appear anomalous rather than systemic. Stories that ignore the intense battles Black Americans fought against racism and Jim Crow segregation on the home front make it appear that World War II was a simpler and more unified time in America, when in reality it was anything but.

Today, America is still fighting battles from World War II. Centering Black Americans in the history of the war is about more than simply setting the story straight. The stories we tell about the past also matter because they can equip us to better understand and navigate the present and future.

The experiences of Black Americans during World War II, for example, are an important example of what it means to dissent in a democracy. FBI director J. Edgar Hoover accused Black newspapers of sedition for their reporting on racial violence at military bases, and many white Americans viewed the Double Victory campaign as an expression of black disloyalty to the United States. For Black Americans, though, "patriotism" meant dealing with America's problems head-on rather than pretending they did not exist. "It's hard to be a patriot when you don't even feel like a citizen," argued Joseph LaNier, who served at Iwo Jima in the Seabees, 23rd Naval Construction Battalion.

It is impossible to understand activist and former National Football League quarterback Colin Kaepernick's decision to protest police violence by kneeling during the national anthem and the uproar that followed without first understanding the history of Black protest during World War II. Throughout the war, Black Americans expressed outrage that they were fighting to secure freedom on far-flung battlefields while being denied freedom in their own country. Every day brought new evidence that they were fighting for a country that did not regard them as fully human. With these lived experiences, the flag has always carried different meanings across racial lines. Generations of Black Americans have proudly saluted the flag while also demanding that the country not treat them as half American. "It's amazing why we keep loving this country, and this country does not love us back," National Basketball Association coach Doc Rivers said after Jacob Blake was shot by police in Kenosha, Wisconsin, in the summer of 2020. "It's really so sad."

In July 2020, the Department of Defense effectively banned the Confederate flag from military installations. This fight, too, has its roots in World War II. When white Southern troops went overseas during the war, some of them carried Confederate flags with them. As American forces took over Pacific islands or European towns, the troops would sometimes raise the Confederate flag alongside or instead of the U.S. flag to celebrate their victory. The Baltimore *Evening Sun* described this as a "recurring phenomenon which has been observed in areas as widely separated as the Southwest Pacific, Italy and France."

The white troops who raised the Confederate flag during World War II argued that they were honoring the military service of their forefathers. "In its day, this flag stood for much and waved over the heads of the same type of men that made America great," the *Charlotte Observer* argued. "Deep in the hearts of all Americans, the Confederacy now is merely a part of 'One nation indivisible.'"

Not all Americans agreed. When army lieutenant general Simon Buckner Jr., himself the son of a Confederate general, saw a Marine unit flying the flag above Okinawa, he ordered it removed. "Americans from all over are involved in this battle," he said.

For Black Americans especially, the Confederate flag was a symbol of decades of racism, hate, and white supremacy. They fought against it being displayed before, during, and after the war. Before Pearl Harbor, for example, the *Baltimore Afro-American* successfully protested a plan to use the flag as the insignia of army quartermasters stationed in Virginia at the base named for Confederate general Robert E. Lee.

While white officers and enlisted men had no difficulty displaying the Confederate flag at home or overseas, Senator Millard Tydings, a Maryland Democrat, wanted to ensure they could do so officially. In 1943, he introduced a bill to allow army units to carry Confederate battle streamers. "The sons of those who fought on the southern side in the Civil War . . . at least should have the right to carry these streamers as a matter of maintaining military morale," he argued. The *Chicago Defender* struck back immediately, calling the bill a "master stroke of hypocrisy" that proposed to have "American troops carrying the banner under which bitter war was waged for the perpetuation of slavery, into a so-called fight for democracy." Among Tydings's opponents, the *Defender* reported, there was talk of amending the bill to call for German Americans "to enter battle under the swastika, right next to the old Confederacy's Stars and Bars."

Tydings's bill was eventually signed by President Harry Truman in March 1948, which opened the door for the official display of Confederate symbols in the U.S. military. The policy was implemented just four months before Southern segregationists formed the Dixiecrats and put forward Strom Thurmond as their presidential candidate.

The Dixiecrats displayed the Confederate flag prominently at campaign events, which sent sales of Confederate flags skyrocketing nationally. "The Confederacy fought to destroy the United States . . . how in heaven's name can those who profess loyalty to the United States of America be loyal to the Confederacy?" asked E. Washington Rhodes, publisher of Philadelphia's largest black newspaper. "Thousands of men suffered and died to make the stars and stripes supreme in the U.S. There is but one American flag. We are either Americans or something else."

I thought of these words when I saw the image of a rioter carrying a Confederate flag inside the U.S. Capitol during the insurrection in Washington, D.C., on January 6, 2021. The flag flourished during and after World War II not only because it was embraced by people who supported the ideals of the Jim Crow South, but also because too few people were willing to call a symbol of slavery, treason, and disunity by its name. Black Americans were seldom shy about calling the Confederate flag and related symbols "racist," but large numbers of white Americans were comfortable soft-pedaling or distorting the history of slavery and its legacies.

This reticence to speak honestly about white supremacy also tracks back to World War II. The war era shaped how Americans talk about, or avoid talking about, race and racism. While Black Americans waged the Double Victory campaign against racism at home and fascism abroad, white politicians and social scientists turned their attention to what they came to call "race relations." Influenced by Gunnar Myrdal's *An American Dilemma: The Negro Problem and Modern Democracy* (1944), dozens of local committees formed to educate themselves and their communities about racial prejudice. They prioritized education and moral persuasion and published hundreds of articles and study guides about race. But there was a fundamental flaw with this strategy and the studies and reports that underpinned it. Despite all of the words spilled, they had little to say about white supremacy or which specific policies and legislation would challenge racist structures.

This "hearts and minds" approach to racial discrimination still frames how race is discussed in mainstream media, political discourse, and the public sphere. It was only a few years ago that the Associated Press updated its style guide to encourage journalists to stop using the euphemisms "racially motivated" or "racially charged" when "the terms *racism* and *racist* can be used . . . to describe the hatred of a race, or assertion of the superiority of one race over others." Whereas Black newspapers in the 1930s and '40s were able to describe Nazism, fascism, and white supremacy as "racist," contemporary news coverage of white nationalism has struggled to break free from World War II–era "race relations" language.

Advocates of closing the racial wealth gap would also be well served by looking at the legacy of World War II–era policies. On Veterans Day in 2021, Congressmen Seth Moulton of Massachusetts and James Clyburn of South Carolina introduced the GI Bill Restoration Act. The legislation is named after Sergeant Isaac Woodard Jr., who was blinded in an attack by police in South Carolina, and Sergeant Joseph Maddox, who was denied VA benefits for a master's degree program at Harvard University. The legislation acknowledges the racially discriminatory outcomes of the original GI Bill and would extend housing and education assistance programs administered by the Secretary of Veterans Affairs to surviving spouses and direct descendants of Black World War II vets. The inability of many Black World War II veterans to access GI Bill benefits and generate wealth for their children and future generations contributed significantly to the vast racial wealth gap in America. As of 2019, for instance, Black families' median wealth is less than 15 percent of that of white families—$24,100 compared with $188,200. The GI Bill Restoration Act would be a step toward repairing the damage and inequity wrought by the denial of benefits decades ago.

All of these contemporary battles, and many others, have their roots in World War II. Stories of the war that do not reckon with the Black American experience leave us ill prepared to understand the present, and rudderless as we try to navigate the future. Ignorance is a luxury we cannot afford. If we tell the right stories about the war, we can meet the resurgence of white supremacy as a deeply entrenched aspect of our country's political history and cultural life, rather than as a surprise or anomaly. If we tell the right stories about the war, we can see modern racial justice activism as the continuation of a decades-long struggle to make America an actual functioning democracy. If we tell the right stories about the war, we can finally honor the sacrifices of the Black veterans, defense industry workers, and citizens who fought on foreign battlefields and in their own cities and towns so that no one would ever again be treated as half American.

ACKNOWLEDGMENTS

This book would not have been possible without a lot of help.

At Dartmouth, I've found a wonderful place to research and teach history and African American studies. Thank you to my colleagues and to President Phil Hanlon and Dean Elizabeth Smith for supporting my research. Thank you to the Dartmouth students who worked as research assistants on this project: Jasmine Abidi, Olivia J. Audsley, Zach Cohen, Daniel Fishbein, Rachel Hobart, Hayden Kim, Alexander Klein, Markus Lake, Khonza Masuku, Coalter Palmer, Darley Sackitey, Elizabeth Simms, Hye Rine Uhm, David Velona, and Raniyan Zaman.

This project started at Arizona State University, where I was also fortunate to have excellent colleagues and students. Thank you to the ASU students, both in Tempe and online, who worked as research assistants during the early stages of this book: Shugri Abdulle, Jeffery Austin Brooks, Julian Burgan, Carlos Castro, Amber Catt, Allen

Crowder, Sarah Harris, Zoe Harrison, Jackeline Herrera, Muneeb Mohiuddin, Sami Omais, Felix Santoyo-Nino, Stephanie Williamson, and Zane Whitney.

Thank you to the graduate students who helped with archival research in Washington, D.C., New York, and Atlanta: Anayeli Nunez Almengor, Henry Balas, Jasmine Cannon, Kelly Duquette, Maria Ferraguto, Brendan Hornbostel, Matthew Kautz, Joseph Loyacono-Bustos, Elizabeth Pigott, Carmen Turner, and Mira Warmflash.

Thank you to Joey Balfour, Gemma Birnbaum, and Emily Hindin at the National WWII Museum, as well as to the archivists and librarians at the Schomburg Center for Research in Black Culture, the National Archives, Emory University Archives and Special Collections, and Yale University's Beinecke Rare Book and Manuscript Library.

Thank you to Jeanne Theoharis for talking through ideas with me and to Jonathan Beard for reading the draft manuscript and offering helpful suggestions.

Thank you to the team at Viking for helping to bring this book into the world: senior editor Georgia Bodnar supported this project from its earliest proposal and through the first two years of the pandemic. Associate editor Gretchen Schmid helped sharpen the chapters through multiple revisions. Thank you to executive editor Ibrahim Ahmad for embracing this project and bringing it to the finish line. Thank you to editorial assistant Marissa Davis for guiding this book through production, to Jane Cavolina for her careful copyediting, and to Laura Ogar for indexing the book. To the publicity and marketing team, including Lindsay Prevette, Kate Stark, Rebecca Marsh, LeBria Casher, and Christine Choi, for helping this book reach readers.

Thank you to Michelle Tessler, my literary agent, for being the first person to see the full potential of this project.

Thank you to the John Simon Guggenheim Memorial Foundation

and the National Endowment for the Humanities for supporting this research at critical junctures.

Thank you to my mom, Diane Delmont, for teaching me the importance of history and for buying me that Tuskegee Airmen T-shirt when I was a teenager.

Finally, thank you to Jacque Wernimont, Xavier, and Simone for their love.

NOTES

INTRODUCTION

xv **"Should I sacrifice"**: James G. Thompson, "Should I Sacrifice to Live 'Half-American'?," *Pittsburgh Courier*, January 31, 1942.

xvii **"taking a leaf"**: "Germans Adopt U.S. Jim Crow," *New York Amsterdam News*, December 31, 1938.

xvii **"the practice of jim-crowism"**: "Hitler Adopts U.S. Jim Crow Laws in Germany," *Chicago Defender*, January 7, 1939.

xviii **"I can truthfully report"**: Dan Burley, "New York Goes Wild on V-J Day," *New York Amsterdam News*, August 18, 1945.

xix **"There are thousands of Black ex-GIs"**: Mary Motley, *The Invisible Soldier: The Experience of the Black Soldier, World War II* (Detroit: Wayne State University Press, 1987), 269–70.

xix **"The veteran from Okinawa"**: Burley, "New York Goes Wild on V-J Day."

xix **from the "European Theater of Operations"**: Maria Höhn and Martin Klimke, *A Breath of Freedom: The Civil Rights Struggle, African American GIs, and Germany* (New York: Palgrave Macmillan, 2010), 35–37.

xx **he would "personally shoot"**: Ulysses Lee, *The Employment of Negro Troops* (Washington, D.C.: U.S. Government Printing Office, 1963), 104.

xx **"The whites think"**: Paul Howard, letter to Walter White, September 10, 1942, NAACP Papers, folder 001537-012-0334.

xx   **"White folks would rather lose"**: Roy Wilkins, "Watchtower," *New York Amsterdam News*, April 18, 1942.

xxi   **"raised in my mind"**: John Hope Franklin, *Race and History: Selected Essays, 1938–1988* (Baton Rouge: Louisiana State University Press, 1989), 289.

xxi   **"The treatment accorded the Negro"**: James Baldwin, *Notes of a Native Son* (1955: repr., Boston: Beacon Press, 2012), 102–3.

xxii   **"It was as if we were the slaves"**: Robert F. Jefferson, *Fighting for Hope: African American Troops of the 93rd Infantry Division in World War II and Postwar America* (Baltimore: Johns Hopkins University Press, 2008), 162.

xxv   **"I saw this great big volume"**: Robert P. Madison interview, April 14, 2010, National WWII Museum.

CHAPTER 1: BLACK AMERICANS FIGHTING FASCISM IN SPAIN

1   **"If democracy is to be preserved"**: "Langston Hughes Delivers Stirring Chicago Message," *Atlanta Daily World*, April 11, 1938.

2   **a headline in the *Chicago Defender***: "World War Seen as Duce, Hitler Aid Fascists in Wartorn Spain," *Chicago Defender*, August 29, 1936.

4   **"we Negroes in America"**: Langston Hughes, "Too Much Race," *The Crisis*, September 1937, 272.

4   **"The racial policy of the Hitler movement"**: Kelly Miller, "Hitler—the German Klu [*sic*] Klux," *Norfolk Journal and Guide*, April 1, 1933.

4   **"If the Swastika is an emblem"**: Editorial, "No Time for Hypocrisy," *New York Amsterdam News*, July 27, 1935.

5   **they arrived in Barcelona**: Langston Hughes, *I Wonder as I Wander* (New York: Rinehart & Co., 1956), 321–22; Langston Hughes, "Hughes Bombed in Spain," *Baltimore Afro-American*, October 23, 1937; Langston Hughes, "Madrid Getting Used to Bombs; It's Food Shortage That Hurts," *Baltimore Afro-American*, November 20, 1937.

6   **"The crack of rifle fire"**: Hughes, "Madrid Getting Used to Bombs."

6   **in Madrid, Hughes's accommodations**: Hughes, *I Wonder as I Wander*, 334.

6   **The meals were far less lavish**: Hughes, *I Wonder as I Wander*, 337–39; Arnold Rampersad, *The Life of Langston Hughes, Volume I: 1902–1941* (New York: Oxford University Press, 2002), 354.

7   **"When we see"**: Langston Hughes, "Howard Man Fighting as Spanish Loyalist," *Baltimore Afro-American*, February 5, 1938.

8   **Rucker offered Hughes**: Faith Berry, *Before and Beyond Harlem: A Biography of Langston Hughes* (New York: Wings Books, 1995), 266.

8   **he felt an artillery bombardment:** Hughes, "Hughes Bombed in Spain"; Hughes, "Madrid Getting Used to Bombs."

8   **"Sounded like the devil's 4th of July!":** Langston Hughes, letter to Louise Thompson, n.d. [ca. 1937], Louise Thompson Patterson papers, box 17, folder 7 (Emory University).

8   **"The Spanish situation":** "Our Stake in Spain," *Baltimore Afro-American*, October 30, 1937.

9   **twenty-three-year-old nurse, Salaria Kea:** "Negro Nurse Leaving for Spanish Service," *New York Amsterdam News*, March 27, 1937; Hughes, *I Wonder as I Wander*, 382; John Gerassi, *The Premature Antifascists: North American Volunteers in the Spanish Civil War, 1936–39: An Oral History* (New York: Praeger, 1986), 43; Bob August, "Salaria Kea and John O'Reilly: Volunteers Who Met and Wed in Spain, 1938," *Cleveland Magazine*, 1975.

10   **she had been in Spain for six months:** "Race Nurse Back from Spanish War Front Says Fascists Won't Win," *Chicago Defender*, May 28, 1938.

11   **"a kind of preview":** Hughes, *I Wonder as I Wander*, 326–28, 347–48.

11   **The officer was Walter Garland:** Hughes, *I Wonder as I Wander*, 366; "Hero of Spanish War Tells Story," *New York Amsterdam News*, November 27, 1937.

12   **"He instilled in me":** Joe Brandt, ed., *Black Americans in the Spanish People's War against Fascism 1936–1939* (New York: New Outlook, n.d., 52–53.

12   **"I have the greatest admiration":** Langston Hughes, "Lieutenant Walter Garland in Command," November 1937, Louise Thompson Patterson papers, box 18, folder 28 (Emory University).

12   **"I couldn't help but think":** Hughes, "Lieutenant Walter Garland in Command."

13   **"Without a declaration of war":** Franklin D. Roosevelt, "Quarantine" speech, October 5, 1937.

13   **Hughes wrote constantly in Spain:** Langston Hughes, "Fights from Other Lands Look to Ohio Man for Food," *Baltimore Afro-American*, January 8, 1938; Langston Hughes, "Pittsburgh Soldier Hero, but Too Bashful to Talk," *Baltimore Afro-American*, January 15, 1938; Langston Hughes, "Harlem Ball Player Now Captain in Spain," *Baltimore Afro-American*, February 12, 1938; Hughes, "Howard Man Fighting as Spanish Loyalist"; "Back from Spain," *New York Amsterdam News*, August 20, 1938; "Harlem Man First of Race Killed in Spain," *Norfolk Journal and Guide*, May 29, 1937; Antony Beevor, *The Battle for Spain: The Spanish Civil War 1936–1939* (New York: Penguin Books, 2006), 274–86; Adam Hochschild, *Spain in Our Hearts: Americans in the Spanish Civil War, 1936–1939* (Boston: Houghton Mifflin Harcourt, 2016), 223–35.

15 **Hughes's poems and profiles:** Langston Hughes, "Love Letter from Spain Addressed to Alabama," Louise Thompson Patterson papers, box 18, folder 12 (Emory University); Langston Hughes, "Postcard from Spain: Addressed to Alabama," Louise Thompson Patterson papers, box 17, folder 17 (Emory University); "Our Stake in Spain."

15 **"wide-awake men of color":** Langston Hughes, "Langston Hughes Tells Poignant Tale of Spain," *Norfolk Journal and Guide*, October 30, 1937.

15 **"all of them here":** Langston Hughes, "Negroes in Spain," October 1937, Louise Thompson Patterson papers, box 18, folder 28 (Emory University).

15 **Wearing uniforms with the insignia:** Langston Hughes, "'Organ Grinder's Swing' Heard above Gunfire in Spain," *Baltimore Afro-American*, November 6, 1937.

15 **"These Negroes in Spain":** Hughes, *I Wonder as I Wander*, 384.

17 **"Unless there is a succession":** Editorial, "Onward Christian Soldiers," *Norfolk Journal and Guide*, July 27, 1935.

17 **"From New York to California":** D. W. McCoy, "Ethiopia," *Atlanta Daily World*, March 14, 1935.

17 **"The Ballad of Ethiopia":** Langston Hughes, "Ballad of Ethiopia," *Baltimore Afro-American*, September 28, 1935.

17 **"I wanted to go to Ethiopia":** Robin D. G. Kelley, *Race Rebels: Culture, Politics, and the Black Working Class* (New York: Free Press, 1994), 124.

17 **"tighten more the chains":** "Spanish Volunteer Returns to U.S.A.," *Chicago Defender*, December 4, 1937.

17 **"Give Franco a hood":** Langston Hughes, "Soldiers from Many Lands United in Spanish Fight," *Baltimore Afro-American*, December 18, 1937.

18 **"to strike a blow":** Ted Poston, "Negroes Heroes in Spanish War, Says I.W.O. Head," *Pittsburgh Courier*, October 9, 1937.

18 **These poems were included:** Langston Hughes, *A New Song* (New York: International Workers Order, 1938).

19 **embarked on a twenty-city:** "300 Welcome Salaria Kee at Reception," *Chicago Defender*, June 18, 1938; Thyra Edwards, "Salaria Kee Returns from Spanish Front," *Chicago Defender*, June 4, 1938; "150 Nurses Attend Banquet Honoring Salaria Kee," *New York Amsterdam News*, May 28, 1938; Marvel Cooke, "'I Would Return to Spain If I Could,' Nurse Says," *New York Amsterdam News*, May 21, 1938.

19 **"Can you imagine that?":** Cooke, "'I Would Return to Spain If I Could,' Nurse Says"; "Race Nurse Back from Spanish War Front Says Fascists Won't Win."

19 **"What is happening there":** Cooke, "'I Would Return to Spain If I Could,' Nurse Says."

19   **"I could not go South"**: Nancy Cunard, "Salaria Kee Plays Hero Role," *Pittsburgh Courier*, January 8, 1938.

20   **peace march in New York City**: "From Negro Americans to the People of Republic Spain," *Call & Post*, September 1, 1938; "Ambulance for Spain to Sail from New York," *New York Amsterdam News*, October 29, 1938; "'Holy War' Row Mars Peace March at 15,000 Parade to Rally in Park," *New York Times*, August 7, 1938.

21   **"Four gangsters met"**: "Four Gangsters Met," *New York Amsterdam News*, October 8, 1938.

21   **"We do not want any secondary Americans"**: Langston Hughes, "Democracy and Me," June 1939, in *The Collected Works of Langston Hughes, Volume 9*, ed. Christopher C. De Santis (Columbia: University of Missouri Press, 2002), 206.

21   **"We do not want a weak"**: Langston Hughes, "Song for Ourselves," Louise Thompson Patterson papers, box 18, folder 22 (Emory University).

22   **Hughes was shocked**: Rampersad, *The Life of Langston Hughes, Volume 1*, 374.

23   **"No men ever"**: Ernest Hemingway, "On the American Dead in Spain," *New Masses*, February 14, 1939.

23   **"if you were against"**: Hochschild, *Spain in Our Hearts*, 351, 355.

23   **"looked and acted as if"**: James Yates, *Mississippi to Madrid: Memoir of a Black American in the Abraham Lincoln Brigade* (Seattle: Open Hand Publishing, 1989), 159.

CHAPTER 2: FIGHTING FOR A CHANCE TO FIGHT

25   **"What, in the final analysis"**: Robert Vann, "Because!: Ten Cardinal Points in Courier's Campaign for Army and Navy Equality," *Pittsburgh Courier*, March 26, 1938.

26   **Davis knew that Black Americans**: Benjamin O. Davis, Jr., *American: An Autobiography* (Washington, D.C.: Smithsonian Institution Scholarly Press, 2000), 65.

26   **Army War College published a report**: Army War College Report, *The Use of Negro Manpower in War* (1925).

28   **"akin to well-meaning"**: Graham Smith, *When Jim Crow Met John Bull: Black American Soldiers in World War II Britain* (London: I. B. Tauris, 1987), 113.

28   **"Leadership is not imbedded"**: Henry Stimson diary entry, September 22, 1941, *Henry L. Stimson, 1867–1950*. The Henry Lewis Stimson

Diaries in the Yale University Library (New Haven: Manuscripts and Archives, Yale University Library, 1973).

28   "If it were a question": Bernard C. Nalty, *The Right to Fight: African-American Marines in World War II* (Washington, D.C.: Marine Corps Historical Center, 1995), 1.

28   "There is no question": Maggie M. Morehouse, *Fighting in the Jim Crow Army: Black Men and Women Remember World War II* (New York: Rowman & Littlefield, 2000), 37.

28   "White officers in general": Mary Penick Motley, *The Invisible Soldier: The Experience of the Black Soldier, World War II* (Detroit: Wayne State University Press, 1987), 75.

29   The army used these attitudes: Ulysses Lee, *The Employment of Negro Troops* (Washington, D.C.: Office of the Chief of Military History, United States Army, 1966), 25–38; Alan L. Gropman, *The Air Force Integrates, 1945–1964* (Washington, D.C.: Smithsonian Institution Scholarly Press, 1998), 3.

29   President Roosevelt asked Congress: Wesley Frank Craven and James Lea Cate, eds., *The Army Air Forces in World War II, Volume Six: Men and Planes* (Washington, D.C.: Office of Air Force History, United States Air Force, 1983), 172–73.

29   "This huge force": "Will a Negro Ever Fly Them?," *Pittsburgh Courier*, December 3, 1938.

29   reprinted a rejection letter: "Barred from U.S. Air Corps," *Baltimore Afro-American*, March 4, 1939.

30   "create an impossible social condition": J. Todd Moye, *Freedom Flyers: The Tuskegee Airmen of World War II* (New York: Oxford University Press, 2010), 14.

30   The *Courier* called the Air Corps: "Will Army Air Corps Continue to Be 'Lily-White'?," *Pittsburgh Courier*, February 4, 1939; "When War Comes!," *Pittsburgh Courier*, February 4, 1939.

30   a handful of Black colleges: Patricia Strickland, *The Putt-Putt Air Force: The Story of the Civilian Pilot Training Program and the War Training Service (1939–1944)* (Washington, D.C.: Department of Transportation, 1970), 39; Robert J. Jakeman, *The Divided Skies: Establishing Segregated Flight Training at Tuskegee, Alabama, 1934–1942* (Tuscaloosa: University of Alabama Press, 1996), 129.

31   Davis envied the pilots: Davis, Jr., *American*, 14.

31   "The Army has consistently discriminated": "Houston, M'Arthur Clash on Army Jim Crow," *Pittsburgh Courier*, September 8, 1934; "Houston Attacks Army Jim-Crowism," *Pittsburgh Courier*, August 18, 1934.

31–32 **"not again silently endure"**: Bernard C. Nalty, *Strength for the Fight: A History of Black Americans in the Military* (New York: Free Press, 1986), 134.

32 **In the first six months**: David F. Krugler, *1919, The Year of Racial Violence: How African Americans Fought Back* (Cambridge: Cambridge University Press, 2014).

32 **"The very uniform"**: Carter G. Woodson, *The Negro in Our History* (Washington, D.C.: Associated Publishers, 1922), 527.

32 *Courier* **readers on February 19, 1938**: Robert Vann, "Courier Letter Starts Drive," *Pittsburgh Courier*, February 19, 1938.

33 **NAACP leaders were divided**: Andrew Buni, *Robert L. Vann of the Pittsburgh Courier: Politics and Black Journalism* (Pittsburgh: University of Pittsburgh Press, 1974), 299–312.

34 **Logan told a congressional committee**: "Text of Statement by Dr. Rayford Logan before Committee," *Pittsburgh Courier*, August 24, 1940; "Dr. Logan Sounds Warning," *Pittsburgh Courier*, August 3, 1940; "Negroes Want Democracy," *Atlanta Daily World*, August 21, 1940.

34 **"want some of the democracy"**: Rawn James, Jr., *The Double V: How Wars, Protest, and Harry Truman Desegregated America's Military* (New York: Bloomsbury Press, 2013), 86–89.

34 **prompted thousands of Black Americans**: Lee, *The Employment of Negro Troops*, 52.

35 **"serve in the same companies"**: James, Jr., *The Double V*, 87.

35 **had finally cracked open**: Gail Buckley, *American Patriots: The Story of Blacks in the Military from the Revolution to Desert Storm* (New York: Random House, 2001), 262.

36 **Draft boards also thwarted**: George Flynn, "Selective Service and American Blacks during World War II," *Journal of Negro History* 69, no. 1 (Winter 1984): 17; "No Negro Draft Board Members in Many States, Says NAACP Survey," *The Crisis*, January 1941, 22; Pete Daniel, "Going among Strangers: Southern Reactions to World War II," *Journal of American History* 77, no. 3 (December 1990): 891.

37 **The** *Courier* **reported**: "Secret Army Order Bared," *Pittsburgh Courier*, November 23, 1940.

37 **"This is a white man's country"**: "Tennessee Governor Asserts Negroes Did Nothing for U.S.," *Atlanta Daily World*, October 29, 1940.

37 **the Army General Classification Test**: Phillip McGuire, "Desegregation of the Armed Forces: Black Leadership, Protest and World War II," *Journal of Negro History* 68, no. 2 (Spring 1983): 148–49.

37   **"the Army had adopted":** Stimson diary entry, May 12, 1942; Phillip Mc-
      Guire, "Desegregation of the Armed Forces."

37   **Secretary of the Navy Frank Knox:** Dennis D. Nelson, *The Integration of
      the Negro into the U.S. Navy* (New York: Farrar, Straus and Young, 1951),
      12–13.

38   **Fifteen mess attendants:** "Mess Attendants Write," *Pittsburgh Courier*,
      October 5, 1940.

38   **"REMEMBER THE THIRTEEN":** "Committee for Participation of Ne-
      groes in the National Defense," *Pittsburgh Courier*, December 21, 1940.

39   **"There is more to all this":** Roy Wilkins, "The U.S. Navy Is for White
      Men," *The Crisis*, September 1940, 279.

39   **Complaints over racial discrimination:** James L. H. Peck, "When Do We
      Fly?," *The Crisis*, December 1940, 376.

40   **"cannot FLY Uncle Sam's planes":** Editorial, "Grounded," *Pittsburgh
      Courier*, December 7, 1940.

40   **sued the War Department:** "Secretary of War Sued by D.C. Youth," *Nor-
      folk Journal and Guide*, February 1, 1941.

40   **"The sooner we learn":** "The Army Again," *Chicago Defender*, February 1,
      1941.

41   **"The catering by our National Party":** William E. Leuchtenburg, *The
      White House Looks South: Franklin D. Roosevelt, Harry S. Truman, Lyndon
      B. Johnson* (Baton Rouge: Louisiana State University, 2005), 127; Richard
      M. Dalfiume, "Military Segregation and the 1940 Presidential Election,"
      Phylon 30, no. 1 (1969); James, Jr., *The Double V*, 82.

41   **"What chance have colored draftees":** "What Chance Have Colored
      Draftees," *Baltimore Afro-American*, October 19, 1940.

42   **"the Negroes are taking advantage":** Stimson diary entry, October 22,
      1940; Richard M. Dalfiume, *Desegregation of the U.S. Armed Forces: Fight-
      ing on Two Fronts, 1939–1953* (Columbia: University of Missouri Press,
      1969), 42.

42   **the "lukewarm" reception:** Davis, Jr., *American*, 67–69.

42   **Davis reported to Tuskegee:** Davis, Jr., *American*, 67–69.

43   **He closely followed:** Davis, Jr., *American*, 67.

43   **"In 1941 the Army":** Davis, Jr., *American*, 69.

CHAPTER 3: MARCH ON WASHINGTON

45   **"If Negroes are going to get anything":** A. Philip Randolph, "Let's March
      on Capital 10,000 Strong, Urges Leader of Porters," *Pittsburgh Courier*,
      January 25, 1941.

45   "My friends, this is not": Franklin D. Roosevelt, "Fireside Chat," December 29, 1940.

46   "The people of Europe": Roosevelt, "Fireside Chat," December 29, 1940.

46   "There was no other group": Jervis Anderson, *A. Philip Randolph: A Biographical Portrait* (New York: Harcourt Brace Jovanovich, 1973), 224–27.

47   Randolph's success as a labor leader: Anderson, *A. Philip Randolph*, 30; David Welky, *Marching across the Color Line: A. Philip Randolph and Civil Rights in the World War II Era* (New York: Oxford University Press, 2014), 15.

48   Alongside another young radical: Anderson, *A. Philip Randolph*, 77, 83, 98.

48   "to forget our special grievances": W. E. B. Du Bois, *The Crisis*, July 1918, 111.

48   Randolph and Owen struck a very different tone: Welky, *Marching across the Color Line*, 22–23.

48   He initially felt the same way about World War II: Lee Finkle, *Forum for Protest: The Black Press during World War II* (Rutherford, NJ: Fairleigh Dickinson University Press, 1975), 199–200.

49   Black workers would be left out: Herbert Garfinkel, *When Negroes March: The March on Washington Movement in the Organizational Politics for FEPC* (Glencoe, IL: Free Press, 1959), 17.

49   "When these dark-skinned craftsmen": Lester Granger, "Barriers to Negro War Employment," *Annals of the American Academy of Political and Social Science* 223 (September 1942): 74.

50   While defense work: Garfinkel, *When Negroes March*, 17; Beth Tompkins Bates, *Pullman Porters and the Rise of Protest Politics in Black America, 1925–1945* (Chapel Hill: University of North Carolina Press, 2001), 151.

50   "Negroes are not getting anywhere": Randolph, "Let's March on Capital 10,000 Strong."

51   "Power is the active principle": Randolph, "Let's March on Capital 10,000 Strong."

51   "To get 10,000 Negroes": "A. Philip Randolph," *Chicago Defender*, February 8, 1941.

51   "It was Randolph's immense prestige": Garfinkel, *When Negroes March*, 39.

51   The march idea gained momentum: David Lucander, *Winning the War for Democracy: The March on Washington Movement, 1941–1946* (Urbana: University of Illinois Press, 2014), 22–30.

52   "Let the Negro masses speak!": A. Philip Randolph, "Let the Negro Masses Speak," *The Black Worker* 7, no. 3 (March 1941).

52   "Is Jim-Crow in Washington?": Welky, *Marching across the Color Line*, 56.

53   "We are simply fighting": Randolph, "Let the Negro Masses Speak."

53   "We will fight for Uncle Sam!": Randolph, "Let the Negro Masses Speak."

53   **"We call not upon"**: Randolph, "Let the Negro Masses Speak."

54   **"Nobody expects 10,000 Negroes"**: Randolph, "Let's March on Capital 10,000 Strong."

54   **"One individual marching"**: Opinion, *Baltimore Afro-American*, August 23, 1941.

54   **By the end of May**: A. Philip Randolph, letter to Franklin D. Roosevelt, May 29, 1941, Official File 391: Marches on Washington, Franklin D. Roosevelt Presidential Library; Anderson, *A. Philip Randolph*, 251–56; Bates, *Pullman Porters and the Rise of Protest Politics in Black America*, 154.

55   **Randolph also pressured the White House**: Anderson, *A. Philip Randolph*, 251–57; Bates, *Pullman Porters and the Rise of Protest Politics in Black America*, 152–54; "100,000 in March to Capital," *New York Amsterdam News*, May 31, 1941.

55   **Roosevelt agreed to meet**: Anderson, *A. Philip Randolph*, 251–57; Bates, *Pullman Porters and the Rise of Protest Politics in Black America*, 152–54.

56   **"'Mr. President, time is running on'"**: Anderson, *A. Philip Randolph*, 256–58.

59   **"you gotta stop Randolph"**: Lucander, *Winning the War for Democracy*, 36.

59   **Executive Order 8802 was warmly received**: Bates, *Pullman Porters and the Rise of Protest Politics in Black America*, 148; Lionel Kimble Jr., *A New Deal for Bronzeville: Housing, Employment and Civil Rights in Black Chicago, 1935–1955* (Carbondale: Southern Illinois University, 2015), 82; Lucander, *Winning the War for Democracy*, 6, 38; Anderson, *A. Philip Randolph*, 261; Garfinkel, *When Negroes March*, 63; "A. Philip Randolph, Leader," *New York Amsterdam News*, July 12, 1941.

60   **Black applicants continued to be turned away**: Andrew Kersten, *Race, Jobs, and the War: The FEPC in the Midwest, 1941–46* (Urbana: University of Illinois Press, 2000), 22, 98.

60   **they often faced resistance**: Kersten, *Race, Jobs, and the War*, 22, 98.

61   **the FEPC lacked the people**: Welky, *Marching across the Color Line*, 84–5; Kersten, *Race, Jobs, and the War*, 19; "The Negro's War," *Fortune*, June 1942, 79; Earl Brown, "American Negroes and the War," *Harper's Magazine*, April 1942, 552.

61   **"the most dangerous force in existence"**: James Wolfinger, *Philadelphia Divided: Race and Politics in the City of Brotherly Love* (Chapel Hill: University of North Carolina Press, 2007), 161.

62   **"the presence of the Negro"**: Bates, *Pullman Porters and the Rise of Protest Politics in Black America*, 151–52; Glenda Elizabeth Gilmore, *Defying*

Dixie: The Radical Roots of Civil Rights, 1919–1950 (New York: W. W. Norton, 2009), 364.

62   **"This victory cannot be overestimated"**: Gilmore, *Defying Dixie*, 364.

62   **"You possess power"**: Randolph, "Let the Negro Masses Speak."

63   **"A New Negro has arisen"**: Bates, *Pullman Porters and the Rise of Protest Politics in Black America*, 6.

63   **"The Negro masses awakened"**: Lucander, *Winning the War for Democracy*, 25.

CHAPTER 4: AT WAR DOWN SOUTH

65   **"Unless some action"**: Thurgood Marshall, "Ask Conviction in Gurdon, Ark. Soldiers Case," *Chicago Defender*, January 3, 1942.

66   **"I am taking it upon myself"**: Sydney Rotheny, letter to Walter White, September 19, 1941, NAACP Papers, group II, series B, folder 001537-011-0301.

67   **Marshall saw seeking justice:** Juan Williams, *Thurgood Marshall: American Revolutionary* (New York: Three Rivers Press, 1998), 17–20, 36; Larry S. Gibson, *Young Thurgood: The Making of a Supreme Court Justice* (Amherst, NY: Prometheus Books, 2012), 36–38, 67–73; Ron Cassie, "Justice for All," *Baltimore*, https://www.baltimoremagazine.com/2017/8/7/justice-for-all-50-years-after-thurgood-marshall-supreme-court-confirmation.

68   **Houston's goal was to:** Williams, *Thurgood Marshall*, 53–60; Oliver Allen, "Chief Counsel for Equality," *Life*, June 13, 1955.

68   **Being a civil rights lawyer:** Howard Ball, *A Defiant Life: Thurgood Marshall and the Persistence of Racism in America* (New York: Crown, 1998), 72; Williams, *Thurgood Marshall*, 106–8.

69   **Marshall's appearance in these small towns:** Ball, *A Defiant Life*, 72; Williams, *Thurgood Marshall*, 106–8.

69   **the men of the 94th Engineer Battalion:** Ulysses Lee, *The Employment of Negro Troops* (Washington, D.C.: Office of the Chief of Military History, United States Army, 1966), 352–53; Mary Penick Motley, *The Invisible Soldier: The Experience of the Black Soldier, World War II* (Detroit: Wayne State University Press, 1987), 42.

70   **Sensational stories spread:** Lee, *The Employment of Negro Troops*, 352–53; Motley, *The Invisible Soldier*, 42.

71   **Unlike many white army officers:** Motley, *The Invisible Soldier*, 40; see affidavits in NAACP Papers, group II, series B, folder 001537-024-0811.

73 **the example of Felix Hall:** "Clarence Woods Jr. affidavit," September 8, 1941, NAACP Papers, group II, series B, folder 001537-024-0811; "Identify Body of Soldier Found Hung Near Camp," *Chicago Defender*, April 19, 1941; Alexa Hall, "A Lynching Kept Out of Sight," *Washington Post*, September 2, 2016.

73 **By daybreak, over two hundred:** "Clarence Woods Jr. affidavit"; Motley, *The Invisible Soldier*, 46–47.

74 **Within the NAACP office:** "Clarence Woods Jr. affidavit"; "Twist," letter to Aunt Mildred, August 17, 1941, NAACP Papers, group II, series B, folder 001537-024-0811; Theodis Gay, letter to Walter White, August 19, 1941, NAACP Papers, group II, series B, folder 001537-024-0879.

75 **NAACP chapter in Detroit organized:** "Stop Army Brutality!!" flyer, August 24, 1941, NAACP Papers, group II, series B, folder 001537-024-1045; office memorandum, August 27, 1941, NAACP Papers, group II, series B, folder 001537-024-0879.

75 TERROR REIGN SWEEPS: "Terror Reign Sweeps Nation's Army Camps," *New York Amsterdam News*, August 23, 1941.

75 **"The wave of beating":** "The Negro Soldier," *Chicago Defender*, August 30, 1941.

75 **"While you were on the high seas":** "An Open Letter to the President of the United States," *Pittsburgh Courier*, August 23, 1941.

76 **"I am ashamed of you":** "William K. Moseley affidavit," October 22, 1941, NAACP Papers, group II, series B, folder 001537-024-0811.

76 **"understanding the attitude":** James Burran, "Racial Violence in the South during World War II" (PhD diss., University of Tennessee, 1977), 54.

76 **"unjustified demonstration" by Black troops:** Henry Stimson, letter to Walter White, November 7, 1941, NAACP Papers, group II, series B, folder 001537-024-0879.

77 **The troops were fortunate:** "5 Appointed to Ft. Custer Court Martial Body," *Chicago Defender*, December 20, 1941.

77 **Two years after surviving Gurdon:** Motley, *The Invisible Soldier*, 40.

79 **The three Black messmen:** Charles Hurd, "Reuben James Hit," *New York Times*, November 1, 1941; "Men Describe Loss of Reuben James," *New York Times*, November 25, 1941; "Reuben James' Men Killed by Destroyer's Depth Bombs," *Washington Post*, November 26, 1941; Robert Cressman, "Reuben James I (DD-245)," Naval History and Heritage Command, October 26, 2016, https://www.history.navy.mil/research/histories/ship-histories/danfs/r/reuben-james-i.html; Ken Ringle, "The Friends on the Good Reuben James," *Washington Post*, October 5, 1991.

79   **"I am grieved"**: Winston Churchill, telegram to Franklin D. Roosevelt, November 2, 1941, in *Churchill and Roosevelt, Volume 1: The Complete Correspondence*, ed. Warren Kimball (Princeton, NJ: Princeton University Press, 2015), 265.

80   **"Have you heard of a ship"**: Woody Guthrie, "Sinking of the Reuben James," 1942, MCA Music Publishing.

80   **Annie Johnson had just come home:** "Mother Says She 'Felt' Son Lost on Reuben James," *Norfolk Journal and Guide*, November 15, 1941.

81   **"Nazi torpedoes make no distinction"**: "Exclusive! Courier Cameraman Visits with Relatives of First American Negroes to Die Defending Nation," *Pittsburgh Courier*, November 15, 1941.

81   **"The Navy has made flunkies of Negroes"**: "Navy 'Cries' for Recruits: Knox, Nimitz Won't Change Color Policy," *Pittsburgh Courier*, December 6, 1941.

82   **Writing back to Walter White:** Thurgood Marshall, memoranda to office, November 17, 22, and 25, 1941, NAACP Papers, group II, series B, folder 001455-005-0243; Williams, *Thurgood Marshall*, 106.

82   **"I am complaining"**: W. F. R., letter to editor, *Chicago Defender*, October 11, 1941.

CHAPTER 5: REMEMBER PEARL HARBOR, REMEMBER SIKESTON TOO

85   **"Is it fair"**: Editorial, "A Hero from the Galley," *Pittsburgh Courier*, January 3, 1942.

86   **Miller rushed to his battle station:** Thomas Cutrer and T. Michael Parrish, *Doris Miller, Pearl Harbor, and the Birth of the Civil Rights Movement* (College Station: Texas A&M University Press, 2018), 18–25; Juliete Parker, *A Man Named Doris* (Maitland, FL: Xulon Press, 2003); Walter Lord, *Day of Infamy* (New York: Henry Holt, 1957); Gordon W. Prange, *At Dawn We Slept: The Untold Story of Pearl Harbor* (New York: McGraw-Hill, 1981).

87   **"It wasn't hard"**: Cutrer and Parrish, *Doris Miller, Pearl Harbor, and the Birth of the Civil Rights Movement*, 22.

88   **24 Black messmen:** Richard E. Miller, *The Messman Chronicles: African-Americans in the U.S. Navy, 1932–1943* (Annapolis: Naval Institute Press, 2004), 181.

88   **"a date which will live in infamy"**: Franklin D. Roosevelt, "Joint Address to Congress Leading to a Declaration of War Against Japan," December 8, 1941.

89   **"These men want to fight"**: "NAACP Asks Navy to End Segregation,"
      Chicago Defender, December 20, 1941; "A Plea to Sec'y Knox," *Chicago
      Defender*, December 27, 1941.

90   **"The Army did not create the problem"**: Ulysses Lee, *The Employment of
      Negro Troops* (Washington, D.C.: Office of the Chief of Military History,
      United States Army, 1966), 142.

90   **"The War Department has been arbitrary"**: "War United All America,"
      Baltimore Afro-American, December 13, 1941.

91   AWAKE WHITE AMERICA: "Awake White America, the Hour Is at Hand!,"
      Chicago Defender, December 13, 1941.

91   **"Don't you accept American citizens"**: "Army Rejects Negroes, First to
      Volunteer in Chicago," *Chicago Defender*, December 13, 1941.

91   **fighting for "a new world"**: Roy Wilkins, "Now Is the Time Not to Be
      Silent," *The Crisis*, January 1942, 7.

92   **Walter White wrote to Secretary Knox**: Walter White, letter to Frank
      Knox, December 26, 1941, NAACP Papers, folder 001535-017-0464.

92   **The sacrifices Black messmen made**: Jim Hewlett, "Brothers in Navy
      Lose Lives at Pearl Harbor," *Chicago Defender*, January 17, 1942; Emory
      O. Jackson, "Jap Bombs Claim Life of Birmingham," *Atlanta Daily World*,
      December 20, 1941; "Birmingham Honors Pearl Harbor Hero," *Chicago
      Defender*, January 17, 1942; "Memorial Services at Church Tribute to
      Ellsberry's Life," *Birmingham News*, January 5, 1942; Jesse Chambers,
      "Pearl Harbor Day: Remembering the First Black Alabamian to Die in
      World War II," *Birmingham Real-Time News*, December 7, 2014, https://
      www.al.com/news/birmingham/2014/12/post_158.html.

93   **The memorial for Private Robert Brooks**: "Honor the Brave," *Philadel-
      phia Tribune*, January 24, 1942.

94   **"In death there is no grade or rank"**: "The Voice of Real Democracy,"
      Norfolk Journal and Guide, January 24, 1942.

95   **"Would you run over a soldier?"**: H. T. S., letter to Walter White, January
      13, 1942, NAACP Papers, folder 001459-026-0709.

95   **"You would think Japan"**: "Night of Horror Vividly Recalled," n.d.,
      NAACP Papers, folder 001459-026-0709.

96   **In the early morning hours**: Dominic J. Capeci, Jr., *The Lynching of Cleo
      Wright* (Lexington: University Press of Kentucky, 1998); Dominic J. Capeci,
      Jr., "The Lynching of Cleo Wright: Federal Protection of Constitutional
      Rights during World War II," *Journal of American History* 72, no. 4 (March
      1986): 859–87.

97   **the lynching of Cleo Wright**: Walter White, telegram to FDR, January 26,
      1941, NAACP Papers, folder 001527-027-1043; "Sikeston Disgraces Itself,"

New York Times, January 27, 1942; "Missouri Savages Set Negro Afire in Sabbath Lynching," *Call & Post*, January 31, 1942; "Don't Forget Missouri," *New York Amsterdam News*, February 21, 1942.

97 **In Missouri, local NAACP branches:** Capeci, Jr., *The Lynching of Cleo Wright*, 38–66; "Remember Pearl Harbor . . . and Sikeston Too!," *Chicago Defender*, March 14, 1942.

98 **In Detroit, tensions boiled over:** LeRoy White, "Hundreds Stand Guard as Tenants Move at Detroit," *Atlanta Daily World*, May 1, 1942; "Tenants Win Fight for Detroit Project," *Chicago Defender*, February 14, 1942; "U.S. Backs Race Claim to Housing Project," *Chicago Defender*, March 14, 1942.

98 **"I will take my fighting and dying":** "Negroes Tore Up Draft Cards after Detroit Riot," *Call & Post*, March 21, 1942.

98 **"Detroit serves as a lesson":** "The Lesson of Sojourner Truth," *Pittsburgh Courier*, May 9, 1942.

CHAPTER 6: DOUBLE VICTORY

101 **"White folks would rather lose":** Roy Wilkins, "Watchtower," *New York Amsterdam News*, April 18, 1942.

101 **"I suggest that while":** James G. Thompson, "Should I Sacrifice to Live 'Half-American'?," *Pittsburgh Courier*, January 31, 1942.

102 **launched the Double V campaign:** "The Courier's Double V for a Double Victory Campaign Gets Country-Wide Support," *Pittsburgh Courier*, February 14, 1942.

102 **"double battle, against slavery":** Philip S. Foner and Yuval Taylor, eds., *Frederick Douglass: Selected Speeches and Writings* (Chicago: Chicago Review Press, 2000), 533.

102 **"battle against the forces of hell":** W. E. B. Du Bois, "Returning Soldiers," *The Crisis*, May 1919, 13.

103 **53 percent of Americans:** Elizabeth D. Samet, *Looking for the Good War: American Amnesia and the Violent Pursuit of Happiness* (New York: Farrar, Straus and Giroux, 2021), 55.

103 ***Life* magazine noted:** Kenneth D. Rose, *Myth and the Greatest Generation: A Social History of Americans in World War II* (New York: Routledge, 2007), 64.

103 **"we were fighting Germany":** Arthur Miller, "The Face in the Mirror: Anti-Semitism Then and Now," *New York Times Book Review*, October 14, 1984.

103 **"You, who have roots in Europe":** A. J. Liebling, "Picture of Ernie," *Esquire*, May 1, 1947, 164.

103   **"99 of 100 people"**: Mary Jarrell, ed., *Randall Jarrell's Letters: An Autobiographical and Literary Selection* (Boston: Houghton Mifflin, 1985), 103; Paul Fussell, *Wartime: Understanding and Behavior in the Second World War* (New York: Oxford University Press, 1989), 137–39.

104   **"as they have been in America"**: Pete Daniel, "Going among Strangers: Southern Reactions to World War II," *Journal of American History* 77, no. 3 (December 1990): 892.

104   **"White men are so fixed"**: Charles W. Eagles, "Two 'Double V's': Jonathan Daniels, FDR, and Race Relations during World War II," *North Carolina Historical Review* 59, no. 3 (July 1982): 255.

105   **"would rather not have a vital radio message"**: Wilkins, "Watchtower."

105   **At training camps**: Thomas A. Guglielmo, *Divisions: A New History of Racism and Resistance in America's World War II Military* (New York: Oxford University Press, 2021), 216.

105   **the Red Cross's policy**: Thomas A. Guglielmo, "'Red Cross, Double Cross': Race and America's World War II–Era Blood Donor Service," *Journal of American History* 97, no. 1 (June 2010): 63–90.

105   **In a poem dedicated to Doris Miller**: Gwendolyn Brooks, "Negro Hero (To Suggest Dorie Miller)," *Common Ground* 5 (1945): 45.

106   **the Double Victory campaign demanded**: Jonathan Daniels, "New Patterns for Old," *Survey Graphic* XXI (November 1942): 487; Patrick S. Washburn, *A Question of Sedition: The Federal Government's Investigation of the Black Press during World War II* (New York: Oxford University Press, 1986), 80–81.

106   **Hoover tried to indict**: "Cowing the Negro Press," *Pittsburgh Courier*, March 14, 1942.

107   **President Roosevelt shared**: Franklin D. Roosevelt, "Fireside Chat: On Sacrifice," April 28, 1942; Washburn, *A Question of Sedition*, 80–81; Wilkins, "Watchtower"; Rawn James, Jr., *The Double V: How Wars, Protest, and Harry Truman Desegregated America's Military* (New York: Bloomsbury Press, 2013), 142.

107   **Pegler accused the *Chicago Defender***: Westbrook Pegler, "Fair Enough," *New York World-Telegram*, April 28, 1942.

107   ***Chicago Defender* publisher John Sengstacke**: Washburn, *A Question of Sedition*, 87–97; Ethan Michaeli, *The Defender: How the Legendary Black Newspaper Changed America* (Boston: Houghton Mifflin Harcourt, 2016), 245–49.

108   **He told the attorney general**: Washburn, *A Question of Sedition*, 87–97; Michaeli, *The Defender*, 245–49.

109   **Black editors felt the burden**: Lee Finkle, *Forum for Protest: The Black Press during World War II* (Rutherford, NJ: Fairleigh Dickinson University Press, 1975), 118–22, 148–154; Gerald Gill, "Afro-American Opposition to the United States' Wars of the Twentieth Century: Dissent,

Discontent and Disinterest" (PhD diss., Howard University, 1985), 282; "Reveal Race War Apathy," *New York Amsterdam News*, January 17, 1942; E. Washington Rhodes, "The Negro Press Takes Up Its Burden," *Brown American*, Spring–Summer 1942, 10.

110 **Morehouse College graduate Lewis Jones:** Finkle, *Forum for Protest*, 122.

110 **Almost overnight, Doris Miller became:** "'Messman Hero' Identified," *Pittsburgh Courier*, March 14, 1942; "How About Dorie Miller?," *New York Amsterdam News*, June 20, 1942; Juliete Parker, *A Man Named Doris* (Maitland, FL: Xulon Press, 2003), 88–89; Thomas Cutrer and T. Michael Parrish, *Doris Miller, Pearl Harbor, and the Birth of the Civil Rights Movement* (College Station: Texas A&M University Press, 2018), 42.

111 **Miller received the Navy Cross:** Cutrer and Parrish, *Doris Miller, Pearl Harbor, and the Birth of the Civil Rights Movement*, 43; "Dorie Miller Given Navy Cross," *Pittsburgh Courier*, June 6, 1942.

CHAPTER 7: DIRTY WORK IN DISTANT LANDS

113 **"When some people decry":** John Virtue, *The Black Soldiers Who Built the Alaska Highway: A History of Four U.S. Army Regiments in the North, 1942–1943* (Jefferson, NC: McFarland & Co., 2013), 158–60.

113 **"This war is a new kind of war":** Franklin D. Roosevelt, "Fireside Chat," February 23, 1942.

114 **"The Pacific situation is now very grave":** William Kimball, *Churchill and Roosevelt: The Complete Correspondence, Volume 1* (Princeton, NJ: Princeton University Press, 2015), 390.

115 **the 96th Engineer General Service Regiment:** "Veteran Says It's Pure Hell in New Guinea," *Chicago Defender*, November 27, 1943; "Negro Troops in New Guinea Win General's Praise," *Call & Post*, June 5, 1943.

115 **Aboard the USS *Lexington*:** "Heroic Sailor in Coral Sea Battle Wins Navy Medal," *Chicago Defender*, February 13, 1943.

116 **"You've had a part":** Ulysses Lee, *The Employment of Negro Troops* (Washington, D.C.: Office of the Chief of Military History, United States Army, 1966), 602; "Negro Troops in New Guinea Win General's Praise."

117 **"The effective defense of Alaska":** Douglas Brinkley, "The Alcan Highway," in William E. Griggs, *The World War II Black Regiment That Built the Alaska Military Highway: A Photographic History*, ed. Philip J. Merrill (Jackson: University of Mississippi Press, 2002), 8.

117 **Black soldiers would "remain and settle":** Virtue, *The Black Soldiers Who Built the Alaska Highway*, 57–58; Charles Hendricks, "Race Relations and the Contributions of Minority Troops in Alaska: A Challenge to the Status

Quo?," in *Alaska at War, 1941–1945: The Forgotten War Remembered*, ed. Fern Chandonnet (Fairbanks: University of Alaska Press, 2007), 277.

118   **Sturdevant, too, did not want:** Virtue, *The Black Soldiers Who Built the Alaska Highway*, 57–58; Hendricks, "Race Relations and the Contributions of Minority Troops in Alaska."

119   **"It was modern-day slavery":** Virtue, *The Black Soldiers Who Built the Alaska Highway*, 130–31, 141; Christine and Dennis McClure, *We Fought the Road* (Fairbanks, AK: Epicenter Press, 2017).

119   **"Have trouble getting them to work":** Kenneth S. Coates and William R. Morrison, "Soldier-Workers: The U.S. Army Corps of Engineers and the Northwest Defense Projects, 1942–1946," *Pacific Historical Review* 62, no. 3 (August 1993): 294.

119   **"a sword pointed":** Virtue, *The Black Soldiers Who Built the Alaska Highway*, 158–60.

119   **"the world's greatest monument":** Claude Albert Barnett, "4,000 Negro Heroes Brave Arctic Blasts to Build U.S. 'Glory Road' to Alaska," *Chicago Defender*, February 6, 1943; "Reveal Negroes Help Build Alaska Highway," *Atlanta Daily World*, November 20, 1942.

120   **"try to imagine a modern highway":** Herbert Frisby, "Frisby Bumps 1600 Miles up Alcan Hi-way," *Baltimore Afro-American*, September 4, 1943; Herbert Frisby, "Alaska Calls Highway We Built 'The Negro Road,'" *Baltimore Afro-American*, September 30, 1944.

CHAPTER 8: TUSKEGEE TAKES FLIGHT

121   **"The nation can no longer":** "The Army Air Corps," *Chicago Defender*, April 17, 1943.

122   **"In past wars":** "First Negro Class Given Commissions at Tuskegee School," *Southeast Air Corps Training Center News*, March 14, 1942.

124   **von Kimble ordered white officers:** J. Todd Moye, *Freedom Flyers: The Tuskegee Airmen of World War II* (New York: Oxford University Press, 2010), 85–88; Benjamin O. Davis, Jr., *American: An Autobiography* (Washington, D.C.: Smithsonian Institution Scholarly Press, 2000), 75–77; "George S. 'Spanky' Roberts," CAF Rise Above, https://cafriseabove.org /george-s-spanky-roberts.

125   **When news of the beating:** Moye, *Freedom Flyers*, 87–88.

125   **It was also hard work:** Moye, *Freedom Flyers*, 59–60; Davis, Jr., *American*, 84–86.

126   **Black women playing a central role:** "Kitchen Aprons 'Packed Away' for Duration," *Pittsburgh Courier*, February 13, 1943.

127   **pilots turned to Black meteorologists:** Gerald A. White Jr., "Tuskegee
       (Weather) Airmen: Black Meteorologists in World War II," *Air Power History* 53, no. 2 (Summer 2006): 20–31.

127   **Lieutenant Norma Greene:** Davis, Jr., *American*, 91.

128   **"The race question is getting worse":** "Tony" (Almeria Plaskett Roberts),
       letter to Mother and Dad, September 17, 1942, NAACP Papers, folder
       0015737-025-0604; Richard B. Collins, letter to Walter White, September
       26, 1942, NAACP Papers, folder 0015737-025-0604.

128   **"They are soul-sick":** "Blame Command for Low Morale at Tuskegee
       Base," *Pittsburgh Courier*, February 20, 1943.

129   **They recorded the bloodshed:** William Hastie, "A Report on Civilian
       Violence against Negro Soldiers," May 29, 1943, NAACP Papers, folder
       001457-021-0485; William H. Hastie and Thurgood Marshall, "Negro
       Discrimination and the Need for Federal Action," *Lawyers Guild Review*
       2, no. 6 (November 1942): 21–23.

130   **"You have embarked":** Paul Sparrow, "A Veterans Day to Remember: 11/11/
       42," Franklin D. Roosevelt Presidential Library and Museum, https://fdr
       .blogs.archives.gov/2017/11/08/a-veterans-day-to-remember-11-11-42; Nor-
       man Gelb, *Desperate Venture: The Story of Operation Torch, the Allied Inva-
       sion of North Africa* (New York: William Morrow & Co., 1992).

130   **"Now this is not the end":** Winston Churchill, "The End of the Begin-
       ning" speech, November 10, 1942.

131   **"The success of the combat unit":** "Flying 99th Anxious to Clash with
       Foe," *Chicago Defender*, December 19, 1942.

131   **"The racial impositions":** William Hastie, memo to Secretary of War,
       January 5, 1943, NARA Record Group 107, Dec. file 291.2, box 95.

131   **"the sincerity and depth":** Hastie, memo to Secretary of War, January 5,
       1943; Ulysses Lee, *The Employment of Negro Troops* (Washington, D.C.:
       Office of the Chief of Military History, United States Army, 1966), 172;
       Moye, *Freedom Flyers*, 90–91.

132   **Hastie's anger with the military:** Charlie and Ann Cooper, *Tuskegee's
       Heroes* (Osceola, WI: MBI Publishing, 1996), 69; Lee, *The Employment of
       Negro Troops*, 433.

CHAPTER 9: WAR WORK

133   **"We want the whole world":** Andrew Kersten, *Race, Jobs, and the War:
       The FEPC in the Midwest, 1941–46* (Urbana: University of Illinois Press,
       2000), 101.

134   **Randolph entered the arena:** Herbert Garfinkel, *When Negroes March:*

The March on Washington Movement in the Organizational Politics for FEPC (Glencoe, IL: Free Press, 1959), 86–96; Beth Tompkins Bates, *Pullman Porters and the Rise of Protest Politics in Black America, 1925–1945* (Chapel Hill: University of North Carolina Press, 2001), 164–65; "18,000 People Jam Madison Square Garden to Bury Race's 'Uncle Toms,'" *Philadelphia Tribune*, June 27, 1942; George McCray, "12,000 in Chicago Voice Demands for Democracy," *Chicago Defender*, July 4, 1942.

135   **"We found unfair employment practices"**: Louis Ruchames, *Race, Jobs, and Politics: The Story of the FEPC* (Westport, CT: Negro Universities Press, 1952), 31.

135   **"war order, and not a social document"**: Ruchames, *Race, Jobs, and Politics*, 29.

135   **"There is no power"**: Roi Ottley, *New World A-Coming: Inside Black America* (Boston: Houghton Mifflin, 1943), 303.

136   **"The old slave masters"**: "Ask Ethridge Ouster," *Chicago Defender*, July 25, 1942.

136   **"very definitely that the South"**: "Ask Ethridge Ouster."

136   **Roosevelt dealt a severe blow**: Ruchames, *Race, Jobs, and Politics*, 46–47; Kersten, *Race, Jobs, and the War*, 38–41.

137   **Randolph had reason to be angry**: Ruchames, *Race, Jobs, and Politics*, 46–47; Kersten, *Race, Jobs, and the War*, 38–41; John Beecher, "This Is the Picture," *Common Ground* 4 (Summer 1943): 16.

138   **"This is our war"**: Quintard Taylor, *In Search of the Racial Frontier: African Americans in the American West, 1528–1990* (New York: W. W. Norton, 1998), 260–61.

138   RACIAL DISCRIMINATION IS SABOTAGE: David Lucander, *Winning the War for Democracy: The March on Washington Movement, 1941–1946* (Urbana: University of Illinois Press, 2014), 109–10.

139   **The barriers to defense work**: Robert C. Weaver, *Negro Labor: A National Problem* (New York: Harcourt, Brace and Company, 1946), 80, 121.

140   **Each of these numbers**: Ronald Takaki, *Double Victory: A Multicultural History of America in World War II* (New York: Little, Brown and Company, 2001), 43; "Local Veterans Honored on 75th Anniversary of D-Day," *Daily Local News*, June 6, 2019, https://www.dailylocal.com/2019/06/06/local-veterans-honored-on-75th-anniversary-of-d-day; Sherma Berger Gluck, *Rosie the Riveter Revisited: Women, the War and Social Change* (Boston: Twayne Publishers, 1987), 23.

141   **A *Chicago Defender* profile**: "WAACS Make First Public Bow in Style at Fort Des Moines, Iowa," *Chicago Defender*, August 15, 1942; "Segregation Rules WAAC Training Camp," *Chicago Defender*, January 16, 1943.

141   "I wanted to prove": Sandra M. Bolzenius, *Glory in Their Spirit: How Four Black Women Took On the Army during World War II* (Champaign: University of Illinois Press, 2018), 23.

141   "We WACs are": George McCray, "The Labor Front," *Chicago Defender*, November 28, 1942.

142   "Negroes on one side!": Bolzenius, *Glory in Their Spirit*, 26, 28; Charity Adams Earley, *One Woman's Army: A Black Officer Remembers the WAC* (College Station: Texas A&M University Press, 2000), 44, 187.

142   Black WACs were allowed: Bolzenius, *Glory in Their Spirit*, 26, 28.

142   Pauli Murray termed "Jane Crow": Rosalind Rosenberg, *Jane Crow: The Life of Pauli Murray* (New York: Oxford University Press, 2017).

142   "I survived in a state": Earley, *One Woman's Army*, 44, 187.

143   bathrooms at the Western Electric Company: Alexander Allen, "Western Electric's Backward Step," *Opportunity* 22 (Summer 1944): 108–11, 140–43.

144   more than one hundred strikes: James Wolfinger, "World War II Hate Strikes," *The Encyclopedia of Strikes in American History*, ed. Aaron Brenner et al. (New York: Routledge, 2009), 126; "War Plant Squelches Hate Strike by White Women," *Chicago Defender*, July 31, 1943; Kersten, *Race, Jobs, and the War*, 53; "1200 White Workers at Timken Roller on Strike over Promotion of Negroes," *Call &Post*, March 20, 1943; James Reid, "War Labor Board's Appeasement Policy Scored," *Pittsburgh Courier*, March 27, 1943.

144   "The mouldering old Gulf seaport": John Dos Passos, *State of the Nation* (Boston: Houghton Mifflin, 1944), 92.

145   "It is pitiful to see": Bruce Nelson, "Organized Labor and the Struggle for Black Equality in Mobile during World War II," *Journal of American History* 80, no. 3 (December 1993): 952–88; James Albert Burran, "Racial Violence in the South during World War II" (PhD diss., University of Tennessee, 1977), 117.

145   a mob of four thousand: Nelson, "Organized Labor and the Struggle for Black Equality in Mobile during World War II"; Burran, "Racial Violence in the South during World War II," 104–28; Shirley Ann Moore, "Getting There, Being There: African-American Migration to Richmond, California, 1910–1945," in *The Great Migration in Historical Perspective: New Dimensions of Race, Class, and Gender*, ed. Joe William Trotter Jr. (Bloomington: Indiana University Press, 1991), 115.

146   Although the separate shipways: Nelson, "Organized Labor and the Struggle for Black Equality in Mobile during World War II"; "Surrender in Mobile," *Pittsburgh Courier*, June 19, 1943; John LeFlore, "Workers Defy Threat of Riot, Break Record," *Chicago Defender*, June 10, 1944.

147 **Packard stood out:** Harvard Sitikoff, *Toward Freedom Land: The Long Struggle for Racial Equality in America* (Lexington: University Press of Kentucky, 2010), 46; Charles K. Hyde, *Arsenal of Democracy: The American Automobile Industry in World War II* (Detroit: Wayne State University Press, 2013), 182–84; Robert Shogan and Tom Craig, *The Detroit Race Riot: A Study in Violence* (Philadelphia: Chilton Books, 1964), 28.

147 **Black war workers in Detroit:** Beth T. Bates, "'Double V for Victory' Mobilizes Black Detroit, 1941–1946," in *Freedom North: Black Freedom Struggles outside the South, 1940–1980*, eds. Jeanne F. Theoharis and Komozi Woodard (New York: Palgrave Macmillan, 2003), 26–30; Hyde, *Arsenal of Democracy*, 184; Walter White, *A Man Called White* (Athens and London: University of Georgia Press, 1995), 225.

148 **"White anger must be reckoned with":** "Hitler's Helpers," *Baltimore Afro-American*, June 10, 1943; Harry McAlpin, "Nazis Find 'Soft Underbelly' of U.S.," *Chicago Defender*, June 12, 1943.

148 **"American boys will die":** "Blames Packard Motor Officials for Recent Strike," *Norfolk Journal and Guide*, June 12, 1943; "Packard Strike Hit at Negro Rally," *Detroit Free Press*, June 4, 1943.

CHAPTER 10: RIOT

151 **"What shall it profit us":** John Robert Badger, "Hitlerism in America," *Chicago Defender*, July 3, 1943.

151 **past midnight on June 21, 1943:** James Hosking, "Who Started the Race Riot?," *Detroit Free Press*, October 24, 1943; Robert Shogan and Tom Craig, *The Detroit Race Riot: A Study in Violence* (Philadelphia: Chilton Books, 1964).

152 **"We didn't know him":** Alfred McClung Lee and Norman Daymond Humphrey, *Race Riot* (New York: Dryden Press, 1943), 38.

152 **"disarm the residents":** Michael Jackman, "Forgotten History: Detroit's 1943 Race Riot Broke Out 75 Years Ago Today," *Detroit Metro Times*, June 20, 2018, https://www.metrotimes.com/news-hits/archives/2018/06/20/forgotten-history-detroits-1943-race-riot-broke-out-75-years-ago-today.

153 **the white mobs grew:** Shogan and Craig, *The Detroit Race Riot*, 61.

154 **"Men, women, and even children":** Langston Hughes, "Fight for Freedom: The Story of the NAACP," in *The Collected Works of Langston Hughes, Volume 10*, ed. Christopher C. De Santis (Columbia: University of Missouri Press, 2001), 105.

154 "I saw from my stoop": "Susie Mae Ransom affidavit," June 29, 1943, NAACP Papers, folder 001527-029-0757.

155 "There was evidenced a desire": "J. H. Forniss affidavit," June 22, 1943, NAACP Papers, folder 001527-029-0757.

155 "Perhaps most significant": Shogan and Craig, *The Detroit Race Riot*, 105–7.

155 "Much of the blood spilled": Thurgood Marshall, "The Gestapo in Detroit," *The Crisis*, August 1943, 247.

156 "Why are you silent": Walter White, telegram to President Roosevelt, July 2, 1943, NAACP Papers, folder 001459-027-0202; Doris Kearns Goodwin, *No Ordinary Time: Franklin and Eleanor Roosevelt: The Home Front in World War II* (New York: Simon & Schuster, 1994), 447.

156 "We cannot fight to crush": John R. Williams, "50,000 Hear Wallace," *Pittsburgh Courier*, July 31, 1943; "Text of Vice President's Speech at Detroit," *New York Times*, July 26, 1943.

156 A week later in Beaumont: James Albert Burran, "Racial Violence in the South during World War II" (PhD diss., University of Tennessee, 1977), 175–76.

157 "Star Spangled Banner in Beaumont": "Star Spangled Banner in Beaumont," *Baltimore Afro-American*, July 3, 1943.

157 Some Black homeowners in Beaumont: Burran, "Racial Violence in the South," 175–76; John Thompson, "Mob Destruction Sweeping Nation," *New York Amsterdam News*, June 26, 1943; Robert A. Hill, ed., *The FBI's RACON: Racial Conditions in the United States during World War II* (Boston: Northeastern University Press, 1995), 290.

157 The racial violence that swept across the country: "Navy Paper Here Blames Whites for Race Clashes," *Chicago Defender*, July 10, 1943; Eustace Gay, "Facts and Fancies," *Philadelphia Tribune*, July 3, 1943; A. Philip Randolph, "Need for Race Political Bloc Seen," *Chicago Defender*, July 17, 1943.

158 "Beaumont to Detroit: 1943": Langston Hughes, "Beaumont to Detroit: 1943," in Arnold Rampersad, ed., *The Collected Poems of Langston Hughes* (New York: Vintage, 1995), 281.

159 the violence came to Harlem: Farah Jasmine Griffin, *Harlem Nocturne: Women Artists and Progressive Politics during World War II* (New York: Basic Civitas, 2013), 119; Dominic J. Capeci, Jr., *The Harlem Riot of 1943* (Philadelphia: Temple University Press, 1977).

159 The incident that sparked: "6 Dead in Harlem Riot," *Chicago Defender*, August 7, 1943; Keneth Kinnamon and Michel Fabre, eds., *Conversations with Richard Wright* (Jackson: University Press of Mississippi, 1993), 75.

160   **Aspiring writer James Baldwin:** James Baldwin, *Notes of a Native Son* (Boston: Beacon Press, 2012), 102–3; J. Milton Yinger, *A Minority Group in American Society* (New York: Berkley Books, 1965), 52.

161   **"It may well be":** Walter White, "Behind the Harlem Riot," *New Republic*, August 16, 1943, 221.

161   **the army "is aggressively engaged":** White, "Behind the Harlem Riot," 221; Burran, "Racial Violence in the South," 133; Phillip McGuire, ed., *Taps for a Jim Crow Army: Letters from Black Soldiers in World War II* (Santa Barbara, CA: ABC-Clio, 1983), 187.

162   **Marshall successfully appealed:** Juan Williams, *Thurgood Marshall: American Revolutionary* (New York: Three Rivers Press, 1998), 128.

162   **white MP was questioning Private William Walker:** "3 Slain at Miss. Camp," *Chicago Defender*, June 12, 1943; Burran, "Racial Violence in the South," 136–37; Mary Penick Motley, ed., *The Invisible Soldier: The Experience of the Black Soldier, World War II* (Detroit: Wayne State University Press, 1987), 127.

163   **"The negro soldiers":** Burran, "Racial Violence in the South," 138–39.

163   **The War Department investigated:** Burran, "Racial Violence in the South," 139; Robert Suro and Michael Fletcher, "Mississippi Massacre, or Myth?," *Washington Post*, December 23, 1999.

164   **The tiny village of Duck Hill:** Burran, "Racial Violence in the South," 158; Amy Louise Wood, *Lynching and Spectacle: Witnessing Racial Violence in America, 1890–1940* (Chapel Hill: University of North Carolina Press, 2011).

164   **The army court-martialed:** "Soldiers Found Guilty in Duck Hill Shooting," *Pittsburgh Courier*, September 18, 1943; "The Attack on Duck Hill," *Time*, September 13, 1943; Grant Reynolds, "What the Negro Soldier Thinks about This War," *The Crisis*, September–November 1944, 289–91, 299, 316–18, 328.

165   **other army camps witnessed serious racial battles:** Charley Cherokee, "National Grapevine," *Chicago Defender*, June 19, 1943; "The Camp Stewart Rebellion," *Baltimore Afro-American*, June 26, 1943.

165   **President Roosevelt remained silent:** Maria Höhn and Martin Klimke, *A Breath of Freedom: The Civil Rights Struggle, African American GIs, and Germany* (New York: Palgrave Macmillan, 2010), 25; Linda Hervieux, *Forgotten: The Untold Story of D-Day's Black Heroes, at Home and at War* (New York: HarperCollins, 2015), 119; Charley Cherokee, "National Grapevine," *Chicago Defender*, November 20, 1943.

166   **the War Department saw:** Ulysses Lee, *The Employment of Negro Troops* (Washington, D.C.: Office of the Chief of Military History, United States

Army, 1966), 380–404; Langston Hughes, "Here's a Film Everyone Should See, Writes Defender Columnist," *Chicago Defender*, February 26, 1944.

167 **three hundred thousand more Black men:** Lee, *The Employment of Negro Troops*, 406

167 **"We were all angry":** M. Dion Thompson, "A Matter of Honor Medals," *Baltimore Sun*, January 14, 1997.

CHAPTER 11: COMBAT

169 **"The Nazis have maintained":** "Black Angels," *London Stars and Stripes*, July 9, 1943.

170 **the first time Black American pilots:** Benjamin O. Davis, Jr., *American: An Autobiography* (Washington, D.C.: Smithsonian Institution Scholarly Press, 2000), 98; John B. Holway, *Red Tails: An Oral History of the Tuskegee Airmen* (Mineola, NY: Dover Publications, 1997), 63; Charles W. Dryden, *A-Train: Memoirs of a Tuskegee Airman* (Tuscaloosa: University of Alabama Press, 1997), 125.

171 **On June 11, 1943:** Herman S. Wolk, "Pantelleria, 1943," *Air Force Magazine*, June 1, 2002; Edith Rodgers, "The Reduction of Pantelleria and Adjacent Islands," *Army Air Forces Historical Studies*, no. 52 (May 1942): 58.

172 **Hall's triumph was front-page news:** "99th Pilot Downs Nazi Plane," *Pittsburgh Courier*, July 10, 1943; J. Todd Moye, *Freedom Flyers: The Tuskegee Airmen of World War II* (New York: Oxford University Press, 2010), 99; "Hall, Pilot Hero, Kept His Promise," *Pittsburgh Courier*, July 17, 1943; "Black Angels."

172 **"I would like to meet":** Thomas Young, "Eisenhower, Spaatz, Doolittle, and RAF Air Marshall Praise Hall," *New Journal and Guide*, July 17, 1943; Joseph D. Caver, Jerome A. Ennels, and Wesley Phillips Newton, "Setting the Record Straight Regarding Lieutenants White and McCullin," *Air Power History* 55, no. 3 (Fall 2008): 4–11.

173 **"If all Americans could see":** Ollie Stewart, "99th Squadron Suffers First Losses," *Baltimore Afro-American*, July 17, 1943.

173 **"War is terrible":** Moye, *Freedom Flyers*, 100.

173 **"Cheering is for those":** Ollie Stewart, "Yanks Don't Cheer," *Baltimore Afro-American*, August 28, 1943.

174 **With recognition came pressure:** Truman K. Gibson Jr., *Knocking Down Barriers: My Fight for Black America* (Evanston, IL: Northwestern University Press, 2005), 123–24.

175 **Momyer played petty tricks:** Lynn M. Homan and Thomas Reilly, *Black*

Knights: The Story of the Tuskegee Airmen (Gretna, LA: Pelican Publishing, 2012), 101–4; Holway, *Red Tails*, 63; Moye, *Freedom Flyers*, 100–101.

175   **"It is my opinion that":** Homan and Reilly, *Black Knights*, 101–2; Davis, Jr., *American*, 103.

175   **Momyer's report made its way:** Homan and Reilly, *Black Knights*, 101–2; Davis, Jr., *American*, 103.

176   **"By publishing an article":** "Experiment Proved?," *Time*, September 20, 1943; Agatha Jo Scott Davis, "Experiment in Segregation," *Time*, October 18, 1943.

176   **Davis got his opportunity:** Davis, Jr., *American*, 105–6; Gibson Jr., *Knocking Down Barriers*, 125–26.

177   **"I was proud":** Holway, *Red Tails*, 78.

178   **"Any outfit would have been proud":** Moye, *Freedom Flyers*, 104–5; "Sweet Victories," *Time*, February 14, 1944; Holway, *Red Tails*, 92.

179   **"a great bridge of ships":** John Gorley Bunker, *Liberty Ships: The Ugly Ducklings of World War II* (Annapolis: Naval Institute Press, 1972), 15.

179   **Merchant Marine ships suffered higher casualty rates:** Arthur R. Moore, *A Careless Word . . . a Needless Sinking: A History of the Staggering Losses Suffered by the U.S. Merchant Marine, Both in Ships and Personnel, during World War II* (Kings Point, NY: American Merchant Marine Museum, 1983); "Recused S.S. Frederick Douglass Crew in Port," *Norfolk Journal and Guide*, October 9, 1943; Sidney Shalett, "Nazis Sank 17 Ships in Bombing of Bari," *New York Times*, December 17, 1943.

179   **merchant crews were racially integrated:** Ben Burns, "No Color Line in Merchant Marine," *Chicago Defender*, April 1, 1944; Ben Burns, "No Color Line on Ships of Merchant Marine," *Chicago Defender*, May 13, 1944.

179   **Captain Hugh Mulzac:** "Mulzac to Command New Booker Washington Ship," *Norfolk Journal and Guide*, September 26, 1942.

180   **hire a racially integrated crew:** "Mulzac's Mixed Crew Ends Initial Voyage," *Norfolk Journal and Guide*, January 2, 1943; "'Booker T' and Mulzac Complete First Voyage," *Pittsburgh Courier*, January 2, 1943; "Capt. Mulzac Broadcasts 'Democracy' to Latin America," *Call & Post*, January 23, 1943.

181   **When the 10,500-ton *Booker T. Washington*:** "First Negro Skipper," *Time*, October 5, 1942; "Singer Star of Booker T. Washington Launching," *Chicago Defender*, October 3, 1942; C. L. Williams, "Ship in Democracy in Action," *Norfolk Journal and Guide*, August 19, 1944; Hugh Mulzac, *A Star to Steer By* (New York: International Publishers, 1963), 146.

181   **When Mulzac and his crew returned:** "1200 at Banquet in Honor of Capt. Mulzac and His Crew," *Norfolk Journal and Guide*, January 23, 1943; Langston Hughes, "To Captain Mulzac (Negro Skipper of *The Booker T.*

Washington Sailing with a Mixed Crew)" in *The Collected Works of Langton Hughes, Volume 2: The Poems, 1941–1950*, ed. Arnold Rampersad (Columbia: University of Missouri Press, 2001), 86.

182   **After transporting bombs:** Ben Burns, "Democracy Afloat," *The Crisis*, April 1945, 107; Lem Graves, "War Reports from Overseas," *Norfolk Journal and Guide*, May 13, 1944.

182   **He and his crew were harassed:** Lee Davis, "Mrs. Roosevelt Opens Seamen's Club," *Baltimore Afro-American*, January 9, 1943.

182   **At a Greyhound bus station:** John Jasper, "Mulzac Back Home," *Baltimore Afro-American*, October 2, 1943; "Insult to Captain Mulzac," *Baltimore Afro-American*, October 9, 1943.

183   **This second-class status:** Morgen Jensen, "Captain Mulzac Couldn't Purchase Brooklyn Home," *Pittsburgh Courier*, March 25, 1944.

185   **Black soldiers on jungle patrols:** Fletcher Martin, "Enemy Deaths So Great Many Bodies Go Unburied," *Norfolk Journal and Guide*, April 15, 1944.

185   **"During the inky blackness":** Fletcher Martin, "Pacific War Writer in Rescue Party," *Norfolk Journal and Guide*, April 29, 1944; Fletcher Martin, "24th Infantry Avenges Jap Attack," *Norfolk Journal and Guide*, May 6, 1944.

186   **"In the days to come":** Fletcher Martin, "24th Infantry Gets Respite from Battle," *Norfolk Journal and Guide*, July 15, 1944.

187   **"I am glad he was a good soldier":** Fletcher Martin, "Letters Bring Happiness," *Norfolk Journal and Guide*, August 12, 1944.

CHAPTER 12: CIVIL RIGHTS BATTLEFRONTS AT HOME

189   **"Our boys, our bonds":** Flora Bryant Brown, "NAACP Sponsored Sit-Ins by Howard University Students in Washington, D.C., 1943–1944," *Journal of Negro History* 85, no. 4 (Autumn 2000): 279.

190   **"a giant milestone":** "116,000 Georgia Registrants," *The Crisis*, July 1946.

190   **a "time bomb":** "Time Bomb," *Time*, April 17, 1944.

190   **White politicians across the South:** "Time Bomb"; Gary R. Mormino, "GI Joe Meets Jim Crow: Racial Violence and Reform in World War II Florida," *Florida Historical Quarterly* 73, no. 1 (July 1994): 40; Jason Morgan Ward, *Defending White Democracy: The Making of a Segregationist Movement and the Remaking of Racial Politics, 1936–1965* (Chapel Hill: University of North Carolina Press, 2011), 65.

191   **When Congress debated:** "Sen. Langer Says Dixie Democrats Seek to Void 13-14-15 Amendments," *Call &Post*, February 5, 1944.

192   **"place the black heel":** Ward, *Defending White Democracy*, 65.

192   **"It is abundantly and increasingly clear"**: Ward, *Defending White Democracy*, 65.

192   **"We must not be delayed"**: Michael D. Davis and Hunter R. Clark, *Thurgood Marshall: Warrior at the Bar, Rebel on the Bench* (New York: Birch Lane Press, 1992), 117.

193   **"You might just say"**: Jeanne Theoharis, *The Rebellious Life of Mrs. Rosa Parks* (Boston: Beacon Press, 2013), 50.

194   **"I had always been taught"**: Theoharis, *The Rebellious Life of Mrs. Rosa Parks*, 17, 22.

194   **Much of the credit**: Barbara Ransby, *Ella Baker and the Black Freedom Movement: A Radical Democratic Vision* (Chapel Hill: University of North Carolina, 2003), 22–23, 82.

195   **wanted the NAACP to be a people's organization**: Ella Baker, "Report of Other Activities," n.d., ca. 1941, Ella Baker Papers, box 3, folder 4, Schomburg Center for Research in Black Culture, New York Public Library; Ella Baker, letter to Roy Wilkins, March 12, 1942, Ella Baker Papers, box 14, folder "field secretary notes."

195   **"shareholders in a huge firm"**: "N.A.A.C.P. Spearhead of Democracy," 1943, Ella Baker Papers, box 3, folder 2.

196   **"We are making a sacrifice"**: Frank Carmen, Jr., letter to NAACP, February 9, 1945, Ella Baker Papers, box 4, folder 5; Ernest Perry, letter to NAACP, November 11, 1944, Ella Baker Papers, box 4, folder 5; L. G. Kramp, letter to NAACP, Ella Baker Papers, box 4, folder 5; Irvin Lytle, letter to NAACP, January 24, 1945, Ella Baker Papers, box 4, folder 5; Lennie Fuller, letter to NAACP, November 8, 1944, Ella Baker Papers, box 4, folder 5; "Weekly News Digest Headquarters 366th Infantry Regiment," September 23, 1944, Lawrence Reddick WWII collection, box 4, folder 18, Schomburg Center for Research in Black Culture, New York Public Library.

197   **"Instead of the leader"**: Ransby, *Ella Baker and the Black Freedom Movement*, 140–42, 188.

198   **"curdled the morale"**: Alain Locke, "The Unfinished Business of Democracy," *Survey Graphic* 31 (1942).

199   **James Farmer and Bayard Rustin**: John Morton Blum, *V Was for Victory: Politics and American Culture during World War II* (San Diego, CA: Harcourt Brace & Company, 1977), 215–17.

199   **Rustin, a Quaker pacifist**: "Bayard Rustin," in *Black Fire: African American Quakers on Spirituality and Human Rights*, eds. Harold D. Weaver Jr., Paul Kriese, and Stephen W. Angell (Philadelphia: Quaker Press of Friends General Conference, 2011); "Bayard Rustin Defied Draft," *Chicago De-*

fender, March 4, 1944; Gerald R. Gill, "Afro-American Opposition to the United States' Wars of the Twentieth Century" (PhD diss., Howard University, 1985), 153–54; Shaina Destine, "Bayard Rustin: The Inmate That the Prison Could Not Handle," National Archives, Rediscovering Black History, https://rediscovering-Black-history.blogs.archives.gov/2016/08/16/bayard-rustin-the-inmate-that-the-prison-could-not-handle.

200 **Activist and lawyer Pauli Murray:** Pauli Murray, "A Blueprint for First Class Citizenship," *The Crisis*, November 1944, 358–59; Blum, *V Was for Victory*, 217–18; Glenda Gilmore, *Defying Dixie: The Radical Roots of Civil Rights, 1919–1950* (New York: W. W. Norton, 2009), 388–93; Brown, "NAACP Sponsored Sit-Ins by Howard University Students in Washington, D.C., 1943–1944."

CHAPTER 13: MUTINY

203 **"The Navy has a slogan":** Mary Lindsey, *Mutiny?* (New York: NAACP Legal Defense and Educational Fund, 1945), 16.

204 **"Everybody felt at that point":** Robert L. Allen, *The Port Chicago Mutiny: The Story of the Largest Mass Mutiny Trial in U.S. Naval History* (New York: Warner Books, 1989), 59–66.

204 **"I was there the next morning":** Allen, *The Port Chicago Mutiny*, 66; John Robert Badger, "Chaplain Tells Fear of 50 Sailors in 'Mutiny,'" *Chicago Defender*, September 30, 1944.

205 **Black sailors at Port Chicago also chafed:** Allen, *The Port Chicago Mutiny*, 41–48.

206 **"The consensus of opinion":** Allen, *The Port Chicago Mutiny*, 68–72.

207 **"We've got the officers":** Allen, *The Port Chicago Mutiny*, 84.

207 **"As far as we were concerned":** Allen, *The Port Chicago Mutiny*, 85.

207 **"I want to remind you":** Allen, *The Port Chicago Mutiny*, 85.

208 **"It seems to me":** Howard Ball, *A Defiant Life: Thurgood Marshall and the Persistence of Racism in America* (New York: Crown, 1998), 104.

208 **The trial began:** Allen, *The Port Chicago Mutiny*, 92–93.

209 **first U.S. mutiny trial:** Allen, *The Port Chicago Mutiny*, 89–121.

209 **"Those men were no more guilty":** Katherine Bishop, "Exoneration Sought in Mutiny of '44," *New York Times*, August 12, 1990.

209 **The families of the fifty men:** Allen, *The Port Chicago Mutiny*, 119–20.

210 **After six weeks of hearings:** Allen, *The Port Chicago Mutiny*, 126–30; "Thorough Investigation of Naval Mutiny Charge Asked," *Atlanta Daily World*, October 22, 1944.

211   **"It is discouraging"**: "Navy to Ship Seabee 'Strikers' Overseas," *Chicago Defender*, March 31, 1945.

212   **"I'd flown sixty-seven combat missions"**: James Christ, *Memories from Tuskegee: The Life Story of Lieutenant Colonel Clarence C. Jamison* (Happy Camp, CA: Mosaic Press, 2006), 134–35.

212   **"I do not have colored WACs"**: Sandra M. Bolzenius, *Glory in Their Spirit: How Four Black Women Took On the Army during World War II* (Champaign: University of Illinois Press, 2018), 2, 81.

213   **"The driver glanced"**: Jackie Robinson and Alfred Duckett, *I Never Had It Made: The Autobiography of Jackie Robinson* (New York: HarperCollins, 1995), 18–19; John Vernon, "Jim Crow, Meet Lieutenant Robinson: A 1944 Court-Martial," *Prologue* 40, no. 1 (Spring 2008).

213   **"I don't want any unfavorable publicity"**: Jackie Robinson, letter to Truman Gibson, July 16, 1944, Records of the Office of the Secretary of War, RG 107.

213   **"Why do Negro soldiers and sailors mutiny?"**: "The 'Work-But-Not-Fight' Policy," *Chicago Defender*, February 10, 1945.

214   **"It is apparent"**: NAACP, "Minutes of the Meeting of the Board of Directors," September 11, 1944, Ella Baker Papers, box 3, folder 3.

214   **"The Negro will give his life"**: "The 'Work-But-Not-Fight' Policy."

CHAPTER 14: D-DAY AND THE MIRACLE OF SUPPLY

215   **"Although port battalions"**: Ollie Stewart, "Port Battalions Resent White Officers," *Baltimore Afro-American*, January 20, 1945.

216   **The balloons were tethered**: Linda Hervieux, *Forgotten: The Untold Story of D-Day's Black Heroes, at Home and at War* (New York: HarperCollins, 2015), 205.

216   **Other Black units**: Ulysses Lee, *The Employment of Negro Troops* (Washington, D.C.: Office of the Chief of Military History, United States Army, 1966), 637–38.

217   **"I remember watching"**: Stephen E. Ambrose, *D-Day: June 6, 1944: The Climactic Battle of World War II* (New York: Simon & Schuster, 1994), 396.

217   **"Flying balloons looks like kids' play"**: "Barrage Balloon Unit Only Such Men in France," *Norfolk Journal and Guide*, September 9, 1944; Edward Toles, "Crack Troops Catch Nazis in Barrage Balloon Net," *Chicago Defender*, July 15, 1944; Hervieux, *Forgotten*, 225; Francis Yancey, "Four Battalions at Camp Tyson Learn to Fly the Barrage Balloons," *Baltimore Afro-American*, September 11, 1943.

218   **Black newspapers hailed Woodson:** Hervieux, *Forgotten*, 212–13, 220, 241–42; Jack Saunders, "City Hails French Invasion Hero," *Philadelphia Tribune*, September 9, 1944; "D-Day Hero," *Call & Post*, March 17, 1945.

219   **"the most difficult and complicated operation":** Winston Churchill, "Address to the House of Commons," June 6, 1944.

219   **"Almighty God: Our sons":** Franklin D. Roosevelt, "Prayer on D-Day," June 6, 1944.

220   **Black troops were everywhere:** "Unit Removes 2742 Mines, Booby Traps from Normandy Beaches in Eight Days," *Call & Post*, November 18, 1944; Hervieux, *Forgotten*, 236; Edward Toles, "Crack Ack-Ack Outfit Keeps Nazis on Run in Normandy," *Chicago Defender*, July 22, 1944; Allan Morrison, "All Black Dump Truck Driver Battalion Unload on Nazis in Normandy," *Stars and Stripes*, July 17, 1944; "'Paradumpers' Wrote Military History D-Day," *Norfolk Journal and Guide*, July 29, 1944; "Review Combat History of First Negro Company to Land in Normandy on D-Day," *Atlanta Daily World*, June 24, 1945; Edward Toles, "Bake Bread Six Miles behind Normandy Lines," *Chicago Defender*.

221   **"Not many of us were killed":** Joseph Connor, "A Grave Task: The Wartime Job Nobody Wanted," *World War II*, August 2017.

222   **contemporary American officials:** "Negro Casualties in France High among Engineer, Port Troops," *Norfolk Journal and Guide*, July 8, 1944; "Eisenhower Proud of Our Troops in France," *Norfolk Journal and Guide*, July 15, 1944; George Padmore, "'Ike' Lauds Negro Soldiers," *Chicago Defender*, August 5, 1944.

222   **"I got a glimpse":** Raymond Danielle, "Huge U.S. Service Army Rushes Supplies to Front," *New York Times*, August 19, 1944.

222   **"My hat is off":** "Eisenhower Pays Tribute to Supply Men," *Norfolk Journal and Guide*, October 21, 1944.

223   **"miracle of supply":** "Miracle of Supply," *Time*, September 25, 1944.

223   **The heart of the Allies' supply effort:** David P. Colley, *The Road to Victory: The Untold Story of Race and World War II's Red Ball Express* (Washington, D.C.: Brassey's, 2000), xvii, 26, 43, 133–35.

223   **These trucks and the Black men:** Colley, *The Road to Victory*, xvii, 26, 43, 133–35; "German Horse Cavalry and Transport," *Intelligence Bulletin* (U.S. War Department, Military Intelligence Service, March 1946), 53–66; R. L. DiNardo and Austin Bay, "Horse-Drawn Transport in the German Army," *Journal of Contemporary History* 23, no. 1 (January 1988): 129–42.

224   **German army ran on oats as much as oil:** R. L. DiNardo, *Mechanized*

Juggernaut or Military Anachronism? Horses and the German Army of WWII (Mechanicsburg, PA: Stackpole Books, 1991), 119.

224 **General Patton concluded:** Colley, *The Road to Victory*, xvii, 26.

224 **the Red Ball truckers:** Colley, *The Road to Victory*, 49, 58; Arthur Goodwin, "Teamwork Is Smashing Nazi Army," *Stars and Stripes*, August 31, 1944.

225 **"There were dead bodies":** Jennifer Friend, "Red Ball Express: Keeping the Wheels of War Turning," U.S. Army Reserve official website, February 3, 2016, https://www.usar.army.mil/News/Article/649158/red-ball-express-keeping-the-wheels-of-war-turning.

225 **Medgar Evers was nineteen:** Myrlie Evers-Williams and Manning Marable, eds., *The Autobiography of Medgar Evers: A Hero's Life and Legacy Revealed through His Writings, Letters, and Speeches* (New York: Basic Civitas, 2005), 6–7.

225 **truckers in a battle south of Saint-Lô:** Tony Castro, *Looking for Hemingway: Spain, the Bullfights, and a Final Rite of Passage* (Guilford, CT: Lyons Press, 2016), 2; Lee, *The Employment of Negro Troops*, 640; Colley, *The Road to Victory*, 31–33.

226 **Black troops made up:** Lee, *The Employment of Negro Troops*, 629; Edward Toles, "Black Troops Made Path for Invasion," *Chicago Defender*, June 17, 1944.

226 **the women of the all-Black 6888th:** Brenda Moore, *To Serve My Country, to Serve My Race: The Story of the Only African-American WACS Stationed Overseas during World War II* (New York: New York University Press, 1996); Charity Adams Earley, *One Woman's Army: A Black Officer Remembers the WAC* (College Station: Texas A&M University Press, 2000), 164–65; Kathleen Fargey, "6888th Central Postal Directory Battalion," U.S. Army Center of Military History, February 14, 2014, https://history.army.mil/html/topics/afam/6888thPBn/index.html.

227 **Appreciating the vital part:** ASF Manual M-409, March 1, 1946, Logistic Data for Staff Planners, 15–16; James A. Huston, *The Sinews of War: Army Logistics, 1775–1953* (Washington, D.C.: Center of Military History, 1966), 674; Richard M. Leighton and Robert W. Coakley, *Global Logistics and Strategy, 1940–1943* (Washington, D.C.: Center of Military History, 1955); Walter S. Dunn, Jr., *Hitler's Nemesis: The Red Army, 1930–1945* (Mechanicsburg, PA: Stackpole Books, 1994), 64; Lee, *The Employment of Negro Troops*, vii.

228 **"If you could see our boys":** Ollie Stewart, "Our Soldiers Under Fire Sing," *Baltimore Afro-American*, May 1, 1943.

CHAPTER 15: VICTORY IN EUROPE

229 **"Whites treated us like boys":** Mary Penick Motley, *The Invisible Soldier: The Experience of the Black Soldier, World War II* (Detroit: Wayne State University Press, 1987), 269.

230 **"The white man is willing to die":** Rick Atkinson, *The Day of Battle: The War in Sicily and Italy, 1943–1944* (New York: Henry Holt, 2008), 383.

230 **Almond set the tone:** Truman Gibson Jr., *Knocking Down Barriers: My Fight for Black America* (Evanston, IL: Northwestern University Press, 2005), 159, 165; Atkinson, *The Day of Battle*, 383.

231 **"If you would take":** Phillip McGuire, ed., *Taps for a Jim Crow Army: Letters from Black Soldiers in World War II* (Santa Barbara, CA: ABC-Clio, 1983), 53.

231 **"Most times you would see":** Christopher Paul Moore, *Fighting for America: Black Soldiers—the Unsung Heroes of World War II* (New York: Random House, 2007), 261.

231 **"I did not send for you":** Motley, *The Invisible Soldier*, 339.

232 **In August, the 92nd crossed the Arno River:** Lee, *The Employment of Negro Troops*, 539–67; Daniel K. Gibran, *The 92nd Infantry Division and the Italian Campaign in World War II* (Jefferson, NC: McFarland & Company, 2001), 56; John Jordan, "92nd Soldiers Storm Gothic Hill despite Kraut Fire," *Norfolk Journal and Guide*, December 9, 1944.

233 **"Men, you are the first":** Trezzvant W. Anderson, *Come Out Fighting: The Epic Tale of the 761st Tank Battalion, 1942–1945* (Staten Island, NY: 761st Tank Battalion & Allied Veterans Association, 1979), 21.

233 **"Bates gave us the dignity":** Gina M. DiNicolo, *The Black Panthers: A Story of Race, War, and Courage* (Yardley, PA: Westholme, 2014), 216.

234 **"These men were such terrific fighters":** Joe Wilson Jr., *The 761st "Black Panther" Tank Battalion in World War II* (Jefferson, NC: McFarland & Company, 1999), 65–66.

234 **"The 761st was winning":** Wilson Jr., *The 761st "Black Panther" Tank Battalion in World War II*, 126.

235 **"They're coming after us":** Frank Viviano, "Almost-Forgotten Heroes / Italian Town Honors Black GIs Who Were Shunned by Their Own Country," *San Francisco Chronicle*, July 13, 2000.

235 **Fox called for a smoke screen:** Lee, *The Employment of Negro Troops*, 562–67; Viviano, "Almost-Forgotten Heroes."

235 **The 92nd Division's artillery commander endorsed:** Cory Graff, "Lieutenant John Fox's Medal of Honor," National WWII Museum, February

16, 2022, https://www.nationalww2museum.org/war/articles/john-fox-medal -of-honor.

236   **Despite evidence of heroism and resolve:** "The Luckless 92nd," *Newsweek*, February 26, 1945; Milton Bracker, "Americans Lose Ground in Italy," *New York Times*, February 14, 1945; Motley, *The Invisible Soldier*, 314.

236   **"The Glorious Collapse of the 106th":** Stanley Frank, "The Glorious Collapse of the 106th," *Saturday Evening Post*, November 9, 1946.

236   **"Let us make mistakes":** Deton Brooks, "India Troops Hit Slander," *Chicago Defender*, April 7, 1945.

236   **The army dispatched Civilian Advisor:** Gibson, *Knocking Down Barriers*, 164–71; Collins George, "Facts Are Exposed by Aide," *Pittsburgh Courier*, March 24, 1945; "Truman Gibson Makes Probe of Race Division," *Atlanta Daily World*, March 22, 1945; John Chabot Smith, "Army Studying More Effective Negro Training," *New York Herald Tribune*, March 15, 1945; Motley, *The Invisible Soldier*, 346; Lee, *The Employment of Negro Troops*, 575–77.

237   **"It is enough our boys":** "Somebody's Gotta Go!," *Chicago Defender*, March 24, 1945.

238   **"In white officered units":** Lee, *The Employment of Negro Troops*, 588–89.

238   **The Black soldiers' combat performance:** David P. Colley, *Blood for Dignity: The Story of the First Integrated Combat Unit in the U.S. Army* (New York: St. Martin's Press, 2003), 189–90; Lee, *The Employment of Negro Troops*, 688–705.

239   **Sergeant Edward A. Carter Jr. was among the Black volunteers:** Allene Carter and Robert L. Allen, *Honoring Sergeant Carter: A Family's Journey to Uncover the Truth about an American Hero* (New York: Amistad/Harper-Collins, 2003).

239   **Carter, a warrior through and through:** Ernest McPherson, "Staff Sergeant Edward Carter," California Center for Military History, http://www.mili tarymuseum.org/Carter.html; Weston W. Cooper, "Edward A. Carter Jr.," March 9, 2016, BlackPast, https://www.Blackpast.org/african-american -history/edward-carter-jr-1916-1963; CMS Dan Elder, "Remarkable Sergeants: Ten Vignettes of Noteworthy NCOs," NCO Historical Society, https://www.ncohistory.com/files/RemarkableSgts.pdf, November 8, 2008.

240   **Despite everything they endured:** Moore, *Fighting for America*, 268–72.

240   **"writing in blood":** "Colored Troops Face Heavy Nazi Fire in Offensive," *Chicago Defender*, April 14, 1945.

240   NEGRO AMERICA HAILS V-E DAY!: "Negro America Hails V-E Day!," *Chicago Defender*, May 12, 1945.

241 **"The crematory was a large room"**: "Chicago GI Tells Horrors of Nazi 'Murder Factory' Prison Camp," *Chicago Defender*, May 12, 1945.

241 **As the Allies liberated towns**: Max Johnson, "Soldiers Rioting in Europe," *New York Amsterdam News*, August 25, 1945; John Jordan, "Virginian Raises Rebel Flag in Italy," *Norfolk Journal and Guide*, November 4, 1944; Mrs. J. A. Yarbrough, "Confederate Flags in Far-Away Places," *Charlotte Observer*, May 7, 1944; Mrs. J. A. Yarbrough, "Confederate Flags in World War II," *Charlotte Observer*, May 10, 1946; "Confederate Flags," *Baltimore Evening Sun*, July 10, 1944; "'Stars and Bars' in Berlin," *Delhi Dispatch*, January 30, 1946.

242 **"Everywhere our Armed forces go"**: Editorial, *Pittsburgh Courier*, September 9, 1944.

242 **"the American race problem"**: Mark A. Huddle, ed., *Roi Ottley's World War II: The Lost Diary of an African American Journalist* (Lawrence: University Press of Kansas, 2011), 103.

242 **"If the invasion doesn't occur soon"**: Lee, *The Employment of Negro Troops*, 627.

242 **"The first words we heard"**: Hervieux, *Forgotten*, 251

243 **"by far, worse than"**: Gordon Parks, *Voices in the Mirror: An Autobiography* (New York: Doubleday, 1990), 88.

243 **German POWs now joined white American troops**: Matthias Reiss, "Icons of Insult: German and Italian Prisoners of War in African American Letters during World War II," *Amerikastudien/American Studies* 49, no. 4 (2004): 539–62.

CHAPTER 16: VICTORY IN THE PACIFIC

245 **"I can truthfully report"**: Dan Burley, "New York Goes Wild on V-J Day," *New York Amsterdam News*, August 18, 1945.

245 **fighting seven thousand miles away**: Waldo Heinrichs and Marc Gallicchio, *Implacable Foes: War in the Pacific, 1944–1945* (New York: Oxford University Press, 2017), 91–99.

246 **the Corps began accepting Black recruits in June 1942**: Melton A. McLaurin, *The Marines of Montford Point: America's First Black Marines* (Chapel Hill: University of North Carolina Press, 2007), 5–9; Edgar Cole interview, National WWII Museum; Nathan Hodge, "Pioneering Marines Get Their Due," *Wall Street Journal*, August 26, 2011; Ian Shapira, "He Saw the Flag Raised at Iwo Jima. Now, at 94, He Watches the Nation Fight a Deadly Virus," *Washington Post*, April 12, 2020.

247   **The Black Marines who came ashore:** James Campbell, "Pride and Preju-
       dice: The Montford Point Marines on Saipan," HistoryNet, August 10,
       2012, https://www.historynet.com/pride-and-prejudice-the-montford-point
       -marines-on-saipan.htm; "Combat Report," *Time*, July 24, 1944.

248   **"Until then, I'd never had":** Martin Evans, "Montford Point Marines
       Talk Discrimination, Earning Congressional Gold Medal," *Newsday*,
       May 2, 2013; Ken Holliday, "Veterans Legacy Program: Pfc. Kenneth
       Tibbs, the Sacrifice of One of the First African-American Marines in
       WWII," February 27, 2018, VAntage Point, https://www.blogs.va.gov
       /VAntage/45721/veterans-legacy-program-pfc-kenneth-tibbs-the
       -sacrifice-of-one-of-the-first-african-american-marines.

248   **"Negro marines, under fire for the first time":** "Combat Report," *Time*,
       July 24, 1944.

248   **"When the battle of Saipan is recorded":** "Our Black Marines," *Chicago
       Defender*, August 19, 1944.

249   **The Black press described the Montford Point Marines:** "Yank Writer
       Finds Good Report on Negro Marines," *Norfolk Journal and Guide*,
       March 25, 1944; Fred Feldkamp, "Negro Marines Fought Bravely on
       Saipan," *Norfolk Journal and Guide*, August 5, 1944; Fletcher Martin,
       "Marines in Pacific Draw High Praise from U.S. Commanders," *Norfolk
       Journal and Guide*, January 8, 1944; Bernard C. Nalty, *The Right to Fight:
       African-American Marines in World War II* (Washington, D.C.: Marine
       Corps Historical Center, 1995), 21.

249   **no sooner was the island secured:** Thomas A. Guglielmo, *Divisions: A New
       History of Racism and Resistance in America's World War II Military* (New
       York: Oxford University Press, 2021), 301.

250   **Victory on Saipan gave the Allies:** Heinrichs and Gallicchio, *Implacable
       Foes*, 91–137.

250   **"Iwo Jima probably is":** Robert Sherrod, "World Battlefronts: Battle of
       the Pacific," *Time*, February 26, 1945, 26.

250   **Black Marines had experienced combat:** Heinrichs and Gallicchio, *Im-
       placable Foes*, 263–85; Dan Glaister, "Absent from History: The Black
       Soldiers at Iwo Jima," *The Guardian*, October 20, 2016; "Former J. C.
       Smith Student Says Iwo Jima Was 'Hell,'" *Norfolk Journal and Guide*,
       June 16, 1945; Clarence E. Willie, *African American Voices from Iwo Jima:
       Personal Accounts of the Battle* (Jefferson, NC: McFarland & Company,
       2014), 80.

251   **ran circuits between ship and shore:** Ulysses Lee, *The Employment of
       Negro Troops* (Washington, D.C.: Office of the Chief of Military History,

United States Army, 1966), 637; Larry Schylenburg, "Duck Drivers Back Up Marines on Iwo Jima," *Atlanta Daily World*, March 28, 1945.

252 **"made the difference":** "Negro Truck Unit Solidified Yanks' Win on Iwo Jima," *Call & Post*, April 7, 1945.

252 **"Among the men who fought":** Heinrichs and Gallicchio, *Implacable Foes*, 271.

252 **"There is no supermarket":** Joseph LaNier interview, June 13, 2013, National WWII Museum.

252 **"There were holes":** Willie, *African American Voices from Iwo Jima*, 81, 95.

253 **"We were still in the heat of battle":** Yvonne Latty, *We Were There: Voices of African American Veterans from World War II to the War in Iraq* (New York: Amistad/HarperCollins, 2004), 24.

253 **"We were all Americans":** Shapira, "He Saw the Flag Raised at Iwo Jima."

253 **"The Marines who climbed Mt. Suribachi":** Willie, *African American Voices from Iwo Jima*, 95–96.

253 **"delete any and all scenes showing the Negro":** "Newsreels and the Negro in the War," *Norfolk Journal and Guide*, January 15, 1944.

254 **"All of us are deeply concerned":** "Walter White in Britain as Correspondent," *Chicago Defender*, January 15, 1944.

255 **"White America was convinced":** "Frank E. Bolden, 90; Journalist Became Historian of Black Life," *Los Angeles Times*, September 4, 2003; Jinx Coleman Broussard, *African American Foreign Correspondents: A History* (Baton Rouge: Louisiana State University Press, 2003), 109.

255 **"The spirit of Negro troops":** "Tan GIs Praised by Stilwell," *Norfolk Journal and Guide*, May 19, 1945.

256 **"They have fought not with guns":** Chas. L. Miller, "Engineers Beat Obstacles to Build Ledo Road in India," *Baltimore Afro-American*, July 22, 1944.

256 **Dan Burley compared Ledo Road:** Dan Burley, "Backdoor Burley Finds Ledo Road Like 7th Ave.," *New York Amsterdam News*, June 30, 1945.

256 **Twenty-six thousand trucks:** Donald M. Bishop, "The United States and China during World War II," September 15, 2005, website of U.S. Embassy in Beijing, China, https://web.archive.org/web/20060211143928 /http://beijing.usembassy-china.org.cn/ww2operationaloutline.html; Deton Brooks, "Ledo Road Job by Negro Troops Key to Jap Defeat," *Chicago Defender*, November 11, 1944; Frank Bolden, "GI's on Ledo Road Happy War's Over," *Philadelphia Tribune*, August 18, 1945.

257 **Like all U.S. citizens:** Harry Truman, "Statement by the President Announcing the Use of the A-Bomb at Hiroshima," August 6, 1945; J. A. Rogers,

"Rogers Says," *Pittsburgh Courier*, September 1, 1945; George Schuyler, "Views and Reviews," *Pittsburgh Courier*, August 18, 1945; Gerald R. Gill, "Afro-American Opposition to the United States' Wars of the Twentieth Century" (PhD diss., Howard University, 1985), 291–92.

258 **"Was this destructive missile":** "A New Low in Thinking," *Chicago Defender*, September 15, 1945.

258 **"Uh-umm! No":** Langston Hughes, "Here to Yonder," *Chicago Defender*, August 18, 1945.

258 **many lauded the Black scientists:** George Schuyler, "Negro Scientists Played Important Role in Development of Atomic Bomb," *Pittsburgh Courier*, August 18, 1945; Richard Durham, "Negro Scientists Help to Split Atoms," *Chicago Defender*, August 18, 1945; "William Jacob Knox," Atomic Heritage Foundation, https://www.atomicheritage.org/profile /william-jacob-knox; "J. Ernest Wilkins Jr.," Atomic Heritage Foundation, https://www.atomicheritage.org/profile/j-ernest-wilkins-jr.

259 **seven thousand Black workers:** Paul Henderson, "7,000 Employed at Atomic Bomb Plant," *Baltimore Afro-American*, August 18, 1945; "Behind the Men Who Made the Atomic Bomb Were These Women," *Baltimore Afro-American*, August 18, 1945.

260 **"As I sat above the surrender stage":** Deton Brooks, "Brooks Relates Drama of Nip Debacle," *Chicago Defender*, September 8, 1945.

260 **The news spread quickly:** Francis Yancey, "Yanks on Ledo Road Jubilant Over Jap Surrender," *Baltimore Afro-American*, August 25, 1941; Bolden, "GI's on Ledo Road Happy War's Over."

260 **"The Saga of Supply":** Dan Burley, "45th Engineers Won Fame Building Vital Ledo Road," *New York Amsterdam News*, July 21, 1945.

CHAPTER 17: HOMECOMING

263 **"I had been on Omaha Beach":** Juan Williams, "Men Changed by War Fight to Be Equals," *Washington Post*, July 26, 1995.

263 **"The Negro soldier was an utter":** U.S. Senate, *Congressional Record*, 79th Cong., 1st sess., 1945, 6992–995.

264 **"The beating which FEPC":** Roy Wilkins, letter to Ewart Guiner, July 3, 1945, NAACP Papers, folder 001537-012-0263.

264 **"The Negro race is an inferior race":** U.S. Senate, *Congressional Record*, 79th Cong., 1st sess., 1945, 6992–995.

265 **"Thank God, the white soldier":** U.S. Senate, *Congressional Record*, 79th Cong., 1st sess., 1945, 6992–995; "Negro Troops Fail, Eastland Asserts," *New York Times*, June 30, 1945.

265   **Eastland was a racist:** John W. Jeffries, *Wartime America: The World War II Home Front* (Lanham, MD: Rowman & Littlefield, 2018), 186–91.

266   **"struggle to take democracy":** "For Manhood in National Defense," *The Crisis*, December 1940.

267   **Black veterans encountered white counselors:** David H. Onkst, "'First a Negro . . . Incidentally a Veteran': Black World War Two Veterans and the G.I. Bill of Rights in the Deep South, 1944–1948," *Journal of Social History* 31, no. 3 (Spring 1998): 520–21.

268   **organized resistance and violence:** "San Mateo NAACP Branch Protests Burning of Vet's House," December 13, 1946, NAACP Papers, folder 001535-018-0701; "Area Limited to White Veterans," *Albuquerque Tribune*, August 6, 1946; "Aryans Only Neighborhood," Seattle Civil Rights & Labor History Project, https://depts.washington.edu/civilr/covenants _Aryans.htm.

268   **homeownership remained out of reach:** Howard Johnson, "The Negro Veterans Fights for Freedom," *Political Affairs*, May 1947, 430; Onkst, "'First a Negro,'" 522–23; "GI Loans: Colored Vets Who Borrow Cash Prove Sound Business Investments," *Ebony*, August 10, 1947; Ira Katznelson, *When Affirmative Action Was White* (New York: W. W. Norton, 2005), 139–140; Lizabeth Cohen, *A Consumers' Republic: The Politics of Mass Consumption in Postwar America* (New York: Random House, 2003), 171; Neil Bhutta et al., "Disparities in Wealth by Race and Ethnicity in the 2019 Survey of Consumer Finances," FEDS Notes, Federal Reserve Board, September 28, 2020.

269   **opportunities differed dramatically along racial lines:** Katznelson, *When Affirmative Action Was White*, 129–34; Edward Humes, "How the GI Bill Shunted Blacks into Vocational Training," *Journal of Blacks in Higher Education*, no. 53 (Autumn 2006): 92–104.

269   **While 28 percent of white veterans:** Humes, "How the GI Bill Shunted Blacks into Vocational Training," 97.

269   **"the veterans' program":** Truman Gibson, "Gov't Fails Negro Vets," *Pittsburgh Courier*, April 13, 1946.

270   **"blue discharges" from the army:** "Blue Discharge," *Pittsburgh Courier*, November 24, 1945; Allan Bérubé, *Coming Out Under Fire: The History of Gay Men and Women in World War Two* (New York: Free Press, 1990), 233.

270   **"He told me not to wear":** Neil McMillen, "Fighting for What We Didn't Have: How Mississippi's Black Veterans Remember World War II," in *Remaking Dixie: The Impact of World War II on the American South*, ed. Neil McMillen (Jackson: University Press of Mississippi, 1997), 97–99.

271   **"As we walked"**: Yvonne Latty, *We Were There: Voices of African American Veterans from World War II to the War in Iraq* (New York: Amistad/Harper-Collins, 2004), 42.

271   **"Whites to the right"**: Alexander Jefferson, *Red Tail Captured, Red Tail Free: Memoirs of a Tuskegee Airman and POW* (New York: Fordham University Press, 2017), 118; Alexander Jefferson interview, March 28, 2012, National WWII Museum.

272   **"I sat down on one of the benches"**: Richard E. Miller, *The Messman Chronicles: African-Americans in the U.S. Navy, 1932–1943* (Annapolis: Naval Institute Press, 2004), 276.

272   **"tear down the sign"**: Oliver Harrington, "Frontiers Still Left in America: The Negro's Part," in *The Struggle for Justice as a World Force: Report of the New York Herald Tribune Annual Forum, 1946* (New York: *New York Herald Tribune*, 1946), 52.

272   **found WHITES ONLY signs**: Fred Atwater, "Legionnaires Beat Negro Vets," *Chicago Defender*, October 12, 1946.

272   **"Every Negro with his country's uniform"**: "A Soldier Is Murdered," *New York Amsterdam News*, April 14, 1945.

272   **Black newspapers carried grim news**: Equal Justice Initiative, *Lynching in America: Targeting Black Veterans* (Montgomery, AL: Equal Justice Initiative, 2017); Tameka Bradley Hobbs, *Democracy Abroad, Lynching at Home: Racial Violence in Florida* (Gainesville: University of Florida Press, 2016); Lucius Jones, "War Veteran Lynched by Mississippi Farmers," *Pittsburgh Courier*, June 29, 1946; John Rousseau, Jr., "Year-Old Lynching of War II Veteran Revealed by Survivor," *Los Angeles Sentinel*, June 27, 1946; "Overseas Vet Slain," *Chicago Defender*, March 23, 1946; "The Price of Voting," *New York Amsterdam News*, August 10, 1946; Martin Luther King, Jr., letter to the editor, "Kick Up Dust," *Atlanta Constitution*, August 6, 1946, Stanford University Martin Luther King, Jr., Research and Education Institute, https://kinginstitute.stanford.edu/king -papers/documents/kick-dust-letter-editor-atlanta-constitution; Erica Sterling, "Maceo Snipes," Georgia Civil Rights Cold Cases Project at Emory University, https://coldcases.emory.edu/maceo-snipes/#f6; "A Veteran Unavenged," *Pittsburgh Courier*, March 15, 1947; Major Robinson, "Woodard Tells Bitter Story," *Chicago Defender*, July 27, 1946; Richard Gergel, *Unexampled Courage: The Blinding of Sgt. Isaac Woodard and the Awakening of President Harry S. Truman and Judge J. Waties Waring* (New York: Farrar, Straus and Giroux, 2019); Laura Wexler, *Fire in a Canebrake: The Last Mass Lynching in America* (New York: Scribner, 2004); James

Albert Burran, "Racial Violence in the South during World War II" (PhD diss., University of Tennessee, 1977); "NAACP Asks Grand Jury Probe in Burns Killing," *Los Angeles Sentinel*, September 30, 1948; "Pair Acquitted in Fatal Shooting of Alston Voter," *Atlanta Daily World*, November 5, 1948; Civil Rights Congress, *We Charge Genocide* (New York: Civil Rights Congress, 1951); "Remembering Black Veterans Targeted for Racial Terror Lynchings," Equal Justice Initiative, November 11, 2019, https://eji.org/news/remembering-Black-veterans-and-racial-terror-lynchings.

276 **"They're exterminating us":** Jennifer E. Brooks, *Defining the Peace: World War II Veterans, Race, and the Remaking of Southern Political Tradition* (Chapel Hill: University of North Carolina Press, 2004), 24.

276 **"The veteran from Okinawa":** Dan Burley, "New York Goes Wild on V-J Day," *New York Amsterdam News*, August 18, 1945.

CHAPTER 18: WE RETURN FIGHTING

277 **"No nation is so great":** W. E. B. Du Bois, ed., *An Appeal to the World!: A Statement on the Denial of Human Rights to Minorities in the Case of Citizens of Negro Descent in the United States of America and an Appeal to the United Nations for Redress* (New York: NAACP, 1947), 1–14.

277 **fifteen thousand protesters:** "15,000 March to Lincoln Shrine to Mourn Victims of Mob Rule," *Norfolk Journal and Guide*, August 17, 1945; Carol Anderson, *Eyes Off the Prize: The United Nations and the African American Struggle for Human Rights, 1944–1955* (Cambridge: Cambridge University Press, 2003), 61–63.

278 **Du Bois and White regarded the UN with suspicion:** Anderson, *Eyes Off the Prize*, 40–55, 93–4.

279 **Fifth Pan-African Congress:** Anderson, *Eyes Off the Prize*, 40–55, 93–4.

279 **"Peoples of the World":** Du Bois, ed., *An Appeal to the World!*, 1–14.

280 **"As long as Great Britain":** Du Bois, ed., *An Appeal to the World!*, 1–14.

280 **"It is not Russia":** Du Bois, ed., *An Appeal to the World!*, 1–14.

281 **The fallout from the NAACP's appeal:** Anderson, *Eyes Off the Prize*, 58–112; Carol Anderson, *Bourgeois Radicals: The NAACP and the Struggle for Colonial Liberation, 1941–1960* (Cambridge: Cambridge University Press, 2014).

281 **Du Bois and other Black internationalists:** W. E. B. Du Bois, "As the Crow Flies," *New York Amsterdam News*, August 19, 1944; "The Charter of the United Nations: Hearings before the Committee on Foreign Relations, United States Senate, Seventy-Ninth Congress, First Session, on the

Charter of the United Nations for the Maintenance of International Peace and Security, Submitted by the President of the United States," July 2, 1945, 392; Keisha N. Blain, *Set the World on Fire: Black Nationalist Women and the Global Struggle for Freedom* (Philadelphia: University of Pennsylvania Press, 2018).

281 **"When the mob gangs"**: Harry Truman, letter to Ernest W. Roberts, August 18, 1948.

282 **"Everything's going to be all right"**: William E. Leuchtenburg, "The Conversion of Harry Truman," *American Heritage* 42, no. 7 (November 1991).

282 **Despite Truman's personal prejudices**: Leuchtenburg, "The Conversion of Harry Truman"; DeNeen Brown, "How Harry S. Truman Went from Being a Racist to Desegregating the Military," *Washington Post*, July 26, 2018.

283 **"As Americans, we believe"**: Harry Truman, "Address before the NAACP," June 29, 1947.

283 **When the President's Committee:** *To Secure These Rights: The Report of the President's Committee on Civil Rights* (Washington, D.C.: U.S. Government Printing Office, 1947); Steven F. Lawson, ed., *To Secure These Rights: The Report of President Harry S Truman's Committee on Civil Rights* (Boston: Bedford/St. Martin's, 2004); "The Administrator Acts," *Chicago Defender*, November 22, 1947; "The Civil Rights Report," *Baltimore Afro-American*, November 8, 1947; Rawn James, Jr., *The Double V: How Wars, Protest, and Harry Truman Desegregated America's Military* (New York: Bloomsbury Press, 2013), 224.

284 **"If you do away with segregation"**: Lawson, *To Secure These Rights*, 31–32.

285 **"Negroes are in no mood"**: Andrew E. Kersten and David Lucander, eds., *For Jobs and Freedom: Selected Speeches and Writings of A. Philip Randolph* (Amherst: University of Massachusetts Press, 2014), 307–8.

285 **Giving voice to the anger:** Kersten and Lucander, eds., *For Jobs and Freedom*, 307–310; Senate Committee on Armed Services, Hearing on Universal Military Training, U.S. Senate, *Congressional Record*, 80th Cong., 2nd sess., 1948, 685–94.

285 **Randolph renamed his committee:** Andrew E. Kersten, *A. Philip Randolph: A Life in the Vanguard* (Lanham, MD: Rowman & Littlefield, 2007), 79–82; James, Jr., *The Double V*, 225.

286 **"The Southerners want the State right"**: P. L. Prattis, "The Horizon," *Pittsburgh Courier*, March 27, 1945.

287 **Executive Order 9981 was an important:** Jason Lyall, *Divided Armies: Inequality and Battlefield Performance in Modern War* (Princeton, NJ:

Princeton University Press, 2020); Richard M. Dalfiume, *Desegregation of the U.S. Armed Forces* (Columbia: University of Missouri Press, 1969).

287   **"not the same Negroes"**: "The Negro Veteran Tests America," *Ebony*, May 1946; Neil McMillen, "Fighting for What We Didn't Have: How Mississippi's Black Veterans Remember World War II," in *Remaking Dixie: The Impact of World War II on the American South*, ed. Neil McMillen (Jackson: University Press of Mississippi, 1997), 94; Maria Höhn and Martin Klimke, *A Breath of Freedom: The Civil Rights Struggle, African American GIs, and Germany* (New York: Palgrave Macmillan, 2010), 35–37.

288   **"don't scare easy"**: Christopher Parker, *Fighting for Democracy: Black Veterans and the Struggle against White Supremacy in the Postwar South* (Princeton, NJ: Princeton University Press, 2009), 4; Timothy B. Tyson, *Radio Free Dixie: Robert F. Williams and the Roots of Black Power* (Chapel Hill: University of North Carolina Press, 1999).

288   **WAC veteran Dovey Johnson Roundtree**: Katie McCabe, *Justice Older Than the Law: The Life of Dovey Johnson Roundtree* (Oxford: University Press of Mississippi, 2011).

289   **Medgar Evers stood proudly**: John Dittmer, *Local People: The Struggle for Civil Rights in Mississippi* (Champaign: University of Illinois Press, 1995), 1; Myrlie Evers-Williams and Manning Marable, eds., *The Autobiography of Medgar Evers: A Hero's Life and Legacy Revealed through His Writings, Letters, and Speeches* (New York: Basic Civitas, 2005); Michael Vinson Williams, *Medgar Evers: Mississippi Martyr* (Little Rock: University of Arkansas, 2013).

290   **"primarily a moral issue"**: John F. Kennedy, "Civil Rights Address," June 11, 1963.

291   **Myrlie Evers refused**: "Medgar Evers, Whose Assassination Reverberated through the Civil Rights Movement," *New York Times*, July 2, 2016; "Civil Rights in the '60s, Part 1: Justice for Medgar Evers," FBI.gov, https://www.fbi.gov/news/stories/civil-rights-in-the-60s-part-1-justice -for-medgar-evers.

291   **Four thousand mourners**: Dan Day and Ernest Withers, "Full Military Rites for Medgar Evers," *Call & Post*, June 22, 1963; Ernestine Cofield, "Evers' Family Still in 'Shadow of Violence,'" *Chicago Defender*, June 18, 1963.

291   **As an honorably discharged veteran**: Cofield, "Evers' Family Still in 'Shadow of Violence'"; "20,000 See Evers Buried in Capital," *Pittsburgh Courier*, June 22, 1963.

292 "He sacrificed his life for you": Day and Withers, "Full Military Rites for Medgar Evers"; Adolph Slaughter, "Widow Visits JFK," *Baltimore Afro-American*, June 29, 1963.

292 President John F. Kennedy arranged: Slaughter, "Widow Visits JFK."

292 "No soldier in this field": "Slain Negro Buried in Arlington Cemetery," *Chicago Tribune*, June 20, 1963.

293 "He is not dead": Marjorie Hunter, "Evers Is Interred at Arlington," *New York Times*, June 20, 1963.

293 "Medgar Evers believed": Hunter, "Evers Is Interred at Arlington."

293 "The taps played": "Medgar Wiley Evers," Arlington National Cemetery, http://www.arlingtoncemetery.net/mwevers.htm.

CONCLUSION

295 "Thus we lived through": Maya Angelou, *Gather Together in My Name* (New York: Random House, 1974), 5.

295 "History, as nearly no one": James Baldwin, "The White Man's Guilt," *Ebony*, August 1965, 47.

296 write Black Americans out of the history: Lawrence Reddick, letter to the editor, "Race Relations in the Army," *American Journal of Sociology* 53, no. 1 (July 1947): 41; Robert F. Jefferson, *Fighting for Hope: African American Troops of the 93rd Infantry Division in World War II and Postwar America* (Baltimore: Johns Hopkins University Press, 2008), 229–32; Warman Welliver, "Report on the Negro Soldier," *Harper's Magazine* (April 1946); Arthur B. Tourtellot et al., *Life's Picture History of World War II* (New York: Time Inc., 1950); *Collier's Photographic History of World War II* (New York: P. F. Collier & Son Corp., 1946).

297 "If this campaign is not nipped": Reddick, "Race Relations in the Army," 41.

298 In the decades after the war, Black veterans: Jefferson, *Fighting for Hope*, 1; Alexander Jefferson, *Red Tail Captured, Red Tail Free: Memoirs of a Tuskegee Airman and POW* (New York: Fordham University Press, 2017), 127; Brenda L. Moore, *To Serve My Country, to Serve My Race: The Story of the Only African-American WACS Stationed Overseas during World War II* (New York: New York University Press, 1996), 200.

299 After a team of historians and military officers: Elliott V. Converse et al., *The Exclusion of Black Soldiers from the Medal of Honor in World War II: The Study Commissioned by the U. S. Army to Investigate Racial Bias in the Awarding of the Nation's Highest Military Decoration* (Jefferson, NC: McFarland & Company, 2008).

300   **"I thought we'd accomplished something"**: "Mose J. Davie," *The Tennessean*, July 28, 2008; Rudi Williams, "Black WWII Vet Recalls Terrible Time Building 'Ledo Road,'" U.S. Department of Defense, July 7, 2004; Geraldine Seay, *African Americans and the Ledo Road: A Man a Mile* (self-pub., 2000).

301   **"We were flying in the skies"**: John J. Kruzel, "President, Congress Honor Tuskegee Airmen," American Forces Press Service, March 29, 2007, https://www.army.mil/article/2476/president_congress_honor_tuskegee_airmen.

302   **"It's hard to be a patriot"**: Joseph LaNier interview, National WWII Museum.

303   **"It's amazing why we keep"**: Andrew Greif, "Doc Rivers: 'It's Amazing Why We Keep Loving This Country, and This Country Does Not Love Us Back,'" *Los Angeles Times*, August 25, 2020.

303   as a **"recurring phenomenon"**: "Confederate Flags," *Baltimore Evening Sun*, July 10, 1944.

303   **"In its day, this flag"**: Mrs. J. A. Yarbrough, "Confederate Flags in Far-Away Places," *Charlotte Observer*, May 7, 1944.

303   **"Americans from all over"**: Thomas E. Ricks, "Time to Follow Gen. Buckner's Example and Pull Down That Confederate Flag," *Foreign Policy*, August 16, 2017, https://foreignpolicy.com/2017/08/16/time-to-follow-gen-buckners-example-and-pull-down-that-confederate-flag-4.

304   **"master stroke of hypocrisy"**: "Confederate Flag for Dixie Troops, Senator Proposes," *Chicago Defender*, November 27, 1943.

305   **"The Confederacy fought"**: E. Washington Rhodes, "No Place for Confederate Flag!," *Philadelphia Tribune*, May 11, 1948.

306   **GI Bill Restoration Act**: Aaron Morrison and Kat Stafford, "Veterans Day Legislation Targets GI Bill Racial Inequities," AP News, November 11, 2021, https://apnews.com/article/lifestyle-business-veterans-affairs-world-war-ii-discrimination-b2d02e6030ef44e798d4e2d4165ae13e.

307   **Black families' median wealth**: Neil Bhutta et al., "Disparities in Wealth by Race and Ethnicity in the 2019 Survey of Consumer Finances," FEDS Notes, Federal Reserve Board, September 28, 2020.

INDEX